# SECURITY EDUCATION AND CRITICAL INFRASTRUCTURES

# IFIP – The International Federation for Information Processing

IFIP was founded in 1960 under the auspices of UNESCO, following the First World Computer Congress held in Paris the previous year. An umbrella organization for societies working in information processing, IFIP's aim is two-fold: to support information processing within its member countries and to encourage technology transfer to developing nations. As its mission statement clearly states,

> *IFIP's mission is to be the leading, truly international, apolitical organization which encourages and assists in the development, exploitation and application of information technology for the benefit of all people.*

IFIP is a non-profitmaking organization, run almost solely by 2500 volunteers. It operates through a number of technical committees, which organize events and publications. IFIP's events range from an international congress to local seminars, but the most important are:

- The IFIP World Computer Congress, held every second year;
- Open conferences;
- Working conferences.

The flagship event is the IFIP World Computer Congress, at which both invited and contributed papers are presented. Contributed papers are rigorously refereed and the rejection rate is high.

As with the Congress, participation in the open conferences is open to all and papers may be invited or submitted. Again, submitted papers are stringently refereed.

The working conferences are structured differently. They are usually run by a working group and attendance is small and by invitation only. Their purpose is to create an atmosphere conducive to innovation and development. Refereeing is less rigorous and papers are subjected to extensive group discussion.

Publications arising from IFIP events vary. The papers presented at the IFIP World Computer Congress and at open conferences are published as conference proceedings, while the results of the working conferences are often published as collections of selected and edited papers.

Any national society whose primary activity is in information may apply to become a full member of IFIP, although full membership is restricted to one society per country. Full members are entitled to vote at the annual General Assembly, National societies preferring a less committed involvement may apply for associate or corresponding membership. Associate members enjoy the same benefits as full members, but without voting rights. Corresponding members are not represented in IFIP bodies. Affiliated membership is open to non-national societies, and individual and honorary membership schemes are also offered.

# SECURITY EDUCATION AND CRITICAL INFRASTRUCTURES

*IFIP TC11 / WG11.8 Third Annual World Conference on Information Security Education (WISE3)*
*June 26–28, 2003, Monterey, California, USA*

*Edited by*

**Cynthia Irvine**
*Naval Postgraduate School, Monterey*
*USA*

**Helen Armstrong**
*Curtin University, Perth*
*Australia*

KLUWER ACADEMIC PUBLISHERS
BOSTON / DORDRECHT / LONDON

**Distributors for North, Central and South America:**
Kluwer Academic Publishers
101 Philip Drive
Assinippi Park
Norwell, Massachusetts 02061 USA
Telephone (781) 871-6600
Fax (781) 681-9045
E-Mail <kluwer@wkap.com>

**Distributors for all other countries:**
Kluwer Academic Publishers Group
Post Office Box 322
3300 AH Dordrecht, THE NETHERLANDS
Telephone 31 78 6576 000
Fax 31 78 6576 254
E-Mail <services@wkap.nl>

 Electronic Services <http://www.wkap.nl>

**Library of Congress Cataloging-in-Publication Data**

A C.I.P. Catalogue record for this book is available from the Library of Congress.

Security Education and Critical Infrastructures
Edited by Cynthia Irvine and Helen Armstrong
ISBN 1-4020-7478-6

*Printed on acid-free paper.*
Printed in the United States of America.

# Contents

# Contributing Authors

Kenneth Alford, Vikram Anantapadmanabhan, Colin J. Armstrong, Helen L. Armstrong, S. Azadegan, Matt Bishop, Justin Brown, Karen L. Burke, Respickius Casmir, Shiu-Kai Chin, Chez Ciechanowicz, Gregory J. Conti, Melissa J. Dark, John Davey, Dorothy E. Denning, Peter J. Denning, George W. Dinolt, Jaroslav Dockal, Paul S. Dowland, Phyllis Frankl, J.D. Fulp, Steven M. Furnell, John Hill, Ji Hu, William Hutchinson, Cynthia E. Irvine, Scott D. Lathrop, M. Lavine, Timothy E. Levin, Anatoli Maljuk, Keith M. Martin, Christoph Meinel, Nasir Memon, Natalia Miloslavskaia, Gleb Naumovich, Susan Older, M. O'Leary, Per Oscarson, Fred C. Piper, Daniel J. Ragsdale, Craig W. Rasmussen, Matthew J. B. Robshaw, Liam Rose, Michael Schmitt, Alexander Tolstoi, Rayford Vaughn, Giovanni Vigna, Teemupekka Virtanen, Alastair G. Warren, M.J. Warren, A. Wijesinha, Christian Willems, Louise Yngström, and M. Zimand

# Preface

Dear Friends and Colleagues in Information Security Education,

Welcome to WISE 3, the third convening of the World Conference on Information Security Education. The theme of this conference is teaching the role of information assurance in an age of critical infrastructure protection. In ways, both obvious and obscure, information technology is transforming our daily lives. We depend upon information systems to ensure that electric power is distributed to our homes and businesses. The financial sector uses extensive systems to manage the world's money and the economies of nations. Water and transportation networks are controlled by underlying networks of distributed computer systems. Health care systems not only contain our medical histories but also control complex, life-saving medical equipment that can ease pain and speed recovery. There are many more examples. Unfortunately, information security is often an afterthought in infrastructure design and implementation.

The vulnerabilities of software products increases with no apparent plateau in sight: in 2000 approximately 1100 software vulnerabilities were reported, but by 2002 that number had increased by close to 300% to over 3,200. These flaws open the door to cyber exploits that run amok across global networks with lightning speed.

The possibility of cyber attack against various infrastructures has received considerable attention in certain government circles and the media. Yet, thus far, no clear mandate to set a new course toward greater security has been articulated. As information technology becomes increasingly embedded in everything we do, our vulnerabilities will only increase. How will protection be designed into the fabric of our new world and maintained so that it remains strong and resilient?

Security is an enabling technology. If our systems are built so that they can be trusted, so that our privacy is maintained, so that transaction integrity can be relied upon, so that resources are there when needed, then we will have succeeded. New paradigms will emerge. For those of us in education, the challenge is to create ways to ensure that those who must construct our enabling technology are equipped with the foundations and knowledge required to do the job.

This is the third time the World Conference on Information Security Education (WISE 3) meets. It is held by Working Group 11.8 under the IFIP Technical Committee 11 (TC11) on Security and Protection in Information Processing Systems. The conference follows in the footsteps of WISE 1, held in Stockholm, Sweden in 1999 and WISE 2, which followed two years later in Perth, Australia. These World Conferences did not emerge from nowhere; instead, they were the result of many information security education workshops held in Capetown, South Africa; Copenhagen, Denmark; Samos, Greece; and at a venue on the Danube between Vienna, Austria, and Budapest, Hungary. We can look forward to WISE 4, to be held in Moscow, Russia. Through these conferences and workshops an international community of security educators is working together toward a common vision.

The conference received a total of thirty submissions. All were reviewed by at least two referees on the international program committee. Twenty-three were selected for presentation at the conference. These papers present important perspectives and ongoing efforts in countries including: Australia, Czech Republic, UK, Germany, Finland, Sweden, Russia, and USA.

Contributions to the conference include the following:

**Refereed papers**. These were papers selected through a process of blind review by an international program committee.

**Invited papers**. Well-known experts in the field of information security and computer science were invited by the program committee to make presentations.

**Panel presentations**. Panel proposals were reviewed by the program committee and selected for presentation.

We hope that the readers of this volume will join the conference organizers, authors and participants for the next conference on information security education, WISE 4 in Moscow, by submitting papers and panel proposals.

There are many who made this workshop possible, but particular thanks goes to National Science Foundation for support of the workshop under Grant Number DUE-0210762. This allowed us to introduce many newcomers to the art and challenges of information security education. We are grateful for the work of the members of the program committee who volunteered their time to review the many excellent submissions for this conference. The organizing committee has provided us with the support in the complexities of conference mechanics. This workshop would not have been possible without the help of those who quietly work behind the scenes. We would especially like to thank Naomi Falby for her invaluable support in helping with the organization of the conference. We are grateful to Matthew Rose whose attention to detail has resulted in this well crafted book. Our thanks extend to David Riebandt and several of our Naval Postgraduate School students, who have provided support during the conference.

June 2003
Cynthia Irvine
Helen Armstrong

Websites:
IFIP TC 11 Working group 11.8
http://www.ifip.tu-graz.ac.at/TC11/WG/index.htm
IFIP TC-11
http://www.ifip.tu-graz.ac.at/TC11
IFIP
http://www.ifip.or.at

# Acknowledgments

## CONFERENCE CHAIR:
Cynthia Irvine, Naval Postgraduate School, USA

## PROGRAM COMMITTEE:
Cynthia Irvine, Naval Postgraduate School, USA
Helen Armstrong, Curtin University, Australia

Colin Armstrong, Curtin University, Australia
Richard Baskerville, Georgia State University, USA
William Caelli, Queensland University of Technology, Australia
Fred Cohen, Sandia National Laboratory and Univ. of New Haven, USA
James Davis , Iowa State University, USA
Lynette Drevin Potchefstroom, University, South Africa
Simone Fischer-Hübner, Karlstad University, Sweden
Deborah Frincke, University of Idaho, USA
Steve Furnell, Plymouth University, UK
Lance Hoffman, George Washington University, USA
William Hutchinson, Edith Cowan University, Australia
Erland Jonsson Chalmers, University of Technology, Sweden
Natalia Miloslavaskaia, Moscow State Eng. Physics Inst., Russia
Karl Posch, Graz University of Technology, Austria
Gerald Quirchmayr, University of Vienna and Univ. of South Australia
Alexander Tolstoi , Moscow State Engineering Physics Inst., Russia
Matthew Warren, Deakin University, Australia
Louise Yngström, Stockholm University, Sweden

## ORGANIZING COMMITTEE:
Cynthia Irvine, Naval Postgraduate School, USA
George Dinolt, Naval Postgraduate School, USA
Craig Rasmussen, Naval Postgraduate School, USA
Naomi Falby, Anteon, USA

## ORGANIZED BY:
IFIP TC-11 Working Group 11.8

The conference wishes to express its gratitude to the National Science Foundation of the USA for support under the Information Assurance Scholarship for Service Program.

# CYBER SECURITY AS AN EMERGENT INFRASTRUCTURE
*Invited Talk*

Dorothy E. Denning
*Naval Postgraduate School, Monterey, California, USA*

When I began studying computer security in late 1972 as a Ph.D. student at Purdue University, the field was in its infancy. There were few academics working in the area, no research conferences or journals devoted to the field, and no professional societies to join. Security papers were presented at conferences and published in journals that covered more established areas of computer science, such as operating systems, or that treated computing and telecommunications broadly. The number of publications and Ph.D. theses relating to computer security was small enough that it was possible to read the entire literature. If there was any security industry at all, I was not aware of it.

The field has changed dramatically in the 30 years that have passed. Now there is a multi-billion-dollar-a-year security industry offering thousands of products and services to everyone from large corporate enterprises to home computer users. There are more security conferences than I can keep track of, let alone attend, and enough publications to fill a library. Thirty-six universities have been declared Centers of Academic Excellence in Information Assurance Education, and numerous companies offer training in computer and network security and forensics. There are professional societies devoted to security, and certification programs for security technologies, operating environments, and security professionals. Information security has become a topic of conversation at board meetings and social gatherings. It is a priority in business and government. It has led to new laws and regulations, to new policies and procedures for handling information, and to a growing cadre of cyber cops and digital forensics specialists. It is on the agenda of Congress, the President, and international bodies.

In short, cyber security has become an infrastructure in its own right. This infrastructure serves to protect computers and networks, and the information that is generated, acquired, processed, transmitted, and stored by them. Like many of the systems it protects, the security infrastructure is global and interconnected. It is growing and evolving, and will continue to do so as long as information technology itself evolves.

The talk explores this emergent infrastructure and the factors that are shaping its development. These factors are divided into five areas: threats, technology developments, economic factors, psychological factors, and social and political factors. These areas will be discussed after first describing the elements of the security infrastructure.

## SPEAKER

Dorothy E. Denning is a professor in the Department of Defense Analysis at the Naval Postgraduate School. Her current work encompasses the areas of conflict and cyberspace, and information operations and iassurance. She has published 120 articles and four books, her most recent being *Information Warfare and Security*. She is an ACM Fellow and recipient of several awards, including the Augusta Ada Lovelace Award and the National Computer Systems Security Award. In November 2001, she was named a *Time* magazine innovator. Dr. Denning received the B.A. and M.A. degrees in mathematics from the University of Michigan and the Ph.D. degree in computer science from Purdue University. She has previously worked at Georgetown University, Digital Equipment Corporation, SRI International, and Purdue University.

# TEACHING NETWORK SECURITY THROUGH LIVE EXERCISES
*Red Team / Blue Team, Capture the Flag, and Treasure Hunt*

Giovanni Vigna
*Department of Computer Science, University of California, Santa Barbara*

**Abstract**:    Live exercises represent a valuable tool to teach the practical aspects of security and the dynamics of network-based attack and defense techniques. However, these exercises are very difficult to organize and execute. For this reason, there are very few courses that offer live exercise as an integral part of the class work. This paper describes a series of live exercises that have been used in a graduate-level Computer Science course on network security. For each exercise, the setup, execution, and lessons learned are discussed. The intended audience of this paper is represented by instructors – especially in colleges and universities – who want to start using this type of instructional tools but have no experience and are unsure of the possible pitfalls in their implementation.

Keywords:    Teaching Security, Live Exercises, Red Team/Blue Team, Capture the Flag

## 1.    INTRODUCTION

Teaching practical computer security is difficult [Bishop, 1997, Bishop, 2000]. First of all, security permeates a wide range of technologies. Addressing a comprehensive set of practical security techniques without getting lost in the details of each technology requires careful selection of the topics and particular attention to the way the topics are presented to the students.

Second, the instructor is faced with the difficult decision of choosing the right balance between a completely theoretical approach and a completely practical one [Bishop, 1999]. Usually, this choice is heavily influenced by the educational curriculum. For example, if there is an existing course that covers the foundational principles of security (e.g., the Bell-LaPadula model), then it is possible to use the course as a prerequisite and focus on more technical issues.

Third, teaching practical security requires substantial effort on the part of both the instructor and the educational institution within which the course is given. This makes it difficult to organize practical security courses, particularly in higher education public institutions, like universities, where resources are scarce.

In addition, if the class has a high-impact technical content (e.g., the class covers break-in techniques), then there is a general concern that the class may get "out-of-hand" or that a particular institution may be flagged as a " hacker school."

This paper describes the instructor's experience in teaching a graduate-level course on "Network Security and Intrusion Detection". This course has been taught three times in the past two years. This class differs from traditional courses in security in three ways: a strong practical and technical emphasis, the support for hands-on experience, and the use of live exercises. These three aspects are discussed in the following three sections.

## 1.1    Teaching How To Break In

The goal of the course is to describe in detail the techniques used to violate the security of computer systems and the techniques used to both prevent and detect the attacks. The description of attack and defense techniques is detailed to the point that the attacks and the defense techniques can be reproduced. For example, the lack of boundary checks in software is not just covered from a theoretical, general viewpoint: Buffer overflow attacks are examined in detail, showing exactly how to create the necessary conditions for an attack to be successful and the tools needed to build and deliver the attack. The rationale behind this approach can be summarized by the well-known saying: "The Devil is in the details." That is, only by understanding the low-level details of vulnerabilities and attacks it is possible to avoid the introduction of similar flaws in software and to design protection and detection mechanisms that are actually effective.

A possible argument against this approach is that students are taught "How to break in". Some instructors (and some administrators) fear that by teaching how attacks are actually designed and delivered will create a new generation of hackers that will wreak havoc and take control of the planet.

The obvious counter-argument is that locksmiths know how to break into a house or a car. Locksmiths are not considered criminals and the best locksmiths are those who design the safes where we store our most valuable items. In addition, even though the information about how to violate the security of a system was once in the hands of a few knowledgeable and skilled programmers, nowadays the same knowledge is accessible to the public through the Internet.

The key here is an ethical approach to security. It is the responsibility of the instructor to sensitize the students to the ethical aspects of security and to inform them of the possible consequences of their actions. Therefore, the class included a detailed, in-depth discussion of computer ethics, of the policies that regulate the department, and the computer crime laws of the United Stated and Europe.

In the past two years, the students in the class didn't create any serious problem to the department or to third parties. The only exception was an experiment whose involuntary side effect caused the disruption of routing in a nearby department for a few hours.

## 1.2    Hands-on Experience and the root Problem

The course's practical approach could not be taught with a blackboard and a few slides. To achieve the goals of the course it was necessary to allow the students to experiment with the security techniques covered in class. The main problem is that most security experiments require privileged access to the operating system – in UNIX lingo, root privileges.

Departments very seldom provide instructional labs where students (even graduate students) have privileged access and can experiment with security tools and techniques. This is mainly because of the possible dangers associated with such activities and because of the complexity that arises in managing an infrastructure with these characteristics.

I was able to obtain the permission of the department to create an instructional network testbed where students were allowed to experiment with various types of attacks and defense techniques without disrupting the normal educational lab activity. For the first edition of the class I built a testbed network composed of ten hosts (PCs and Sun Workstations) configured with a number of different operating systems. The PCs were assembled from the pieces of hardware that were discarded during the upgrade of other departmental instructional labs. The testbed (named "the playground" by the students) was accessible remotely and secured by a firewall, so that only authorized users could use it. This network proved to be an invaluable educational tool: For the first time the students were able to test security tools and attacks in a "safe" environment. The feedback from the students in the class was overwhelmingly positive, and for both the second and third instances of the class the department provided substantial support to improve the testbed network.

Even though the creation, configuration, and maintenance of the testbed required a substantial amount of additional effort from both the instructor and the teaching assistants, this experience proved that it is actually possible to create an instructional tool where students are able to enjoy a hands-on experience with security techniques.

## 1.3    Learning the Hard Way: Live Exercises

Even though the testbed network was an important instructional tool, it didn't provide a realistic experience of the attack/defense process. Each tool and technique was experimented with in an isolated way. Therefore, in the first edition of the course it was decided to create a live exercise that would give the students a feel for the difficulties of both attacking and protecting computer networks. During this exercise, which was conducted at the end of the class, the students were divided into two teams. Then the teams had to perform a coordinated attack and defense process against each other, within a limited time frame (around four hours). The enthusiastic response of the students convinced me to include this type of exercise in every future edition of the course.

## 2.    MOTIVATION AND ROAD-MAP

Live exercises are incredibly difficult to organize and there are many lessons that were learned from conducting these activities. For each edition of the class, the lessons learned suggested a modification in the organization and execution of the exercise. This paper describes in detail the structure and execution of each exercise, explaining the rationale behind it and discussing the lessons learned. The intended audience for this paper is higher-education instructors that may want to reproduce similar exercises and educators in general, which may use some of the experiences described in this paper to enrich their classes.

The rest of this paper is structured as follows. In Section 3, a classic Red Team/Blue Team exercise is described. Section 4 presents the evolution of the first exercise into a "capture the flag" contest. The third exercise, presented in Section 5, is a network-based "scavenger hunt" which represents another evolution of the exercise. Then Section 6 presents some related coursework. Finally, Section 7 concludes the paper.

# 3. RED TEAM/BLUE TEAM

This exercise was carried out during the first edition of the course. In this exercise, the class was divided into two teams: the Red Team and the Blue Team. The Red Team was responsible for attacking and compromising a set of hosts, while the Blue Team was responsible for detecting the attacks and, in a limited form, for protecting the hosts.

The final goal of the Red Team was to obtain a file named secret.txt stored on each victim host. There could be multiple copies of the file and decoy copies could be present too. The only files that had to be retrieved were those whose contents started with the keyword SECRET.

The goal of the Blue Team was to detect the attacks coming from the Red Team. In addition, the Blue Team could execute some counter-measures to slow down or confuse the attackers. In particular, the Blue Team could freely decide where to store the secret file. The only requirement was that the file be on a mounted file system.

Some rules were introduced in order to make the exercise more interesting. First of all, the Blue Team could not filter or block any network traffic. Second, the Blue Team could not patch any vulnerability: The Blue Team had to work with out-of-the-box operating systems. These rules were imposed to prevent the Blue Team from completely patching and locking down the systems. Even though in real-life situations network access to sensitive services is actually heavily filtered, in this case a network filter and the patching of known vulnerabilities would have made the whole exercise uninteresting.

The Read Team also had some limitations. First, the Red Team could not use *a priori* knowledge about the victim hosts. It was clear that some of the hosts in the class testbed would have been used as victims. The students were invited to avoid any use of "testbed-specific" knowledge, e.g., the association of a certain Ethernet address with a certain host in the testbed network. Second, the Red Team could not disrupt services, bring down hosts, and delete files. This rule was introduced to avoid actions from the Red Team that would have jeopardized the effectiveness of the detection tools of the Blue Team.

Participation in the Blue Team/Red Team exercise accounted for 20% of the final grade. The students had to break into sub-teams with specific tasks. At the end of the exercise, each team had to submit a report.

The report format was specified in detail so that the instructor could evaluate a number of parameters, such as the ability to plan in advance both attack and defense, the ability to deploy protection/detection mechanisms and to prepare automated attack scripts, the ability to cooperate with other sub-teams, and the ability to maintain a log of the activities (both attacks and detections).

## 3.1    Setup

The setup for this exercise required the configuration of two sets of hosts, one set for each team. Both teams needed root access to the hosts in order to set up attack and defense tools. The teams were told to prepare and test their tools on the class testbed network and to be ready to move their tools to different hosts right before the exercise. This was done to push student to develop portable software.

It was decided that the Blue Team hosts would be four of the hosts in the class testbed. The IP addresses of the hosts where changed, to make identification of the hosts not completely trivial. In addition, the operating systems on these hosts were re-installed to avoid the possibility of Trojan-ed software left by components of the Red Team. The network was instrumented so that a complete dump of the traffic could be collected.

The Red Team was given privileged access to a set of hosts located in an instructional lab, where the exercise took place. These hosts were the main concern for the administrators, because the students could use their privileged access to attack other hosts in the instructional lab and access the departmental file server. It was decided that the advantage in terms of management overcame the risks, and that the students could be trusted (at least for a four-hour period).

## 3.2    Execution

The exercise included a two-hour preparation, where the two teams set up their tools, and a two-hour execution phase, where the actual competition took place.

The day of the exercise, an instructional lab was completely reserved for the exercise. The room was divided into two zones, one for each of the teams.

The preparation phase was carried out without surprises. The testbed hosts were made accessible to the members of the Blue Team who installed their tools and decided the location of the secret files. The Red Team installed the attack tools on the hosts that were placed in the instructional lab.

When the actual attack phase started, the atmosphere in the lab heated up. The students were very excited and there was a general feel that a competition had started. The competition was not just about getting a good grade in the class. The students actually felt that they were part of a team, and they had a sort of team pride.

The Blue Team had developed a number of network-based decoy tools, which were supposed to confuse the adversaries. These tools were simple but very effective. They ranged from sniffers that would respond to ICMP requests even when directed to non-existent hosts, to tools that would simulate the existence of multiple hosts by "mirroring" the behavior of one. In addition, the Blue Team created host monitoring software that acted as a form of host-based intrusion detection.

The Red Team also developed a number of tools. Most of them were filters to translate the outputs of scanning tools into a format that was usable by tools developed by other teammates. The attack process had been organized in detail: the attackers had an "attack pipeline" where the results from one team were given as input to the following team in a continuous process.

During the execution of the attack a few incidents occurred. A couple of times the scanning activity of the Red Team crashed a victim host. The hosts were then rebooted and restored. In a small number of instances the monitoring systems developed by the Blue Team overloaded the monitored hosts to the point that they were unresponsive and, in two instances, they had to be rebooted.

Apart from these events the exercise progressed smoothly. The Red Team was able to successfully compromise all the hosts and access the secret files. Most of the attacks of the Red Team were successfully detected by the Blue Team. In addition, the decoys and the defense tools developed by the Blue Team successfully slowed down the attackers.

## 3.3    Lessons Learned

– Having a team that is responsible for defending only and a team that is responsible for attacking only has a number of disadvantages. First of all, the members of the defense team think they are having "less fun" than the members of the attack team. In addition, they feel that protecting and detecting requires much more work than attacking. This last observation was confirmed by comparing the tools developed for the exercise. The Blue Team developed tools that were much more sophisticated than the Red Team tools. This is mostly because of the restrictions imposed on the defenders in terms of network filter configuration and OS patching.
– The development of original tools should be required, or at least rewarded more. The Red Team members downloaded most of their attack tools from the network and concentrated most of their efforts on coordinating the activities of different sub-teams. It would have been

preferable to have more of the Red Team's effort devoted to developing new attack tools.

- It is necessary to specify a precise format for both the description of the attacks and the detection logs. The reports from the students contained very imprecise descriptions of both. Often, basic information (e.g., correct timestamps and TCP ports involved) was missing. This made it impossible to correctly match the descriptions of the attacks performed by the Red Team with the detections reported by the Blue Team. In addition, no automated processing was possible.
- It is important to stress the importance of a process. Students tend to take shortcuts (e.g., an attempt to run a known exploit blindly against the 255 addresses of a subnet) in order to win the competition. Instead, it is important to foster the preparation and the execution of a well-defined process.
- It is important that the two teams work in different rooms. Having the two teams sharing the same lab space causes a number of problems. First of all, some of the students' energy is devoted to checking if some members of the other team are trespassing. Second, noise and cheering from a team may disturb or irritate the other team.
- The Blue Team and the Red Team need to be on different IP subnets. This makes management and filtering simpler. In addition, by having attackers and defenders separated by intermediate routers it is possible to create a more realistic setup.

## 4.　　CAPTURE THE FLAG

This exercise was carried out as part of the second edition of the class. The goal was to modify the Red Team/Blue Team exercise to take into account the lessons learned in the previous editions of the class.

The exercise was organized in a way similar to the Red Team/Blue Team exercise, with the difference that there was an attempt to balance the attack and defense responsibilities between the two teams.

The class was divided into two teams: The Alpha Team and the Omega Team. Both Teams were responsible for both attacking the other team and defending their own assets. More precisely, each team was responsible for protecting a set of hosts and hiding a flag (the secret file described in Section 3) on every hosts. The team's goal was not to prevent the other team from breaking into the host. Instead, the priority was to detect the attacks of the opponents. In addition, each team had to attack the other team's hosts and retrieve the flags for each of the attacked hosts.

The rules that were imposed to the two teams were similar to those described in the previous exercise: the teams could not use *a priori* knowledge about the testbed network; the teams could not disrupt services, bring down hosts, or delete files; they could not filter/block network traffic and/or patch vulnerable software.

Participation in the "Capture The Flag" exercise accounted for 20% of the final grade.

## 4.1 Setup

The setup for this exercise was different with respect to the original Red Team/Blue Team exercise. Two different instructional labs, one for each team, were reserved for the exercise. The labs were on different IP subnets. Two sets of hosts different from the ones used for the class testbed were prepared and configured in an identical way. In addition, it was decided to connect all the hosts to a hub and to provide extra connection ports for the students' personal laptops. This way they could pre-install some of the attack/defense software prior to the exercise. A complete dump of the traffic directed to the victim hosts was collected.

## 4.2 Execution

When the exercise started each team gathered in their assigned instructional lab. Then, each team was given the hosts to be protected.

At the beginning of the exercise, the teams had two hours of "truce" to prepare their hosts for the exercise (installation of attack/defense software, hiding of the flags, etc). The truce was actually enforced by a set of rules in the router connecting the two instructional labs. The actual attack was carried out in the following two hours.

This time the students were strongly encouraged to develop their own tools. The results were impressive: the students created complete honeypots using virtual machines (e.g., User Mode Linux and VMware) and built very complex attack tools to improve the resilience to decoy techniques.

## 4.3 Lessons Learned

- It is important to push the students to be precise in identifying their targets. This is mainly to prevent attacks from getting out of hand, but also to make them understand the subtleties of stealthy attacks.
- Collecting data during the attack is an important activity. Extra effort should be devoted to collect host audit trails. These are particularly

valuable for use in future editions of the class (e.g., audit trail analysis assignments) and as research data.

- The creation of unnecessary traffic during an exercise should be penalized. By penalizing the excessive generation of traffic it is possible to prevent the students from launching massive denial-of-service attacks against the opponents' hosts and force them to use advanced techniques that use the least amount of traffic.

- It would be beneficial if the students were required to proceed through a path that would force them to progressively make their way to a complex network. The Red Team/Blue Team and Capture The Flag exercises had a "flat" structure: the same techniques were applied iteratively to a number of targets and there were no changes in the mission's goals during the exercise.

## 5.     TREASURE HUNT

In this exercise, the Alpha and Omega teams competed in a treasure hunt. The treasure hunt goal was to break into a simulated (yet realistic) payroll system and perform a money transfer transaction.

Each team had to perform a number of tasks (e.g., scan a network or break into a host). Each task had to be completed in a limited amount of time (e.g., 30 minutes). The first team that achieved the task got 5 points. If the other team completed the task within the specified time, it received 3 points. If the time elapsed and the team was not able to complete the task, then a cheat-sheet was provided so that the task could be completed, but no points were given. A task was disclosed only after the previous one was completed by both teams. The list of tasks is presented in Table 1.

In this exercise, no detection task was required[1]. The teams had to concentrate on attack techniques only. The goal was to be prepared for the unknown and to be able to deal with unforeseen problems. In addition, a considerable amount of stress was put on the production of truth files, that is files that contain a complete specification of the attacks that were carried out. These files had to be produced in IDMEF [Curry and Debar, 2002] format, for automated processing.

In preparation for the exercise it was suggested that each team build expertise in a list of topics: network scanning techniques, attacks against SQL servers (both local and remote), NIS-based and NFS-based attacks, buffer overflow attacks (both local and remote), privilege escalation

---

[1] An exercise similar to the one described in Section 4 was carried out previously, as a form of midterm.

techniques, password cracking techniques, attacks against Apache web servers, attacks against CGI applications. This list was provided to focus the energy of the teams on techniques that would be useful during the exercise.

*Table 1:* List of tasks used during the Scavenger Hunt exercise.

| Task | Description | Max Duration |
|------|-------------|--------------|
| 1 | Determine the active hosts in subnet X.Y.Z. Also determine each host's OS and the services/applications that are remotely accessible. Scanning techniques that will evade detection by the Snort system will receive additional bonus points. | 20 minutes |
| 2 | Get interactive access to the web server host by exploiting a web-based vulnerability. You must be able to login into the host as a user account other than root. | 30 minutes |
| 3 | Get root privileges on the web server host. | 30 minutes |
| 4 | Determine the hosts that are located in the specified internal subnet. Also determine their OSs and the services/applications that are remotely accessible. Scanning techniques that will evade detection by the Snort system will receive additional bonus points. | 20 minutes |
| 5 | Access the MySQL database on host SQL and obtain the content of the table Employees. | 20 minutes |
| 6 | Get interactive access to the MySQL server host. You have to be able to login with an account that is not root. | 20 minutes |
| 7 | Get root access to the MySQL server host. | 20 minutes |
| 8 | Modify the database table Employees, setting the account number of each employee to an account number of your choosing. | 10 minutes |
| 9 | Obtain access to the transaction service on host TRN. Schedule a paycheck payment that will transfer the employee paychecks to your account. | 30 minutes |

It was made very clear that the ultimate goal of the exercise was to perform a multi-step attack that was as realistic as possible. One of the lessons learned from previous exercises is that the data collected during these exercise is valuable both from the instructional and the research viewpoints. The traces collected in the previous exercises lacked an underlying "plan". That is, it was desirable to have traces of attacks that had a well-defined final goal. This is particularly useful for alert correlation purposes. Therefore, an important by-product of this exercise was the Tcpdump data, BSM data, Windows event logs, and Snare events collected on the networks and hosts used during the exercise. Combined with the truth files produced by the students, these traces are an invaluable resource for researchers in the field of intrusion detection and attack correlation [Lindskog et al., 1999].

## 5.1    Setup

In order to prevent the two teams from interfering with each other, two identical target networks were setup. The topology of the networks used in the exercise is shown in Figure 1. In the following, we describe a single target network.

The web server was placed on a DMZ network. The MySQL server (host SQL), the file server (host NFS), and the transaction server (host TRN) were placed on a separate network, accessible only by the web server host.

The web server was an Apache server, running as user apache, as per default installation. In addition to a fake corporation site, a number of broken CGI scripts were installed on the web server. One CGI script was vulnerable to a phf-style attack. Another CGI script contained information about how to log into the MySQL database, namely a clear text password. A program for checking the syntax of perl files was "erroneously" left around in the CGI directory. This program could be invoked through the web server. The program allowed one to view the source code of all the CGI scripts installed on the server, disclosing important information, such as embedded MySQL passwords.

The file server was configured to export the file system /home to the world. This is a security mistake often present in protected networks where security is more relaxed. In addition, the host NFS was configured to provide password files through NIS.

The MySQL server provided remote access to user dbuser with password bsecret. Note that by default MySQL allows local access to root without having to provide a password. The server mounted the /home file system from the file server.

The transaction server had a service running on port 7979. The transaction application was developed *ad hoc* for this exercise by the instructor.

When connecting to port 7979, the user was dropped into a simple shell application. Typing HELP would show a list of commands, one of which is PAYCHECK. The team was supposed to invoke that function to transfer all the employee paychecks to the attacker's account. That function required a password. The encrypted (but very guessable) password was stored in the password file distributed through NIS.

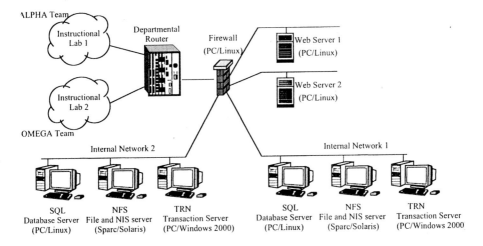

*Figure 1:* Treasure Hunt: Network setup

This setup required a considerable effort. I developed the web site, the code for the CGI scripts and some applications, and the SQL schema for the database with the help of the teaching assistants and some of my students. In addition, the networks had to be physically set up, and a whole set of services were created and configured on each network.

The setup of the exercise and the testing of the network configuration required two days of work for a team of four people.

## 5.2     Execution

The day of the exercise the two teams gathered in two separate (but nearby) instructional labs. The execution of the exercise included a first hour where the teams would prepare their tools and then the actual treasure hunt.

The students were extremely excited about this exercise. In this exercise there was no direct clash of teams. Therefore, there was no fear that a team could do something illegal to jeopardize the mission of the other team. By the same token, the exercise was structured as a race: the first to achieve a given task would get the most points. This motivated the students to organize their subteams effectively.

The exercise progressed seamlessly up to task seven, where one of the team wasn't able to complete the task and had to use a cheat sheet. The same team also had significant problems in performing the final task and needed to be helped (so that the exercise could finish). These difficulties were due to the way the teams were created. The Alpha Team was composed of students whose last names were between A and I, while the Omega Team was composed of students whose last names were between J and Z. This division didn't take into account the skills of the individual students, and by chance the most skillful students ended in the Alpha Team.

## 5.3     Lessons Learned

- Setting up separate targets for the two teams and having them race against each other is a very good way to foster competition without having to deal with the less pleasurable aspects of a direct clash between the teams.
- Building balanced teams is important. It promotes a fair and interesting exercise, and at the same time it supports the morale of the students by letting them know that there is not a "best" team.
- Collecting traces of all the actions performed by the students is important. This activity should not be limited to network traffic, but it should also include host-based audit trails (e.g., Windows events).
- It is important to educate the students to create *good* truth files. These are extremely useful to identify the attacks within the logs.
- This type of exercise requires twice the effort needed to set up exercises like those described in Section 3 and 4.

## 6.      RELATED WORK

The use of hands-on experience in labs is obviously not new. Testbed networks are often used to provide root-level access to students. A different approach is used by a class taught in Stanford [Boneh, 2002] where students can experiment with their techniques on isolated virtual machines. While this approach gives a reasonably precise idea of the working of security attacks, it is different from the "real thing." Only a testbed network can provide a realistic environment.

Even though hands-on experience is advocated by many, there are few graduate and undergraduate courses on computer security that offer live exercises as part of the course. For example, Georgia Tech offers a class [Santos, 2002] where a team has to install a number of services on a Windows host and another team has to perform attacks. In this case, each of the two phases, preparation and attack, lasts a couple of weeks. As another example George Washington University offers a class [Daniel, 2002] that includes the creation of honeypots and some sort of team-based interaction.

In general, live exercises are difficult to organize and conduct, and, therefore, instructors generally prefer other types of educational tools, which are less expensive in terms of time and hardware/software resources. We believe that our experience, especially the adoption of the treasure hunt exercise is rather unique.

## 7. CONCLUSIONS

Live exercises are an important instructional tool in teaching the practical aspects of network security. They motivate the students to give their best because of the competitive nature of the exercise, and because their success is heavily determined by the students' creativity.

Live exercises are also extremely difficult to organize, manage, and execute. They require detailed preparation, and since they are executed in a short time span, if something goes wrong it is difficult to solve problems within such tight schedule.

This paper described the live exercises that have been designed and executed as part of a graduate level course on network security and intrusion detection. The class has a successful history of attendance (the maximum allowed is 40, but classes ranged between 50 and 90). The success of the class is also determined by the use of live exercises. The student feedback was overwhelmingly positive. Some of the students that took a previous edition of the class even came to observe the live exercises of other editions.

This class has received some attention by other instructors. The class materials have always been online and have been used in other courses (with permission of the instructor). In addition, the by-products of the class attracted the interest of research groups. We are currently preparing a web site to distribute the traces collected during the different exercises, in addition to the course material. We hope that this effort will allow other courses to use our experience to build similar live exercises.

## REFERENCES

[Bishop, 1997] Bishop, M. (1997). The State of INFOSEC Education in Academia: Present and Future Directions. In Proceedings of the National Colloquium on Information System Security Education, pages 19–33. Keynote address.

[Bishop, 1999] Bishop, M. (1999). What Do We Mean By "Computer Security Education"? In Proceedings of the 22nd National Information Systems Security Conference.

[Bishop, 2000] Bishop, M. (2000). Academia and Education in Information Security: Four Years Later. In Proceedings of the Fourth National Colloquium on Information System Security Education.

[Boneh, 2002] Boneh, D. (2002). CS155: Computer and Network Security. Stanford University.

[Curry and Debar, 2002] Curry, D. and Debar, H. (2002). Intrusion Detection Message Exchange Format: Extensible Markup Language (XML) Document Type Definition. draft-ietf-idwg-idmef-xml-09.txt.

[Daniel, 2002] Daniel, R. (2002). ECE 297 - Special Topics. Network Security: Honeypots. The George Washington University, School of Engineering and Applied Science, Department of Electrical and Computer Engineering.

[Lindskog et al., 1999] Lindskog, S., Lindqvist, U., and Jonsson, E. (1999). IT Security Research and Education in Synergy. In *Proceedings of the First World Conference on Information Security Education (WISE1)*, pages 147--162, Kista, Sweden.

[Santos, 2002] Santos, A.D. (2002). CS6265 Information Security Lab. Department of Computer Science, College of Computing, Georgia Tech.

# INFORMATION WARFARE IN THE TRENCHES
*Experiences from the Firing Range*

Scott D. Lathrop, Gregory J. Conti, and Daniel J. Ragsdale
*U.S. Military Academy, West Point, NY 10996*

**Abstract:**    With the increased potential of a bona fide cyber terrorist attack and the possibility of a future "war in the wires", we must continue to improve the education and training of individuals responsible for defending our national borders—whether those borders are physical or electronic. The Information Analysis and Research (IWAR) laboratory at the United States Military Academy (USMA) has proven to be an exceptional resource for such an education for our cadets and faculty studying information warfare and information assurance. The laboratory has also been successful in motivating the need for continued education and training in this area on a much larger scope. This paper justifies why information warfare laboratories are necessary, describes the phenomenon that is occurring as a result of the IWAR lab, explains the current configuration, and presents lessons learned that others might use in designing an Information Warfare laboratory. While this paper has a military context, the results apply to any university, corporation, or non-profit organization desiring to increase awareness and improve education in the area of information warfare

**Key words:**    Information warfare, information assurance, education, educational laboratories

## 1.    INTRODUCTION

Two years ago, the Information Technology and Operations Center developed the initial Information Warfare Analysis and Research (IWAR) laboratory to support undergraduate education and faculty research in Information Assurance (IA) at the United States Military Academy (USMA). Since that time, it has matured into a much larger and robust laboratory. What began as a single, isolated network has matured into three separate networks and a library. Each component has a distinct purpose but all are aimed at furthering education in Information Assurance at USMA and throughout the IA community. With the increase in size and scope of the laboratory, technical and social issues in manageability have risen.

The original purpose of the IWAR laboratory focused on providing an isolated laboratory where students enrolled in our Information Assurance course could familiarize themselves with various known computer security exploits and employ technical measures to defend their network against such exploits. Additionally, the laboratory provided a facility for faculty members to conduct research in Information Assurance. [1] Currently, the laboratory serves not only the Information Assurance course which is limited to computer science and electrical engineering majors, but also provides a "clubhouse" atmosphere for our ACM SIGSAC student chapter; supports the annual CyberDefense Exercise (CDX) conducted with the other military institutions of higher learning and in conjunction with the NSA penetration teams, the 1$^{st}$ Information Operations Command, and the Air Force 92d Information Warfare Squadron [2]; is used as a focal point for congressional, academic, military, and other visitors interested in observing or replicating our work; and is used for information warfare demonstrations during a once-per-semester "Tech tour" for the freshman students. The purpose of this demonstration is to motivate the plebes to take advantage of the laboratory and IA course while they are at West Point.

There are several other courses at USMA that use the laboratory in addition to the computer science-based, Information Assurance course. Almost every CS course uses the laboratory for computer security related lessons. A political science course entitled, "The Policy and Strategy of Cyberwar" uses the IWAR laboratory exclusively as their classroom in order to demonstrate the technologies that common hackers and cyber-terrorists use to gain access to computing resources and then to relate those experience to strategic level policy issues. The Cyber Policy course includes hands-on exercises where the students build viruses, worms, and malicious applets. The "Cyber Law" course uses the laboratory for a lesson to give pre-law students an appreciation of the tactics and techniques used by cyber-criminals. Finally, the IWAR laboratory provides faculty with a facility to learn about emerging information warfare. Computing infrastructure upgrades and initiatives often begin in the IWAR laboratory before inflicting them on the user base. For example, the laboratory has been used to install a Windows 2000 Active Directory infrastructure before deploying it on a larger scale. It has been also used to familiarize, test, and validate wireless security solutions prior to decisions being made on whether or not to install a wireless network. What was originally designed primarily for a single undergraduate class has blossomed into an institution-wide resource, but with that has come additional administrative overhead and technical requirements.

The intention of this paper is to provide an overview of the current state of the laboratory, the methodology used to obtain this condition, impart lessons learned to managing the increased overhead of others considering such an endeavor, and discuss future improvements.

## 2.      BACKGROUND AND MOTIVATION

It can be argued that education in information warfare is paramount for the students at the United States Military Academy and the other military institutions of higher learning. Nearly a year ago, the Secretary of Defense summarized a long-standing national discussion when he stated that our dependency on information networks makes attractive targets for new forms of cyber attack. [3] In the recent Department of Defense Report to Congress, the assertion was made that "In the future, the network will be the single most important contributor to combat". Furthermore, the report asserted the *information domain* must be protected and defended in order to generate and sustain combat power in the face of offensive actions taken by an adversary.[4] With the military's increased reliance on information systems coupled with the cyber-coordinated events of September 11th 2001, the reasons for educating our students in information warfare are readily apparent.

Current systems being developed by the Army depend on this network-centric warfare concept. For example, Land Warrior is a wireless networked system of computers. Each infantry solider in a 30-soldier platoon wears a personal computing device that communicates with other soldiers in the platoon through a wireless local area network (LAN). The system enables the exchange of terrain, enemy, and friendly information; digital maps; operations orders; and e-mail messages between the soldiers in order to facilitate information dominance.[5] [6] Such systems also are to provide a "just-in-time" logistics framework, enabling supplies such as ammunition and food to be pushed forward as the information indicating a logistics shortfall is autonomously sent to the supply forces. These systems will connect into the Army's tactical Internet. Without technically savvy soldiers and an information structure designed to protect and defend these critical assets, the Army's reliance on information dominance is a fragile one.

Consider the fact that the Code Red worm infected more than 250,000 systems in approximately nine hours on July 19, 2001.[7] Had even one percent of those computer systems been military end systems such as Land Warrior, rather than commercial or home-based computers, the effects would have been to cripple the unit's reliance on such systems—infrastructures which our doctrine advocates as being a combat multiplier by increasing situational awareness (that is the ability to spatially and temporally know where the enemy is and where friendly units are). If such systems are denied service, or worse compromised, then clearly information dominance is no longer established. The future of the military's information dominance on the battlefield hinges on the security of the networked information systems providing the necessary services—thus, the increased requirement that future officers educated at the military institutions of higher learning become aware of such issues and their potential solutions.

The issues in assuring our information are much larger than just what the military foresees. Our nation's critical infrastructures and economic structure are becoming increasingly reliant on information systems and the Internet that provides connectivity between such systems. Addressing these issues requires an education in information warfare that does not merely theorize and describes such concepts. A hands-on, *active learning* experience entails that we provide an environment where students, employees, and anyone managing or administrating information systems can apply theoretical concepts in an isolated environment [8]. Such an environment allows the unleashing of viruses, worms, and Trojan horses so as not to have an effect on a production network. Kaucher and Saunders found that even for management-oriented graduate courses in Information Assurance, a hands-on, laboratory experience enhances the students understanding of theoretical concepts [9]. The above reasons justified the original creation of the IWAR laboratory and validate continued expansion and improvements to the laboratory.

Recent success in the Cyber Defense Exercise and the educated, yet tough, information assurance questions coming from our former students further justify the usage and improvements to the IWAR laboratory. Our Cyber Defense team showed vast improvement between the first and second years of the competition. The Cyber Defense Exercise (CDX) is an annual competition between the United States Military, Naval, Air Force, Merchant Marine, and Coast Guard Academies. At USMA, the competition serves as the final project for senior-level computer science majors enrolled in the Information Assurance (IA) course. Participating students are required to design, implement, configure, and secure a network of computers. Required services are determined by the exercise's operation's order and allowed red team attacks are controlled by a set of rules. After verifying all services are running, the students must secure that network using open source tools. Each school's network is then attacked by members of the NSA's red team, the Army's 1$^{st}$ Information Operations Command, and the Air Force's 92d Information Warfare Aggressor squadron while the students attempt to maintain the required services; prevent and detect attacks; and then recover and restore any loss of information or services.

The main goal of the CDX is to reinforce the knowledge that students have acquired in academic courses addressing the protection and defense of information systems. To take part in the exercise, the participating students are required to design and implement a security plan for a network comprised of various operating systems, services, and applications. Their plans must address the issue of maintaining confidentiality, integrity, availability, and authentication of all services and resources. The National Security Agency's Director of Information Assurance sponsors the event and awards a trophy to the school with the best overall showing in the competition. The trophy is a traveling award that resides at the winning school for a given year.

In the first CyberDefense exercise, our students struggled to maintain services and provide security simultaneously. Much of their effort was aimed at maintaining the required services leaving little time for analysis and improvements in their defensive plan. [2] In the recently completed 2002 CyberDefense exercise, the students not only maintained the majority of the required services throughout the exercise, but also had a very high success rate in defending their network from the red team. Not only did they secure the network with the tools and technologies learned during their course work, but they also were able to explore various other security options such as Bastille Linux, one-way Ethernet cables for intrusion detection systems, and *honeypots*. A majority of their success is due to the fact that both students and faculty had access to a facility such as the IWAR laboratory and even more of an opportunity to work with the various technologies such as firewalls, vulnerability scanners, system integrity tools, and intrusion detection systems that are required to defend such a network.

Another recent example, which validates the continued usage and improvements to the IWAR laboratory, are the experiences a former student, now an Army second lieutenant, had when attempting to determine a technical solution to a typical information assurance issue in determining the appropriate balance between service and security. The problem the lieutenant was trying to solve was providing access to .mil sites from IP addresses originating from within the Republic of Korea (ROK). Soldiers in the lieutenant's organization were attempting to take continuing education courses offered on-line through the Army's .mil portal. However, the soldiers could not access the sites through their ASDL and cable modem connections from their homes located off Army installations. The problem had existed since the September 11th, 2001 attack on the World Trade Center, when the Army decided to block access to all .mil sites from IP addresses originating from within the Republic of Korea and from several other foreign countries. Therefore, soldiers could only take the online courses from computers, which were on a military installation. The security solution imposed by the Army defeated the purpose of after-hours education for those soldiers living off an Army installation in any oversea location. [10]

The lieutenant, based on his experiences in the IA course and specifically, in the IWAR laboratory, realized that technical solutions should exist (VPN, PKI, proxy servers, etc) that would both provide soldiers with access to .mil URLs while simultaneously protecting the Army servers in Korea. The lieutenant fielded the question with a proposed, well-informed solution to the USMA IA faculty and Computer Emergency Response Team (CERT) who made minor changes to the lieutenant's solution and then proposed an Army-wide recommendation for overseas units.

Such examples highlight that the experiences learned in the IWAR laboratory directly translate to solutions in real world applications. The IWAR laboratory component of the IA educational program at West Point provides a much richer experience for students than what classroom instruction alone could provide.

## 3.    RELATED WORK

Primarily due to the increasing importance of IA education, many colleges and universities are beginning to invest resources towards the construction of information security laboratories. [9, 11, 12] Others have been looking at using simulation-based tools to educate their students. [13] To the best of our knowledge, no one has attempted to design and implement a laboratory on the scale or complexity currently exhibited by the IWAR laboratory. Others have created laboratories, primarily to serve different purposes, but none have the similar heterogeneous nature or scale that the IWAR demonstrates.

Kaucher and Saunders describe an Information Assurance laboratory that they use at the National Defense University for educating information assurance and information security professionals. Their network serves a different purpose and thus does not need to be the same scale or complexity as we have built into the IWAR laboratory. Similar characteristics include a heterogeneous network. One of the unique features of their network is that they expose the entire network to their students. This works well for their particular situation, as their students often need to see the entire network to "demystify the technology." [9] However, for this particular application major portions of the network are not revealed to the computer science and electrical engineering majors taking the IA course. This forces students to conduct reconnaissance using port scanners and similar tools. Exposing the network might be a better idea for Cyber Policy and Cyber Law courses, but the administrative overhead to perform such a task makes it unfeasible.

Others have taken heterogeneous networking to another level by implementing different layer 2 architectures such as Ethernet, Asynchronous Transfer Mode (ATM), and Fiber Distributed Data Interface (FDDI) on a token ring. [12] Their network design is different from ours in that they are using it more for system modeling and simulation, networking, and special projects rather than information warfare. The scope of their network is also much smaller and where our heterogeneous nature consists of multiple operating systems and services, their heterogeneous flavor is a result of different link layer protocols. Some similarities also exist, however. We have begun establishing a wireless network using the 802.11b protocol in order to further investigate the security issues surrounding this wireless protocol.

Yasinsac describes a computer security laboratory project for outreach, research, and education. Their laboratory serves a similar purpose as the IWAR laboratory but on a smaller scale. Similar to the IWAR laboratory, they have been challenged to provide an environment where students are free to explore without creating administratively challenging headaches when systems break because of the use of certain tools. One of their solutions is to use a virtual machine software wrapper created by Vmware. [11] We also use Vmware but more so to provide a heterogeneous environment of operating systems rather than to control computer configuration. We control the configuration by re-imaging the systems or swapping hard drives when a student has applied a technology that causes unrecoverable damage. We place certain machines in an "administrative" mode and specify that these machines are off-limits. While this approach has worked thus far, we realize that in future years we may have to impose further constraints. However, we encourage our students and researchers to attack the various servers that exist in our laboratory.

Others have begun designing or looking at simulation based-tools to educate others in IA. However, to the best of our knowledge, many tools exist that model networks, but no tool exists that accurately models the specific decisions that must be made to simulate an IA education. [14]

The implementation and maintenance of an IWAR type laboratory requires significant investments in terms of hardware, software, and human resources to build and maintain the physical networks of computers and communication components. This is not a unique problem. We agree that a tool or model that can be used by students to assess the quality of their information system design choices prior to (or instead of) a physical implementation is required in an IA education. Simulations also allow the proposed network to be tested by a larger variety of conditions and attacks than would be feasible with a real network. There may also be a number of attacks that are too dangerous to perform on the real system. [13] As is true in military training exercises however, simulation-based tools will always complement, rather than replace a hands-on "live-fire" experience.

## 4.      LABORATORY ORGANIZATION

The design goals for the IWAR laboratory were that it consist of heterogeneous operating systems, networking equipment, defensive security tools, and offensive exploits; contain "soft" and "hard" targets; be large enough to provide a real world signature; and be robust enough to withstand the attacks from students and faculty—that is we wanted to make the laboratory conducive to exploitation experiments without creating a lot of administrative overhead in repairing the network. We selected open-source security tools to allow students to "look under the hood" and identify what each tool is doing. Our requirements were that we have a facility for the IA course and other IA-related courses, a network for the CyberDefense competition, a network for our ACM SIGSAC student chapter, dedicated browsers where users could locate and download exploits posted to hacker websites, and the reference material necessary to build and maintain the laboratory. What evolved were four separate networks: (1) The IA network, (2) the CyberDefense network, (3) the SIGSAC network, and (4) a small "search box" network. Additionally, we began building an IWAR library with reference material gathered during the re-design of the current laboratory.

The remainder of this section will focus on each component separately with emphasis being placed on the IA network.

## 4.1      Information Assurance Network

The Information Assurance (IA) network is the original IWAR laboratory as cited by Schafer.[1] Its primary purpose is to provide a facility for course instruction and hands-on exercises for our Information Assurance course taught in the spring semester each year. Secondary purposes include using the laboratory as the primary classroom for the Social Science's course on "The Policy and Strategy of Cyberwar," provide a resource for other CS courses to use in order to demonstrate information warfare principles, and using the facility to display and provide demonstrations to our many guests from outside of USMA.

The IA network is a completely isolated network that we often compare to a firing range. The Army uses firing ranges to train soldiers on individual weapons and firing systems. Likewise, the IA laboratory is a range where students and faculty may use and experiment with port scanners, vulnerability scanners, Trojan horses, worms, and viruses without running the risk of releasing malicious code onto our production network or into the "wild". Just as a solider would only fire a weapon on the range or in combat, the IA network policy only permits users to use the malicious tools in the controlled confines of the laboratory.

Malicious software that exploits system vulnerabilities is installed on select systems within the laboratory, allowing students and faculty to learn about, and experiment with, the capabilities of potential adversaries. Through experimentation with malicious software, users gain an appreciation of the numerous vulnerabilities existing in currently deployed information systems. With this knowledge IWAR laboratory users are better equipped to protect and defend the information and information systems for which they are, or will be, responsible.

Since the original publication of the IA network, it has been re-designed and refurbished with new equipment. The current configuration is shown in Figure 1. Including the virtual machines, there are approximately 200 nodes in this *isolated* network. The current network consists of two primary LAN segments based on USMA's school colors. The *black* segment contains the classroom machines, "soft" server targets, and a few administrative machines. The *gold* segment, separated from the *black* network by a router and a firewall, consists of a few administrative machines and several "hard" targets. "Soft" targets are computers that have a default operating system installation and configuration with no patches applied. The only "hardening" that has been done to these machines is to insure that all local and domain administrative passwords are strong. Otherwise, the systems are wide open. The "hard" targets are harden using the SANS and NSA guides and applying the current patches to the operating systems.

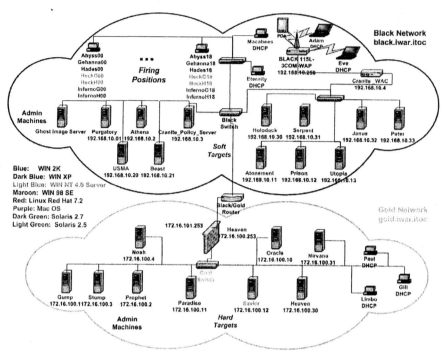

*Figure 1*: IA Network

The *black* network serves as the laboratory's "LAN" while the *gold* network attempts to portray the remaining *Internet* from the perspective of the users on the *black* network. The majority of the *black network* is contained in our IA classroom and consists of the 19 classroom computers (18 for students and one for the instructor), which we refer to as the "firing positions". These computers are the systems from which students may launch offensive exploits against the soft or hard targets that are arrayed throughout the network. Each of the 19 classroom computers is a DTK 733 MHz Intel Pentium with a 750 MB swappable hard drive. The systems contain a standard classroom image consisting of a Windows 2000 Server as the base operating system and VMware 3.0 installed on each machines. VMware is a virtual machine software solution that allows one to run multiple operating systems on one personal computer. By simply switching between windows, the user can switch between host operating systems. The VMware software isolates each virtual machine from the others (including the base operating system). This separation prevents an improper configuration in one system from affecting another virtual machine. VMware allows users to install and configure Windows 2000, Windows XP, Windows NT, and Linux operating systems. Each virtual machine has a unique IP address and a full complement of hardware devices. In our IA network, each virtual machine is registered as an individual node on the *black* network. Additionally, one can establish a "virtual network" between the virtual machines residing on the same computer. [15] We found VMware to be particularly useful in teaching the students both offensive and defensive operations.

Including the virtual machines, each classroom computer effectively has eight machines (Figure 2). Individuals with accounts on these machines have administrative privileges on all the virtual machines on that particular computer. Windows 2000 Server is the base operating system with one Windows XP and Windows 98 virtual machines. We also installed two Windows NT4.0 Servers and two Red Hat Linux 7.2 virtual machines. There are two of these operating systems in order to allow students in each of our two sections to have their own virtual computer with this type of operating system. Finally, we have an additional Red Hat Linux 7.2 virtual machine that we use as a machine on another "external network". This configuration allows gives each student a "virtual network" on their machine and provides some flexibility and creativity for the instructors and the students (Figure 2).

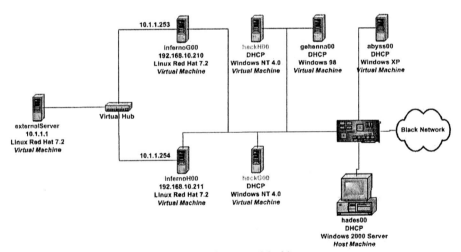

*Figure 2:* Classroom Machine

For example, a student may want to test an exploit against an IIS 3.0 sever running on Windows NT. The individual can create the malicious virus, worm, or applet and launch it from their Linux virtual machine and target the IIS server running on their Windows NT virtual machine. The entire attack sequence is isolated to their classroom PC. Once the student has perfected their exploit, they can then attempt to target the "soft" and "hard" targets existing in the larger network. The virtual network configuration "exposes" a portion of the network, similar to Kaucher and Saunders idea. [9]

From a defensive perspective we have used the virtual machines' to demonstrate the concept of firewalls. The Linux virtual machine running on the "external" network portion serves as the outside world from which the student wants to protect their internal network. The internal network consists of the remaining virtual machines. The student can configure their Linux virtual machine as a firewall between these two networks. Using *ipchains*, a stateless packet-filtering firewall, we can demonstrate the advantages of a packet-filtering firewall. In order to show a stateful packet-filtering firewall we can then use *iptables*. Finally, in order to take the exercise to the final level, we can install a proxy server such as Squid on the student's Linux machine and demonstrate the firewall that separates the *black* and *gold* networks.

Other uses we have found for the virtual machines is using them in a hands-on laboratory where students install, configure, and then harden an operating system using a security checklist such as from SANS or the NSA. The virtual machines enable the student to perform these functions without having to worry about tampering with the base operating system's configuration.

The remainder of the *black* network is contained in a server room next to the classroom and contains six administrative machines, seven "soft" target servers, three additional workstations, and a small wireless network. Additional funding allowed us to purchase Dell Poweredge 1550 rack mountable servers to replace the desktop computers we originally used. Each server is a 1 GHz Intel Pentium processor with two, 8-GB hard drives. All of the servers except for the Solaris servers run on these machines in order to save space in our server room. The operating systems within the *black* network include Solaris 2.8, 2.7, and 2.5; Windows 2000 Advanced Server and Windows NT 4.0 Servers; Linux Red Hat 7.2 servers; and MAC OS 8 and MAC OS 9. Administrative machines include domain controllers, file servers, Samba servers, and a NIS server. Our "soft" targets currently include web servers, ftp servers, SNMP servers, telnet servers, Exchange 5.5 server, and several other wide-open, services without patches. The router currently has unnecessary services running such as an http server, telnet, and SNMP server.

We attempt to provide an "enterprise" appearance to the users of the network. For example, we have a two web servers running on the various machines. The course web page is on an Apache web server running on a Linux operating system and another web server is running on a Windows based Internet Information Server (IIS) 3.0 server. The Exchange Server is used not only for email within the IA network, but also as a "soft" target. Other services are added as required by the instructors, students, or other users of the laboratory. Finally, there are three additional workstations. One is identical to the classroom computers and is used primarily by instructors during class preparation. The other two workstations are Macintosh computers used as other potential targets that can be used as a launching pad for other attacks.

The *black* network also has an IEEE 802.11b wireless basic service set (BSS) infrastructure. The wireless network is tied into the *black* network with a wireless access point. Currently there are two laptops with wireless cards and a personal digital assistant (PDA) device with a wireless card used in the network. Primarily used for familiarization and research, we plan on incorporating wireless security into our IA curriculum. We are also using the wireless network to evaluate current wireless security solutions such as the Cranite Systems' Wireless Wall™ architecture.

The *gold* network is contained entirely in the server room. It consists of five administrative machines and seven "hard" targets. It is similar in setup to the servers running on the *black* network except that the machines are configured with the most recent patches and hardened using the NSA and SANS security checklists. Services similar to those in the *black* network are running with the exception of improved, more secure services running where applicable. For example, instead of running NIS, the *gold* network runs NIS+. The IIS Server 5.0 is running and configured with the latest patches rather than IIS 3.0 or 4.0. Additionally, the *gold* network sits behind a Solaris based firewall product in order to provide increase security. The *gold* network is where small groups of students and faculty working on research projects normally operate because of the added security and less risk of losing their work. However, everyone understands to back up their work and store any important files on the file server that is off limits. For example, we have a group of students working on plug-ins and a Java based client for the Nessus vulnerability scanner. Their work is currently stored on the *gold* network. This gives the laboratory a "real-world" look-and-feel and also provides the individuals working on their projects some additional security. However, all users understand that any node in the laboratory is subject to an attack. Therefore, most computers are configured with a zip disk in order to provide an additional storage method for backing up work.

## 4.2    CyberDefense Network

The CyberDefense network supports the CyberDefense exercise as described in Section II. The CyberDefense network serves as the initial configuration for the CyberDefense exercise. Each school's networks are connected via a VPN to the red team and white cell's observers. This configuration allows the red team to attack each network without fear of repercussions from a stray attack, and allows the white cell evaluators to

verify that required services are running and observe the actions of each of
the schools respective teams. Each year the configuration is changed based
on the students' design within the constraints of that year's exercise
guidance.

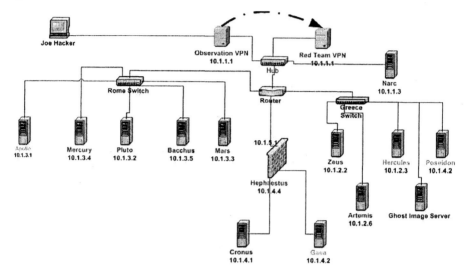

*Figure 3:* CyberDefense Network

The design philosophy of the CDX network is similar to the IA network,
but on a much smaller, more manageable scale. The network is designed to
have heterogeneous operating systems provide services such that an outside
observer would view it as a real-world environment. Unlike the IA network,
however, the students implementing the CyberDefense network wish to
make it secure as possible—thus there are no explicit "soft" targets.

The CyberDefense network consists of platforms running Sun Solaris
8.0, Red Hat Linux 7.2, Windows 2000, and Windows NT 4.0 operating
systems. Internet access is allowed through the VPN for downloading the
latest patches and software updates; however, students are not allowed to
purchase any additional software in order to implement their defense. The
network systems are configured to provide various services such as: web
servers, database servers, file servers, e-mail servers, and the normal
contingent of network utilities.

During the preparation phase of the exercise, students harden the systems
using the SANS and NSA security checklists. They also use a variety of
open-source port scanners, vulnerability scanners, network monitoring tools,
intrusion detection, and host-based and network-based firewalls in order to
establish a defense-in-depth and defense-in-breadth posture. For example, in
the recently completed exercise, the students established an intrusion

detection system using Snort running on a Linux machine. In order to prevent traffic from leaving their network interface card, they built a one-way Ethernet cable that allowed only one-way traffic into their intrusion detection machine, aptly named *Narc*.

The intent of the exercise is to force the students to pull together what they know theoretically and from what they learned using the IA network and apply it to a real network, under attack, in an environment in which mistakes will not cause catastrophic loss of life or information.

Responses to attacks were limited to network reconfiguration. Offensive operations were limited to the Red Team only, and social engineering by either the attackers or defenders is not allowed. Social engineering is a major threat that we face in information assurance; however, it would have introduced undesirable complexity to the CDX without corresponding benefits. As you might imagine in an undertaking of this complexity, the execution of the Cyber Defend Exercise involved a number of lessons learned for future iterations.

## 4.3     SIGSAC Network

The SIGSAC network supports USMA's Special Interest Group for Security, Auditing, and Control (see figure 3.). Designed and built in 2002 by members of SIGSAC, the network, otherwise known as the SIGSAC "clubhouse" supports the group of over 300 members by providing an isolated network of computers from which members of the club may learn and explore both offensive and defensive tools used in cyber warfare. The network equipment co-exists with the CyberDefense Network in order to take advantage of the most recent information technology available to students at West Point. Additionally, the co-location of the two networks facilitates the exchange of ideas between the current CyberDefense team and the future Cyberdefenders that are currently involved in the SIGSAC club. Members of the club learn about the threat of information warfare and how to defend against it--having fun in the process. It is not a hacking clubhouse, per se, although students have the opportunity to learn and apply hacking type tools in an isolated environment.

The advantages to having a network specifically set aside for our SIGSAC club is that it allows them to experiment with offensive and defensive tools, again, in an isolated network without the concern of interfering with our IA classes. Since the individuals using the SIGSAC network are generally less experienced, they work on a smaller network separate from the IA network, minimizing the risk due to a mistake and minimizing the time to rebuild. At a minimum the laboratory provides them with a resource where they can "play" on a network with administrator privileges--something unlikely in a traditional university setting.

Currently, the SIGSAC network consists of seven computers interconnected by a hub. It is also a heterogeneous network with two Windows 2000 servers, and two Windows 2000 workstations, one Windows NT4.0 server, and one Red Hat Linux 7.2 server. The computers share the keyboard, mouse, and monitor with the computers in the CyberDefense network through a KVM (Keyboard, Video, Mouse) switch.

## 4.4    IWAR Library

The final component to the IWAR laboratory is one that we began building slowly, but over time has evolved into a significant resource for our students and faculty. The library provides reference material for faculty to use in their classes, for students to use throughout their various IA course and in the CyberDefense exercise, and most importantly by our SIGSAC student members excited to learn about information warfare. We found that as we built the various networks and installed various services, often times it was useful to have a book explaining, in detail, what it was we were trying to configure. As we acquired books over the past few years, we began receiving requests from students and faculty alike to borrow the references. The library was organized and is currently maintained by members of our SIGSAC club. They are currently building an on-line checkout system for the library.

## 5.    LESSONS LEARNED

There were numerous lessons learned from the creation of the IWAR laboratory. At a larger scale, we found that (1) following an engineering design process, (2) limiting the networks to their specific purpose(s), (3) developing a viable recovery plan, (4) creating a policy, and (5) delegating responsibility to individuals or groups were keys to our success.

As computer scientists, we are trained in engineering thought process, but often times fail to follow such a procedure whether it be creating software or building a laboratory of networks. In the IWAR project we often times began moving equipment, cabling, and software services from machine to machine without thinking of the consequences. Only after sitting down and insuring that we understood the requirements and what functionality we desired, did a design and implementation succeed.

The first step is to understand what your requirements and desired functionality are. We realized that we wanted a network for educational purposes, for our CyberDefense exercise and for the use of our SIGSAC club so the original idea of three separate networks was readily apparent. However, the hardware and software resources were not readily available and had to be acquired over time using "unwanted", older systems, and eventually through acquisition of new systems. The funding for these new systems came only after we were able to demonstrate the potential for the IWAR laboratory and exercises such as the CyberDefense exercise.

The modular design of four separate networks provides us with the flexibility to combine networks, if we determine it would be beneficial in the future. Domain names and IP addresses were carefully chosen so as not to have conflicting namespace issues. If for example, we decide to create a mini-CyberDefense exercise with our SIGSAC club members, we could combine the SIGSAC network and all or portions of the IA network (for example the *gold* network) through either a CAT-V cable or wireless connection. The design of the IWAR laboratory's networks tried to anticipate such future requirements.

Determining requirements also involves how you want your network to appear to the general user, what operating systems and services you wish to provide, and at what level of security. A conscious decision has to be made about where to emplace those services and the administrative burden that you place on the faculty maintaining those systems when a service breaks. There is a point where the number of services to install, configure, and then maintain becomes unmanageable. One has to decide this breaking point based on the number of qualified administrators and faculty you have at your particular location.

Once you have decided on the requirements and functionality you can then design the network. Drawing the network on paper and using a chart to manage the nodes provides a good starting point for your design. An example network node chart is shown in table 1.

*Table 1:* Network Nodes

| NAME | SERVICES | HARDWARE | OS VERSION | IP ADDRESS |
|------|----------|----------|------------|------------|
| Purgatory | Domain Controller | DELL PowerEdge 1550 | Windows 2000 Server | 192.168.10.1 |
| Athena | File Server | DELL PowerEdge 1550 | Windows 2000 Server | 192.168.10.2 |
| Beast | SSH, FTP Server | Sparc LX | Solaris 2.7 | 192.168.10.21 |
| Atonement | Web Server | DELL PowerEdge 1550 | Linux Red Hat 7.2 | 192.168.10.11 |

After finalizing the design, it is essential to discuss its features with those who will implement it. In our case, we were able to leverage the knowledge of the staff and faculty in the USMA Department of Electrical Engineering and Computer Science. In particular, we exploited their knowledge of UNIX and Windows system administrators in installing, configuring, and "hardening" of operating systems and various services. After working together with the administrators, one becomes proficient enough to venture into the systems in more depth. Finally, when building the network, as in any design project, manage it in an incremental fashion.

Developing a viable restore and recovery plan is vital to the long-term maintenance of networks such as the IA network and the CyberDefense network. Although we have not reached our goals in this area we have a plan to implement some of our ideas. Currently, in the IA laboratory, prior to the beginning of the semester, we ghost each of the classroom images and keep an archive on a removable hard disk. Furthermore, we use a disk duplicator device to make backup copies of the master classroom image. When an IA classroom machine crashes we can simply swap the hard drives with a fresh image and manually enter a few configuration changes (IP address, machine names, etc.). Ultimately, we would prefer to have this capability for the *black* and *gold* network servers also. Currently, if one of these machines crashes we have to either troubleshoot the problem or reinstall the software. Neither course of action is suitable for our current operation.

During the CyberDefense exercise the students planned on ghosting their server images, but never put their plan into action. Consequently, when our

Microsoft Exchange 5.5 Sever crashed, we had to re-install not only the service, but also the underlying Windows NT 4.0 Server operating system. Another academy, on the other hand, successfully replicated their images prior to the start of the exercise so when they lost a service, they were able to efficiently re-image their servers.

A written and verbal policy must be created by a few with input from many. Our current policy is mainly communicated through verbal means and is gradually being recorded in written form with the creation of the IWAR laboratory user's guide and Standard Operating Procedures (SOP). Certain policies draw on our analogy to a live fire range. The range (i.e. IWAR laboratory) is used for training individuals on live fire weapons (i.e., offensive and defensive information tools). Individuals are not allowed to take their weapons off of the range.

Other policies address the administrative issues in the laboratory. Certain servers in the IA network are designated "administrative servers" and are off-limits to attack. Viruses, worms, and other exploits that are downloaded using the search boxes are stored on the zip disks and not allowed outside of the IWAR laboratory area. Finally, certain reference material is available for checkout and other is required to stay in the laboratory area. These policies are just the beginning of our user's guide but provide a baseline for general user behavior.

The final lesson learned is more of a leadership or management issue rather than a technical solution. However, delegating the work, following through with supervision and refinement of the delegated task, and then rewarding the individuals involved in the task pays enormous dividends and sets conditions for a successful experience. The IWAR laboratory reached its current state by the dream of a few individuals; the ideas of a few more persons; and the assistance and guidance from many parties. For example, the original vision of the laboratory was created by its original designers. [1] With a fresh crop of faculty and students with new ideas, purchasing of upgraded equipment, a new design, and assistance from the department's system administrators during implementation, the IWAR laboratory has evolved to its current configuration. The current CyberDefense network was designed and primarily implemented by a student working on an Advance Individual Study project. Finally, the library and SIGSAC network was built and organized predominantly by the SIGSAC student body members. Each individual or group was rewarded either through an Army award, a certificate, special priority on SIGSAC sponsored trips, or simply with a time honored pat on the back and public recognition.

## 6.    FUTURE WORK

The key to implementing future work is to make incremental changes and learn from their lessons. We plan to follow this approach as we continue to refine and improve the laboratory so that we continue to provide a quality IA education to our students and sustained research work for our Army.

One of the first issues we must address is the search box network. Because those workstations ultimately connect to our local area network and the Army's backbone, some "hacker" sites are often blocked. What we are proposing is the installation of a cable modem through a local Internet Service Provider along with a small honeynet on the far side of our firewall. This solution provides the students in our programs the ability to scan the Internet freely while still being constrained to a controlled environment. The search box computers will not be on our local area network and will continue to force the students to save downloaded exploits to their zip disks. Second, the honeynet will allow us to capture live attacks enabling us to use that information in the classroom and further our education on forensics analysis.[16] We would also like to add a few more workstations to this search box network to improve the availability for the students.

Our final issue for immediate improvements is to expand the SIGSAC network either by connecting it into the IA network or by adding more nodes to the existing network. Currently, the size of the network only allows a small number of students to work on the network. One way to add more nodes to the network would be to establish a wireless network with a few laptops as thin clients. Since real estate is an issue in the SIGSAC Clubhouse, the mobility provided by the laptops would provide us with more space and also enable us to expand our wireless networking infrastructure. The other alternative is to connect the SIGSAC network to the IA network in order to provide more targets for the club members.

## 7.    CONCLUSION

The IWAR laboratory began as a small experiment, but with continued visibility resulting in funding, the IWAR laboratory continues to grow. The justification for the laboratory is clear—in order to provide a quality Information Assurance education for our students, the hands-on experiences acquired using the laboratory's networks cannot be replaced by PowerPoint presentations or simulations.

Neither Rome nor an IWAR laboratory is built in a day. The influence that Rome had on Western civilization is well documented in history. The long-term influence that the IWAR laboratory will have on the education of students and faculty at the United States Military Academy remains to be determined, but initial signs indicate that the experiences observed in the laboratory will provide a positive impact on the future leaders of our country for years to come. These are the same individuals who will ultimately have to make critical decisions concerning the assurance of information.

# REFERENCES

1. J. Schafer, D. J. Ragsdale , J. R. Surdu, and C. A. Carver, "The IWAR range: a laboratory for undergraduate information assurance education," presented at Consortium for Computing in Small Colleges, Middlebury, Vermont, 2001.
2. D. W. Welch, D. J. Ragsdale, and W. Schepens, "Training for Information Assurance," IEEE Computer, pp. 2-9, 2002.
3. J. Garamone, "Capabilities, Strategy Must Converge to Face New Threats," http://www.defenselink.mil/news/Jun2001/n06222001_200106221.html, accessed on May 9, 2002.
4. Department of Defense Report to Congress, "Network Centric Warfare," http://www.c3i.osd.mil/NCW/, accessed on April 23, 2002.
5. J. Garamone, "Land Warrior Coming to a Grunt Near You," http://www.defenselink.mil/news/May2001/n05092001_200105094.html, accessed on April 15, 2002.
6. G. Blackwell, "802.11's in the Army Now," http://www.80211-planet.com/columns/article/0,4000,1781_1000821,00.html, accessed on April 15, 2002.
7. CERT/CC Advisory CA-2001-23, "Continued Threat of the "Code Red" Worm," http://www.cert.org/advisories/CA-2001-23.html, accessed on April 15, 2002.
8. R. M. Felder, "Reaching the Second Tie--Learning and Teaching Styles in College Science Education," Journal of College Science Teaching, vol. 23, pp. 286-290, 1993.
9. C. E. Kaucher and J. H. Saunders, "Building an information assurance laboratory for graduate-level education," presented at 6th National Colloquium for Information System Security Education, Redmond, WA, 2002.
10. M. Brakewood,"Question," email to D. J. Ragsdale, March 05, 2002.
11. A. Yasinsac, J. Frazier, and M. Bogdanov, "Developing an Academic Security Laboratory," presented at 6th National Colloquium for Information System Security Education, Redmond, WA, 2002.
12. G. A. Francia and R. K. Smith, "The Design and Implementation of a Heterogeneous Computer Networking Laboratory," presented at 6th National Colloquium for Information System Security Education, Redmond, WA, 2002.
13..J. H. Saunders, "Simulation Approaches in Information Security Education," presented at 6th National Colloquium for Information System Security Education, Redmond, WA, 2002.
14. C. A. J. Carver, J. R. Surdu, J. M. D. Hill, D. J. Ragsdale , S. D. Lathrop, and T. Presby, "Military Academy Attack/Defense Network," presented at 3rd Annual IEEE Information Assurance Workshop, West Point, NY, 2002.
15. VMware, VMware Workstation 3.0 User's Manual, 2001.
16. The Honeynet Project, Know Your Enemy Revealing the Security Tools, Tactics, and Motives of the Blackhat Community. Boston: Addison-Wesley, 2002.

# CHANGES IN THE PROFILE OF SECURITY MANAGERS

Teemupekka Virtanen
*Helsinki University of Technology, teemupekka.virtanen@hut.fi*

Abstract: Twelve years ago a development program for security managers was started in Finland. The first program was designed to fulfil the needs of a security manager in an organization. However, the content was an educated guess. During the second program, in 1993, we made a study on how security managers themselves feel the requirements of their work and which part of their work they felt difficult or easy. We were interested in what kind of education security managers would need. These results were used when the following programs were planned and some extra courses were introduced. However, these results were never really published. Now, we try to improve the development program for security managers again. We took the results of the old study and found out the current situation. We noticed that the requirements for a security manager have changed. The security managers have become a manager of a department instead of a single specialist. They do not need as deep specialized knowledge as nine years ago. Instead they need understanding of business processes and managerial skills. Another finding is that security manager is a long term career. Few security managers have proceeded to higher vacancies. Instead many of those security managers who participated the old study as a security manager are now retiring from that very same position.

Key words: security education, areas of security, requirements for security manager

## 1. INTRODUCTION

Security as a word has many different meaning and people understand it several different ways. Louise Yngström presented these questions (applied to information security) in her thesis (Yngstrom, 1996). She proposed a holistic approach and stated that security is not only collection of technical methods but a way to combine several areas into a system to produce a secure system. Another view is presented by Mikko T. Siponen (Siponen, 2000).

Security in general has the same problems. There are several different areas and it is sometimes difficult to combine security functions to the business processes. Perhaps due to this problem it has been difficult for security to find its place in the scientific world. Layne Hesse and Clifton L. Smith have presented some existing placements for security curricula at universities (Hesse and Smith, 2001}. According their study security is closely related to the crime prevention or the law enforcement curricula.

In Finland there has been a trend to take some duties from the governmental officers to the private companies. This far there has not been a need for an officially certified education for security professionals since there has been no special duties either. The guards have had in principle the same rights than any citizen have. The change requires a formal education for all levels of security professional and thus the university level education has to be defined properly (Virtanen, 2001).

In this paper we present some older results, which have been used when the development program for security managers was defined. We also present the current situation; what skills the education security managers think they need to manage their work.

## 2.      TEN YEARS AGO

Almost ten years ago we made a small study on background and knowledge of security managers in Finland. Since the results of the study was published only in Finnish (Virtanen, 1994) we introduce here the main results of the study.

*Figure 1.* The groups in the graphs

## 2.1     Background

The study was made in the end of 1993 and published 1994. It was part of the second development program for security managers. We were interested to find out which were the strong areas of security managers and which should have more lectures in the program.

We selected the participants of the two first development programs as a target group of our questionnaire. The practical reason was that those people were easily available and they were assumed to be willing to participate the study. However, there was another reason, too. These two development programs were the first higher level education on security in Finland. Thus the participants were extraordinary high level security managers. After the initial need was fulfilled there has been also lower level security professionals in these programs.

## 2.2    The Results

As background information we asked some general questions. Over 75% of people were over 40 years old and about 20% between 30 and 40. This was quite natural result since in these first development programs the participants were quite high level managers. About half of people had a university level degree when most of the others had polytechnics degree (now this level is a Bachelor's degree when the university level is a Master's degree). The biggest business areas were industry (35%), services (22%), defence (17%) and consulting (10%).

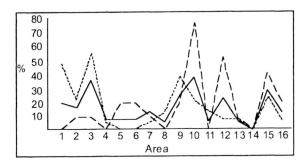

*Figure 2.* The most important duties

When we asked the main education areas we noticed that there were two areas which were much more common than the others. 42% of people had a technical and 31% a military background. The other groups were economics (10%), juristic (3%), police (7%) and others or no education (7%). We decided to concentrate on the two biggest groups: engineers and soldiers.

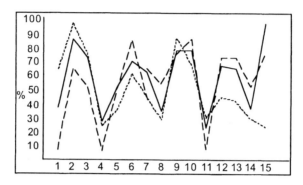

*Figure 3.* All duties

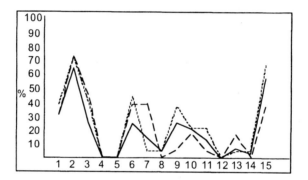

*Figure 4.* Easy duties

Figure 2 presents the most important areas of security according the answers (The different areas are listed in Table 1 and the groups are presented in Figure 1). In Figure 3 are all the areas which are part of people work. There are some natural explanation for the differences between engineers and soldiers. Most of the soldiers were working in the governmental organizations where were no products nor production.

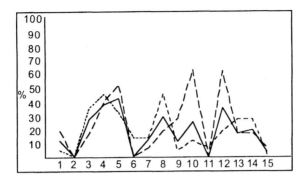

*Figure 5.* Difficult duties

There were no insurance in those organizations either. In the industry where most of the engineers were working were more technical staff and areas like continuance planning belonged to other than security managers.

*Table 1.* Security areas in the questionnaire

| Number | Area | Number | Area |
|---|---|---|---|
| 1 | Working safety | 9 | Fire and rescue |
| 2 | Access control | 10 | Personnel security |
| 3 | Risk management | 11 | Insurance |
| 4 | Product safety | 12 | Information security |
| 5 | Computer security | 13 | Security of transportation |
| 6 | Preparing for war | 14 | Environmental security |
| 7 | Continuance planning | 15 | Physical security |
| 8 | Environmental protection | | |

We asked also how people grade their expertise in these areas. In Figure 6 are the answers in scale 0 to 10. We also asked for easy areas (Figure 4) and difficult areas (Figure 5). The need for education is presented in Figure 7.

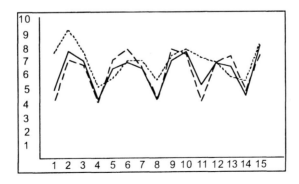

*Figure 6.* How people grade their expertise

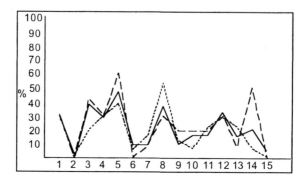

*Figure 7:* The need for more education

## 2.3     Discussion

These results present the situation almost ten years ago. In that time there were still many senior officers who didn't use computers at all. However, the process was already going on. Most of the employees at the offices already use personal computers even if the integration was not complete.

The computer security was something confusing. Also the meaning of information security was changing due to the computer-based systems. The security managers felt they need more information on these areas. There was also a competition that is responsible for these issues. There was a computer department in many organizations and conflicts between computer and security people were common.

The engineers and soldiers worked mainly in different types of organizations. The engineers worked in the industry and they typically had some background in the production. They were more familiar with safety in the working places and insurances than the soldiers who worked mainly in the administration.

## 3.     THE CURRENT SITUATION

In this section we describe the situation in the end of 2002.

## 3.1     Background

In this time we decided to use an interview instead of a questionnaire. We noticed that remarkably many of security managers are still in the same position as nine years ago. These questions were probably familiar to them and thus the interview might give better results.

This time the target group was selected more clearly among the managers than nine years ago. That time there were also some people from security related service providers or manufactures and insurance companies. This time we selected only security managers from public companies and central administration organizations.

We noticed that there were some changes happening. Several "old boys" either have just retired or will retire in the near future. The situation in this study is like it was in the end of 2002.

## 3.2    The Results

When considering security managers (leaving out insurance and security related companies) we notice that about 50% of the security managers are still the same as nine years ago. However, during last year there has been some changes and during the next year there will be several retirements.

In general the requirements for formal education is higher than earlier. The big companies require a Master's degree and smaller ones a Bachelor's degree for a security manager. There is only one self-made-man security manager who has changed a company during last year.

The background of security managers is almost the same as earlier. The percentage of engineer is the same but the number of military people has decreased. The number of lawyers has increased. However, the changes are small.

There are now two Masters of Security in Finland, one with background in engineering and other in military. The first is now working as a professor at the university (security) and the other as the chief security officer of the Finnish Defence Forces. Since Master of Security is not an official degree (yet) we have considered these according their original background.

The working areas of security managers have remain mostly the same. The risk management is a tool, which is now understood in more general way than nine years ago. In that time it means merely insurance management while it is now a general tool to manage risk and security. Thus the risk management is now part of every security manager's work.

The security managers of the new generation have higher formal education and they feel themselves more familiar with computers and information systems. In the same time the traditional guard-and-dog security is more difficult to manage for them. The older generation people manage computers in personal level but the information systems are not familiar. They have a long experience as a leader and manager but managing the new generation is sometimes difficult.

## 3.3      Discussion

The role of security managers has changed during last ten years. When the security manager was a single specialist with perhaps one assistant there is now often a security department with several people in many organizations. The role has changed from a specialist to a manager.

Nine years ago security managers felt they need more information in several security related areas. Now it is not so important any more since they have specialists of their own who managed these areas. Instead they need general managing skills and understanding of business management.

Ten years ago there was a great economic depression in Finland. However, that had no effect on computer departments since information processing was a way to improve efficiency. After another depression after the millennium this attitude has changed. Now computers are only one department among the others and as mortal as the others. Perhaps this has reduced conflicts between computer and security people.

When we compare this results with those Hesse and Smith have presented (Hesse and Smith, 2001), we noticed that there are several similarities. Our study concentrates on security managers while they have several different groups. Perhaps our nine years old results are more like their requirements for experts and our current results are more like their security managers.

These results suggest that we should continue the current education but target it more to the experts than managers. Perhaps we should introduce a security awareness program, like (Warren and Hutchinson, 2001). The security education should be part of normal curricula. In information security area there are such curricula (like (Katsikas, 1999) and (White et al., 1999)) but in security management there are a few curricula (Edith Cowan University, 2001}, (University of Leicester, 2001)).

## 4.      CONCLUSION

Nine years ago we study the background and personal capabilities of security managers in Finland and noticed that there were two main areas of education: engineering and military. Many of the security managers felt that they need more information in several security related areas.

Now the situation has changed. Security managers are more managers than specialists and they felt they need more experience in general management than in some specific areas. The changes in the background are small but we assume that there will be changes in that, too.

There will be more lawyers and economists in the future.

However, security seems to be a long career. Those who have entered this area have stayed there. There have been some movements between industry, insurance, services and education but the area has been the same. This means that it is difficult to get promotion since there is no step after the security manager. Those people who were security managers nine years ago are still in the same position.

# REFERENCES

Edith Cowan University (2001). Security Science, Postgraduate studies. PD-3236-04-01-1000, Australia, Edith Cowan University.

Hesse, L and Smith, C. L. (2001). Core curriculum in security science. In Armstrong, H., editor, *Proceedings of the 5th Australian Security Research Symposium*, pages 87 – 104, Australia, Edith Cowan University.

Katsikas, S. K. (1999). Academic curricula and curricula developments in Europe - The ERASMUS/SOCRATES Approach. In Yngströn, L. and Fischer-Hubner, S., editors, *WISE 1, Proceedings of the IFIP TC11 WG 11.8*, pages 3 – 17, Sweden, DSV.

Siponen, M. T. (2001). A paradigmatic analysis of conventional approaches for developing and managing secure IS. In Dupuy, M. and Paradinas, P., editors, *Trusted Information, The New Decade Challenge, pages 421 – 452, USA.* Kluwer Academic Publisher.

University of Leicester (2002). The Scarman Centre: excellence in the study and teaching of community safety, policing, criminology, security, risk and health & safety. GB.

Virtanen, T. (1994). Tutkimus turvallisuusjohtajan ominaisuuksista (Study on the capabilities of security managers). In Berg, K.-E., editor, 2. *Turvallisuusjohdon kurssi, Kurssijulkaisu*, Finland, HUT.

Virtanen, T. (2001). An information security education program in Finland, In Armstrong, H. and Yngström, L., editors, *Proceedings of WISE2*, Australia, Edith Cowan University.

Warren, M. and Hutchinson, W. (2001). Teaching small and medium sized enterprises about security. In Armstrong, H., editor, *Proceedings of the 5th Australian Security Research Symposium*, pages 207 – 218, Australia, Edith Cowan University.

White, G. B. , Marti, W. and Huson, M. L. (1999). Incorporating Security Issues Throughout the Computer Science Curriculum, In Yngströn, L. and Fischer-Hubner, S., editors, *WISE 1, Proceedings of the IFIP TC11 WG 11.8*, pages 19 – 26, Sweden, DSV.

Yngström, L. (1996). A systemic-holistic approach to academic programmes in IT security. Sweden, Stockholm University/Royal Institute of Technology.

# A TUTORING SYSTEM FOR IT SECURITY

Ji Hu, Michael Schmitt, Christian Willems, and Christoph Meinel
*University of Trier, Research Group "Institute for Telematics", Bahnhofstrase 30-32, 54292 Trier, Germany, (hu, schmitt, willems, meinel)@telematik-institut.de*

**Abstract**:     Due to the many vulnerabilities of today's computer systems, IT security education has become an important topic. For that reason, a new tutoring system is developed at the Institute for Telematics, Trier, that allows users to gain knowledge about security technologies and tools via a web browser interface. Unlike other systems, this tutoring system does not provide a restricted simulation environment. Instead, guided exercises are performed on a real system (Linux). In this paper, the user interface and architecture of the tutoring system as well as some implementation aspects and future enhancements are described.

**Key words**:     IT Security, Tutoring System

## 1.     INTRODUCTION

Today's IT systems are suffering from various kinds of hacker attacks. Pitifully, many of these attacks succeed because people do not know about the vulnerabilities of their systems and how to defend against attacks. Therefore, IT security education has become a hot topic.

Recently, many universities have integrated lectures on computer security into their curricula. For example, teleteaching courses are currently held at the University of Trier, Germany. One of the courses is a joint project of the University of Trier and the Beijing University of Technology, China, in which students of both countries are made familiar with aspects of Internet security.

Besides knowing the theory, practical experience and the acquisition of practical skills are essential. Therefore, the Institute for Telematics develops a tutoring system for IT security, called *Lernplattform IT-Sicherheit* (LPF; English: learning platform IT security). The LPF is based on web technologies so that users can interact with it via a web browser. It offers both a German and an English front end.

The LPF is designed for Linux. This operating system has been chosen because it is freely available and gains increasing popularity. It also provides a vast number of open source security and hacker tools. This makes it possible to ship the LPF as a complete system that does not require additional, commercial software. Currently, the LPF is based on SuSE Linux 8.1, the Apache web server, and the PHP and Perl script languages. For practical exercises, various security tools and auxiliary programs are used such as OpenSSL, the Nmap port scanner, the Nessus security scanner, John-the-Ripper (a password cracker), and the Snort intrusion detection system.

The lectures of the LPF cover general security topics as well as specific aspects of the Linux operating system. The range of topics includes cryptography and secure email, authentication, firewalls, intrusion detection, viruses, and security scanning. In order to follow the course, a user is required to have some rudimentary knowledge about Unix concepts (e.g., how to enter commands in a shell, how to create a subdirectory or delete a file).

For every topic, the LPF provides a set of exercises. These guided exercises are performed on the real Linux system with standard tools rather than in a closed but restricted simulation environment. This approach allows users to easily apply their knowledge to production systems later.

**Document structure.** This paper is structured as follows: Section 2 provides background materials and discusses related work. The system architecture of the LPF and its functional components are described in Section 3. Finally, Section 4 gives a summary and presents future enhancements.

## 2.     RELATED WORK

*Intelligent tutoring systems* (*ITS*) are the next generation of *computer-based tutoring* (CBT) systems (Sleeman and Brown, 1982). An ITS is able to communicate with a user to assess her results and to teach the user in a manner that is appropriate according to her knowledge and skills (Persché, 1997).

There are a few known projects dealing with security training. The Chalmers University of Technology, Sweden, has a long-term project in which users evaluate the security of a target system by attacking it (Lindskog et al., 1999). However, the exercises are guided by an instructor instead of a computer-based training system.

The *ID-Tutor* (Rowe and Schiavo, 1998) and the ITS described in (Woo et al., 2002) are computer-based tutoring systems for becoming acquainted with intrusion detection. They allow users to perform practical tasks in a simulation environment. The user's answers are evaluated by comparison with predefined or fixed criteria.

The ID-Tutor creates audit files with information on user login and executed user commands. The user has to decide whether an intrusion has occurred and, in case of an intrusion, she must resolve the problems. The ID-Tutor provides a simple interactive operating environment in which the student chooses Unix commands from a menu instead of entering commands on a console. Unfortunately, the generated audit files merely cover a few selected problem cases. In addition, the ID-Tutor does not record and analyze the student's performance.

The ITS described in (Woo et al., 2002) is similar to the *ID-Tutor* but it has an intelligent tutoring system architecture and generates its missions from a knowledge base. The ITS provides an interactive, virtual Unix system with a command line interface. However, the virtual operation system provides only a limited set of commands and a simple directory structure. In order to finish a mission successfully, students have to follow a strict prob_lem-resolving path.

## 3.    SYSTEM ARCHITECTURE

The primary tasks of an ITS are the modeling of (1) the knowledge of the domain (domain model), (2) the user (student model), and (3) the pedagogical strategies (tutor model). Furthermore, the development of an ITS must focus on the creation of a powerful user interface (Sleeman and Brown, 1982).

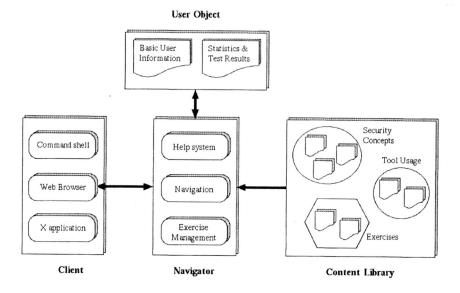

*Figure 1:* System Architecture

The architecture of the LPF is designed according to these ideas. The main components are illustrated in Figure 1. The *content library* corresponds to the domain model. It is an IT security knowledge base represented by a collection of web pages and scripts. The *navigator* is the corresponding entity to the tutor model. It guides the user through security topics in the content library, prepares and assigns exercises to the user, and processes feedback from the user. The *user object* is the counterpart of the user model. It keeps track of the user's knowledge at every stage in the learning process. The web browser provides the student with a user-friendly and uniform interface. In order to perform the exercises, the user must use a command shell or an X window application.

## 3.1    The Content Library

The content library is a knowledge base that consists of three types of contents:
1. descriptions of security concepts
2. descriptions of security tools
3. security exercises

The first two types represent declarative knowledge that is presented to the user in hypertext form mixed with multimedia objects, such as graphics, images, or animations. The security exercises reflect procedural knowledge related to how a security task is performed. The implementation of the procedural knowledge is much more complicated because it must be presented in terms of scenarios. This means, we must carefully design the steps and actions in the exercises.

The organization of the content library is illustrated in Figure 2. The basic unit is a section. A section represents a complete learning item or several closely related items. A section is also the basic unit for measuring the user's performance. Completing a section means the user has succeeded in acquiring the given knowledge or skills. The LPF has three types of sections including concepts, tool usages, and exercises. They correspond to the three types of knowledge described above. Every section consists of one or more pages. The exercise sections comprise some additional scripts.

Multiple sections are combined in a chapter that represents a security topic. In most cases, a chapter introduces some security concepts first. Then it explains some tools or commands. Afterwards, the user is asked to perform some practical exercises.

Technically, for each section, there is a description file that provides the navigator (see below) with meta information, including the section type, the number of pages, the title, etc. A chapter description file specifies how a chapter is organized. Finally, a profile description file defines which chapters are reasonable for which type of user. Based on these description files, the navigator is able to construct a hierarchy of chapters and sections and to produce appropriate hyperlinks. The use of description files makes it very easy to adapt user profiles and the structure of chapters in the future, without having to touch the individual sections. Instead, only items in the description files have to be changed for that purpose. Furthermore, it allows to define several chapters that share some common sections.

## 3.2    The Navigator

The main goal of the navigator is to deliver the materials in the content library in a structured manner to the user. As a gateway to the tutoring system, the navigator is also able to track every communication with the user and analyze her learning process.

The navigator knows exactly which pages belong to a section and which sections belong to a specific chapter. The navigator creates linked web pages that are displayed in the web browser of the user (see Figure 2). It also decides whether the user has finished a section successfully and where to continue at the end of a section.

When starting the LPF, the user must register herself or login into the LPF with a valid account. Then, the navigator provides a list of available chapters from which the user can choose. When the user enters a chapter, the navigator creates a navigation bar on the left side of the web page that lists all sections and represents their type by a small icon (see Figure 3).

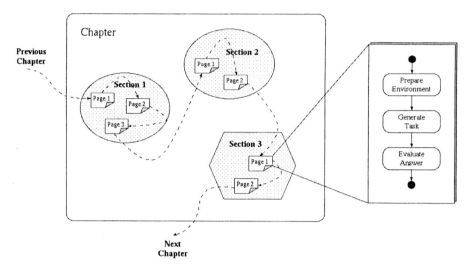

*Figure 2.* Content organization and navigation

Help information is available for each exercise. This information is provided in a popup window as a series of questions and answers (see Figure 4).

## 3.3    Exercise Management

Exercises are specified as Perl and PHP scripts in the content library and interpreted by the navigator. An exercise takes place in three steps (cf. Figure 2):

In the first phase, the working environment, i.e. the Linux operating system, is configured. For example, if the user is to perform security scans, a set of services are activated so that the user gets reasonable results.

The next phase deals with generating questions or tasks and passing them to the user. Where possible, these tasks are created dynamically. I.e., all users do the same type of exercise but with different detailed content. For example, for password cracking, a Unix *passwd* file (that the users must decrypt) is generated at run-time. Exercises must be created in such a way that the degree of difficulty does not vary. For instance, passwords created in the *passwd* file are selected randomly from the same dictionary and can be cracked in similar time.

After the user completes her task, the LPF evaluates her result.

In some cases, it may also be necessary or useful to generate some background load *during* an exercise. For instance, the tutoring system might instantiate a *telnet* session while the user practices network sniffing so that some critical passwords can be observed in the data packets.

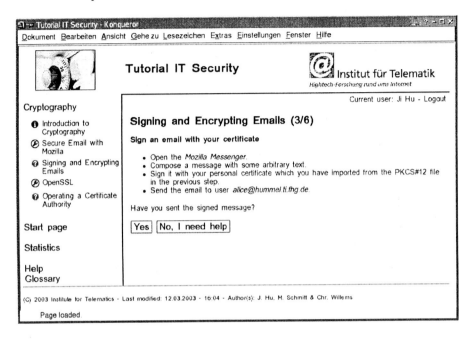

*Figure 3.* Exercise example: Secure email

**Example.** The preparation, execution, and result analysis of exercises in a real system environment is a complicated task for which many technical problems have to be solved. The effort needed to set up a proper environment is illustrated by an exercise for secure email. Its purpose is to make users familiar with certificates so that they can sign and encrypt emails. The LPF user interface for this exercise is shown in Figure 3.

**Phase 1:** Preparation of the working environment:

– clear previous settings and create the necessary working directories
– set up a local mail server
– create a virtual user Alice for email communication with the user, i.e. create a Linux account and configure the email settings
– create a certificate authority by OpenSSL commands
– issue certificates to Alice and the user, install the certificate for Alice, and guide the user to import the certificate to the mail client

**Phase 2:** Generation of exercise:

– create a random message with the signature on behalf of Alice
– send the message to the user

– ask the user to:
1. verify the signature attached to the message, accept and trust Alice's certificate
2. reply to Alice's message with her own signature
3. send a message encrypted with Alice's certificate to Alice

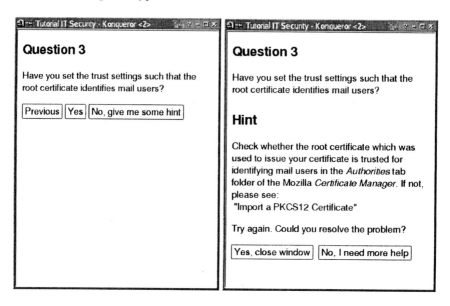

*Figure 4.* Help information

**Phase 3:** Evaluation of the answer:
– fetch a message from Alice's mailbox
– verify its signature to see whether it has been sent from the user and matches with the original
– try to decrypt the message with Alice's private key corresponding to her certificate
– record the (un-)successful completion of the exercise in the user object

## 3.4    The User Object

An important feature that distinguishes an ITS from other tutoring systems is that it "knows" the individual users and tracks their performance. In the LPF, this feature is supported by the *user object*.

The user object contains two types of data: One is static personal information, such as name, password, language, and profile. The profile places the user into one out of (currently) three categories: administrators, end users, and students. The LPF defines different sets of security topics for each category.

The second class of data includes the records of completed sections, the time needed to complete an exercise, the link to the last visited web page, help requests and their frequencies, and so on. In order to complete a topic, the user must pass all exercises in a chapter. A user can repeat an exercise until she finally finds a correct solution. The data in the user object are used to analyze the user's performance and to present statistics on the current status.

Technically, user objects are implemented by a PHP class. When a user logs in or logs out, the user object is read from/written to a floppy. Thus, even if the user corrupts the Linux systems by some exercise, her test results are still accessible.

## 4. SUMMARY AND OUTLOOK

In this paper, we have presented a web-based tutoring system for IT security. The LPF improves the existing security education activities by several features: it offers users a real system environment instead of a limited simulation environment; it has a navigation mechanism that presents contents and creates exercises dynamically; its user interface is based on a web browser interface. The tools and programs needed in the exercises are available via the browser or already installed on the system.

As of April 2003, the main framework of the LPF is completed. In addition, 5 out of 11 planned chapters are available. These chapters deal with authentication, secure email, certificates and PKIs, data security, network services, and port scanning.

The web server requires root rights for the preparation of exercises. Sometimes, even the user needs to execute privileged commands to perform certain exercises. This introduces the risk that the user spoils the system. Since the LPF runs on the same operating system on which the user performs her exercises, this may lead to a complete breakdown. Currently, the LPF must be reinstalled on hard disk in such a case. We plan to combine it with a Linux system that can be booted from CD and does not require any hard disk installation. Another approach that is investigated is the use of virtual machines on top of a base Linux system (Dike, 2000). We are also examining the possibility to provide the LPF as an online tutoring system.

Furthermore, we are looking for a way to provide a pure browser-based user interface where external applications are displayed inside the browser. This would avoid the necessity to switch between different application windows during exercises. A possible solution is to embed a Java applet into the web page that connects to a Linux server (Cao et al., 2002).

## REFERENCES

Cao, Jiannong, Chan, Alvin, Cao, Weidong, and Yeung, Cassidy (2002). Virtual Programming Lab for Online Distance Learning. In *Proceedings of the First International Conference*, ICWL 2002, pages 216-227, Hongkong, China.

Dike, Jeff (2000). A user-mode port of the Linux kernel. In *Proceedings of the 4th Annual Linux Showcase & Conference,* page 63, Atlanta, GA. Usenix.

Lindskog, Stefan, Lindqvist, Ulf, and Jonsson, Erland (1999). IT Security Research and Education in Synergy. In *Proceedings of the 1st World Conference on Information Security Education*, Stockholm, Sweden.

Persché, Richard (1997). Immediate Feedback During Online Lectures. Master's thesis, Institute for Information Processing and Computer Supported New Media of the Graz University of Technology, Graz, Austria.

Rowe, N. C. and Schiavo, S. (1998). An Intelligent Tutor for Intrusion Detection on Computer System. *Computers and Education*, pages 395-404.

Sleeman, D. and Brown, J.S. (1982). *Intelligent Tutoring Systems.* Academic Press Ltd., London.

Woo, Chong-woo, Choi, Jin-woo, and Evens, Martha (2002). Web-based ITS for Training System Managers on the Computer Intrusion. In *Proceedings of the 6th International conference* ITS 2002, pages 311-319, Biarritz, France and San Sebastian, Spain.

# DESIGN OF A LABORATORY FOR INFORMATION SECURITY EDUCATION

Vikram Anantapadmanabhan, Phyllis Frankl, Nasir Memon,
and Gleb Naumovich
*Polytechnic University, Brooklyn, NY 11201*

**Abstract**: It has been recognized for some time now that education in information security is better served by a laboratory component that reinforces principle and theoretical analysis learnt in the class room with a follow-up hands-on component performed in an appropriate laboratory. In this paper we present the design of a highly reconfigurable laboratory for information security education. The design has been implemented successfully in ISIS - The Information Systems and Internet Security Laboratory at Polytechnic University. We also describe the rationale for our design and give examples of a few typical assignments that the laboratory facilitates.

**Key words**: Laboratory Education, Network Security Laboratory, Information Security Laboratory, Network Security Education, Information Security Education, Information Assurance Education

## 1. INTRODUCTION

The recent focus on security education, kindled by the NSA Center of Excellence in Education program [3] has seen a variety of universities add a security component to their computer science and engineering curriculum. As a result, we now have 36 universities that have been designated as Centers of Excellence in education. However, a significant number of programs continue to teach information security in the decades old traditional framework, focusing solely on theoretical principles and their analysis. Although theoretical concepts are essential and need to be taught, it is very important to also show students how to apply the theory they have learnt in very different and important practical situations. Hence, a good part of an information security course should also focus on applications and operational concerns. In order to do this, a supporting laboratory becomes necessary.

Recent years have seen an increased awareness on the importance of a laboratory component in information security education [7,1,5,6]. In [7], Irvine points out that securing a system requires a "marriage" of good science and engineering. And that engineering components are best taught by reinforcing concepts taught in the class by hands-on experiences in the laboratory. She further points out that just as it is unreasonable to expect a student to learn programming only by reading about it, it is also unreasonable to expect students to learn "security engineering" solely from discussions in the class room. Similarly, [5] and [6] also make the case for laboratory based instruction in information security and in fact provide detailed examples of specific courses and lab projects that accomplish this goal.

A laboratory for information security education can be designed in a different manner depending on the nature of the program and the course being serviced. However, there are certain general principles that guide the design of such a laboratory. Specifically, a well-designed laboratory should possess the following characteristics:

- *Reconfigurable:* The lab should be highly flexible and re-configurable. Different topics and assignments require different operating systems and/or network topologies and it should be possible to change the configuration of hosts and networks easily and efficiently.

- *Heterogeneous:* The lab should comprise of multiple platforms from multiple vendors. A lab with homogeneous environment does not effectively train students to cope with real world situations.

- *Scalable:* The lab should be scalable and should be able to sustain many students, and still have enough duties for each student to handle. Student groups should not get large due to lack of resources.

- *Cost Effective:* The cost of setup and maintenance of the lab must be far less them what's being simulated by the lab. For example, the lab should effectively simulate a small to medium enterprise network but the cost for building and maintaining the lab should be far less then the cost of a moderate enterprise network.

- *Robust:* The lab should be able to sustain and handle inadvertent damage by the students. For example, it should be possible to quickly recover the set-up and configuration of a host node even after a student accidentally causes a malicious program to erase the hard disk.

- *Maintainable:* The lab should be easy to maintain. Routine tasks like back-up and application of software patches should be easy to perform and automated to whatever degree possible.

- *Realistic:* The lab should provide practical and first hand experience to students in a network environment that is close, in terms of complexity, to a network that they might encounter in a real world enterprise.

- *Insulated:* Activities in the lab should not affect traffic on the campus network. There should be sufficient amount of separation and isolation enforced between the lab network and the external network. The presence of the lab should not be a cause of concern to campus network authorities.

In the rest of this paper we describe the design of ISIS - An Information Systems and Internet Security Laboratory at Polytechnic University, which aims to achieve the above listed design goals. ISIS was initially started as the result of an NSF CCLI grant to develop a sequence of undergraduate courses in computer and network security and an accompanying laboratory. Initial lab and course design was done with the assistance of ISSL [2] at Iowa State University which has long been an NSA designated Center of Academic Excellence in information assurance education and research. ISIS has been running for more than two years now and the lab and the courses it supports have proved to be immensely successful. In fact the role of ISIS has been significantly expanded beyond its original scope and design and it now serves as a center of education and research in information assurance at Polytechnic University.

The rest of this paper is organized as follows: In the next section we describe the overall architecture of ISIS and two of its smaller components - the student workstation network and the server cluster. In Section 3 we describe in detail the design of the core of ISIS, a secure systems experimental testbed. In Section 4 we describe briefly some typical assignments supported by ISIS and in Section 5 we conclude with a brief discussion on future plans for expanding ISIS.

## 2.    ISIS ARCHITECTURE

ISIS consists of heterogeneous platforms and multiple interconnected networks to facilitate hands-on experimentation and project work in issues related to information security. ISIS lab is divided physically and logically into three areas, namely:

- The Student Workstation Network,
- The Server Cluster,
- A Secure Systems Experimentation Testbed (ASSET).

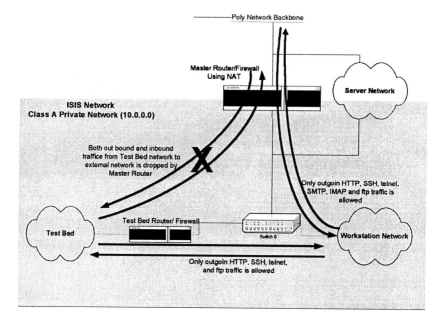

*Figure 1.* ISIS lab architecture overview showing its three main components - 1) ASSET - A Secure Systems Experimentation Testbed, 2) The Student Workstation Network, and 3) The Server Cluster - and their interconnection with each other and with the campus network backbone

Figure 1 shows how these three components are interconnected with each other and also with the external campus network. The student workstation network and the testbed ASSET are inside a class A private network so that they are isolated from traffic on the campus network and the internet. The private network is created using a router with NAT capabilities. This router is shown in Figure 1 labeled as the"Master Router". Usually a private network is created to hide internal network topology and expand the range of available IP address. In our case it is critical to separate our network traffic from the external network in order to stop internal traffic, malicious and otherwise, from reaching the external network. The router will prevent packets from internal traffic to escape out into the external network.

The second advantage that a Class A private network provides is the large number of subnets that can be created within it. We could potentially have $2^{16}$ subnets with 250 hosts in each subnet in the network. This fact is critical to the design of our testbed network, as is explained in the Section 4.

In addition to performing NAT, the master router also is configured to act as a firewall in order to impose restriction on traffic flowing to and from the internal network. Furthermore, traffic from and to the testbed network from the workstation network and the server network is restricted by a second firewall labeled as the Testbed/Router Firewall in Figure 1. This ensures that any attack traffic in the testbed network does not enter the workstation network or the server network.

## 2.1     The Student Workstation Network

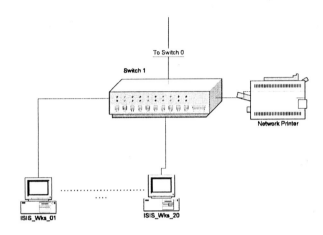

*Figure 2.* Physical network layout of the student workstation network.

The primary purpose of the workstation network is to provide students a means to access the ASSET network. Typically, for most assignments, students have to be physically present in the lab and logged on to a workstation in order to access ASSET. The workstations themselves are Pentium 4, 1.5 GHz general-purpose machines, running Windows 2000 and equipped with standard university lab software, like compilers, editors etc. They are members of the ISIS active directory server present in the server network. Currently there are 20 workstations as shown in Figure 2.

Individual workstations in this network are completely locked down physically by using padlocks on the machines and also by appropriate configuration of BIOS settings and Windows domain policies and restrictions. For example, students cannot reboot these machine using bootable floppies or CD's. They cannot install or remove any software, and connect or disconnect these computers from the network. They are only allowed to use the applications that are installed on the workstations. The software restrictions are enforced using Windows 2000 domain policies and restriction suggested by NSA's Windows 2000 lock down guidelines (http://www.nsa.gov/snac/index.html).

Although students are only allowed to store their files on the file server and not in the workstation they work on, they are still provided some writable space in each workstation. Without user writable space, Windows will not allow any user to log on. This space is very small (10MB) and each workstation is cleaned occasionally by erasing all users temporary directories, and/or re-installing a fresh image, if necessary, during the cleaning process.

## 2.2     The Server Cluster

The server component of ISIS currently is composed of four serves: 1) A Web server, 2) A Solaris server, 3) A Win2k Terminal/File server and 4) An Active Directory server. The web server is used to host lab's and students web pages. The Solaris and Win2k terminal servers are used by the students for compute intensive tasks like password cracking and cryptanalysis. These servers also contain a repository of security related tools that students need for their projects and assignments. The active directory server is used to manage the ISIS lab active directory. The Win2k server is also used as a file server to store student files. Each student is allowed to store up to 5GB's in the file server and their files are automatically backed up by the backup system and also screened for common viruses frequently. The total storage capacity on the server network exceeds half a terabyte.

The server network can facilitate secure remote access to our network via the Windows terminal server. We use a dual homed Win2k terminal server for remote access. The remote access server is also part of the ISIS active directory; so all users in the active directory can potentially access the secure systems experimental testbed from a remote location. This was done to facilitate students who cannot be physically present in the lab.

## 3.     ASSET - A SECURE SYSTEMS EXPERIMENTATION TESTBED

In this section we describe the third component of ISIS - A Secure Systems Experimentation Testbed (in short ASSET). ASSET is the core of the lab and this is where most of the lab activities take place. It consists of a highly reconfigurable network built around a layer 2 switch, 32 computers fitted with two or more NICs and removable hard drives, and two VMware ESX servers as shown in Figure 4.

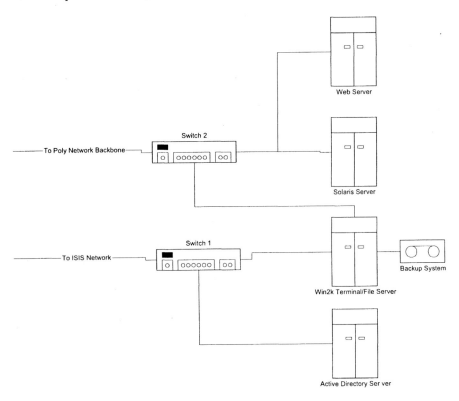

*Figure 3.* Physical network layout of the server network.

ASSET is designed to be flexible and highly reconfigurable. Flexibility in terms of network layout and software running on end nodes is necessary as this allows us to support assignments of vastly different nature and scope with the same resources. The need for flexibility in terms of operating system can be seen in assignments like Linux and Windows hardening.

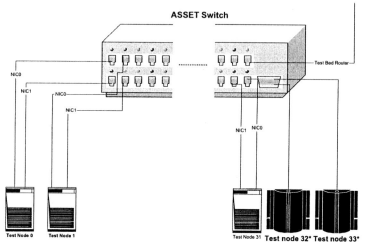

*Figure 4.* Physical layout of ASSET.

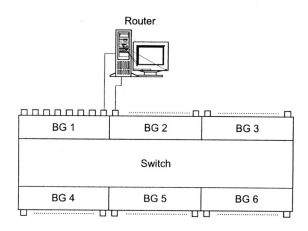

*Figure 5.* A switch divided into 6 bridge groups, each bridge group represents a VLAN. Figure also shows how two bridge groups could be connected using a router.

These assignments follow each other and it's important that we are able to change the operating system on a large number of nodes in a reasonable amount of time (say a few hours). Dual boot architecture will not suffice, as we need the ability to load ASSET hosts with selected versions of an operating system with deliberate misconfigurations for students to discover and fix. It is also important that we have the ability to restore these nodes to a default state in minutes, after inadvertent damage by a student. In order to achieve these goals we use nodes with removable hard drives. This way we can load or restore a node by simple replacing its hard drive. A hard drive duplicator allows us to load the same configuration in multiple hosts. Disk images of different versions of different operating systems, and applications with and without flaws, are stored on the server network and can be copied on to a disk in minutes, and can then be duplicated and loaded in multiple hosts.

The need for flexibility in terms of network layout arises from the variety of network security assignments that students are required to perform, ranging from network fingerprinting, penetration testing, intrusion detection and prevention, and finally war games. Again, such assignments follow each other in a logical sequence and one needs the ability to reconfigure the network topology from one assignment to the other in order to meet the specification of each assignment. Furthermore, in certain more complex assignments it is also desirable to mimic a slowly changing enterprise network and this leads to the need for an ability to automatically change network layout by means of scripts and without human intervention.

To make ASSET flexible in terms of network layout we use Virtual LAN's (VLAN's) and create logical networks. We do this using a switch with VLAN support. In a conventional switch, all ports belong to the same broadcast domain (i.e. one switch represents a network segment) and many networks can be created using multiple switches interconnected with a router to represent an enterprise network. An example of such a network is depicted in Figure 6. With a switch that can support multiple VLAN's, it is possible to create such a network without having multiple switches, and we can change the network layout without changing the physical layout.

With a switch with VLAN support, VLAN's can be created and modified by changing the software configuration of the switch to which all the hosts on the network are physically connected to. Using VLAN's it is possible to create independent virtual broadcast domains within a switch as shown in Figure 5. Also, a switch with VLAN support can have multiple broadcast domains. We could interconnect these domains by having a router between them (Figure 5) and the network in Figure 6 could be created by configuring the switch to have multiple VLAN's and physically it would look like what is shown in Figure 7.

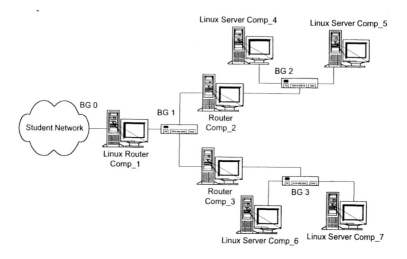

*Figure 6.* An example of small network with 4 network segments, built using an independent switch to support each network segment. Each network segment is interconnected using a Linux router.

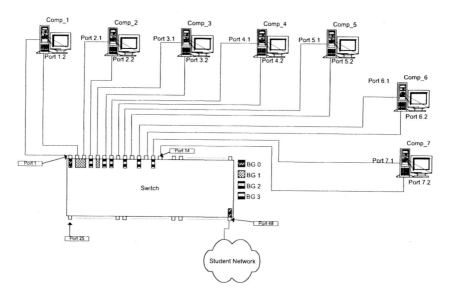

*Figure 7.* The network depicted in Figure 6 implemented in a single switch configured to support 4 bridge groups.

More complicated networks as shown in Figure 8, can be created using test nodes 32 and 33 in combination with the other 32 computers. These two machines can run up 32 virtual computers using VMware's ESX operating system. ESX server is a mainframe class-computing environment, and is capable of having internal networks independent of the external network. Node 32 and 33 can be used to simulate a changing network. There are 16 virtual test networks inside each node and the network topology is dynamic. Using a skillfully crafted script one can periodically change the internal network configuration of the VMware network to simulate a changing network. This kind of a network, for example, could be used in routing vulnerability analysis assignments.

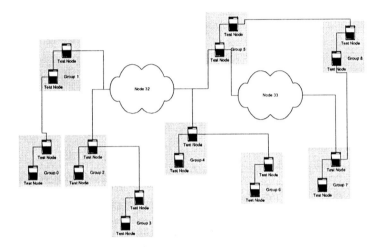

*Figure 8.* An example logical network that can be built in ISIS testbed network. This example can support 8 student groups. Node 32 and 33 simulate a changing network.

From the above discussion, we can see that ASSET meets the design goals of reconfigurability, heterogeneity, maintainability, and robustness. The dual firewalls and private network provide sufficient isolation to yield an insulated environment for experimentation. Since the entire lab can be constructed from cheaply available hardware and open source software, the design is also cost effective. The design is scalable as it allows us to have several networks, thereby facilitating smaller groups even with a class size of 30 or 40 students. Finally, the design allows us to configure different realistic environments for experimentation and exploration.

## 4.      EXAMPLE CLASS ASSIGNMENTS

The laboratory design that we have described facilitates a rich variety of class assignments. A detailed description of the different assignments we have created and their objectives are beyond the scope of this paper.

However, in order to describe what the laboratory makes possible, we give a few brief examples below.

## 4.1     Server Assignments

These assignments only utilize one or more of the servers in the server network. Often they are compute intensive in nature. For example, one assignment makes students explore the confusion and diffusion properties of modern cryptosystems like AES. Another explores the difficulty of a brute force attack as the key length increases. Students are able to successfully attack a 40-bit key using the computing resources of the server. Finally, assignments that involve password cracking also utilize the servers.

## 4.2     Host Assignments

Here the ASSET network is configured as a flat network of hosts and each student or group of students is assigned a host. Assignments for this type of configuration typically explore security vulnerabilities in a stand-alone computer system. One example of such an assignment is to make students harden a poorly configured Windows and/or Linux machine as per security guidelines specified by the NSA. Assignments involving malicious code are also performed with such a configuration. Finally, another example is provided by assignments that involve learning about robust programming techniques in general and exploring buffer overflow, and format string vulnerabilities in particular.

## 4.3     Network Assignments

These assignments require configuration of the ASSET into a collection of networks or clouds of networks and student tasks include exploring, configuring, and defending a network. Example assignments include exploiting and understanding ARP vulnerabilities, such as ARP cache poisoning and denial of service attacks that can be done through ARP in the local subnet. TCP and UDP vulnerabilities such as session hijacking, spoofing, and other DOS attacks in TCP and UDP. Vulnerabilities in routing protocols such as RIP, and OSPF. Use of network mapping utilities. Secure communication using IPSEC, SSL, and other upper layer protocols. Implementation of secure echo and secure HTTP. Configuring firewalls using IP chains. Assignments involving intrusion detection and prevention. And finally, war game like assignments where students attack networks being administered by other students while at the same time defending their own network from attack.

## 5.   CONCLUSIONS AND FUTURE DEVELOPMENT PLAN

In this paper we have described the design of a laboratory for information security education. We argued that the design goals of such a laboratory should include reconfigurability, scalability, robustness, maintainability, cost effectiveness, and heterogeneity. Furthermore the lab should be well insulated from the external network and should provide a realistic environment for student experimentation and learning. The design has been implemented successfully in ISIS - The Information Systems and Internet Security Laboratory at Polytechnic University.

Future plans for expanding ISIS include the addition of a wireless subnet, the addition of VPN and tunneling capabilities, software and hardware for advanced intrusion detection and prevention and finally equipment that will facilitate lab work in computer and network forensics.

## REFERENCES

[1]   M.Bishop. What Do We Mean by Computer Security Education 22nd National Information Systems Security Conference, Oct.1999.

[2]   ISSL: Information Systems Security Laboratory, Iowa State University: http://www.issl.org/

[3]   NSA Centers Of Academic Excellence in Information Assurance Education http://www.nsa.gov:8080/isso/programs/coeiae/index.htm.

[4]   National Coordination Office for HPCC. Committee on Information and Communications (CIC) Strategic Implementation Plan. http://www.whitehouse.gov/WH/EOP/OSTP/NSTC/html/cic/cic_plan.html.

[5]   John M. D. Hill et. al. Using an Isolated Network Laboratory to Teach Advanced Networks and Security. Proceedings of ACM SIGCSE Technical Symposium on Computer Science Education, Charlotte, North Carolina, pp 36-40,Feb.2001.

[6]   Prabhaker Mateti. A Laboratory-Based Course on Internet Security. Proceedings of ACM SIGCSE Technical Symposium on Computer Science Education, Reno, Nevada, Feb.2003. Cynthia E.Irvine. Amplifying Security Education in the Laboratory. Proceedings IFIP TC11

[7]   WC 11.8 First World Conference on Information Security Education, pp 139 146,Kista,Swe-den,June 1999.

# INTEGRATING INFORMATION SECURITY AND INTELLIGENCE COURSES

William Hutchinson
*School of Computer and Information Science, Edith Cowan University, Mount Lawley, Western Australia 6050*

Abstract:       As the Western nations move further into the Information Age, the strategic nature and value of information becomes more apparent. The conventional approach to (corporate) information management, security, and its associated systems has conventionally been narrow, protective and a reactive. However, this paper argues that information security is a part of the information management (rather than the security) function. The contemporary concept of Information Warfare has developed the concept of information as a 'target' and that of a' weapon'. This means an aggressive and dynamic organisational change in the use of information and associated systems. This requires a change in mindset. An integrated information strategy requires an integrated perspective on security (a protective paradigm) and intelligence (an aggressive paradigm). This paper argues that courses for information professionals of the future should integrate these worldviews in their education. A post-graduate course being implemented at an Australian university will be offered as an example.

Key words:     Information warfare, information security training, intelligence training, information superiority, education.

## 1.     INTRODUCTION

It is generally accepted that in the Information Age that information is the defining element in a modern organisation's competitive stance. Ideas of *information superiority* are becoming acceptable concepts for an organisational strategy to be based. Information superiority has been the aim of commanders since the dawn of warfare. However, the contemporary concept derives from the Gulf War in the early 1990s (Campen, 1992). It involves the use of integrated electronic communications and computer networks plus the use of sophisticated satellite and airborne surveillance to totally dominate the battle-space. This is a two way process. Not only is the C4I (command, control, communication, computers and intelligence) system capable of providing better information for one's own actions, but this very advantage often allows the enemy's C4I system to be degraded. This degradation of the opponent's abilities is caused by the capability to monitor and disrupt data communication, and also to manipulate and fabricate data. Thus, the adversary knows 'what you want them to know'. This concept has also been exploited by the US in both the conflicts in Kosovo (Ignatieff, 2000) and Afghanistan. All this tends to lift the 'fog of war' (see Owens, 2000). In other words, the information confusion caused in all dynamic battlefield situations is alleviated to some degree.

Other commentators (Arquilla and Rondfeldt, 1996) have seen this trend merge with the development of networks in the organisational and societal contexts. All this is facilitated by information technology. Hence, there is also a trend for the effective use of networks in a competitive sense to diffuse from the military into the commercial and governmental areas.

A simple version found in Alberts *et al* (1999), and Alberts and Gartska (2000) defines information superiority in terms of timeliness, relevance, and accuracy of the information supplied to the commander (manager). Coupled with this, is the assumption that the information is given to the correct manager, is in an easily comprehensible form, and that the manager acts on the information presented. In conventional, contemporary organisations these concepts are relevant where forms of competition are in play. Hence, it is relevant to almost all organisation and certainly commercial businesses.

All this discussion of information superiority begs the question: what is information? It is in this definition that lies the basis for a modern and rational approach to information management education. The conventional linear definitions of data, information, knowledge, and wisdom with each stage having a greater degree of collation and involvement with context and learning does not appear to be very useful. In fact, this definition appears to delineate many functions such as knowledge management, information management, and, in the author's opinion, propagates confusion around these roles. What is needed is a definition that reflects the integrated nature of the *information* security function. One such definition of data, information, and knowledge was developed from Boisot (1998) - see Hutchinson and Warren (2001a, 2001b). In his model, data is associated with a *thing*, and discriminates between different states of the thing it describes. It consists of attributes of the events or objects it describes. On the other hand, knowledge is an attribute of an *agent*. Knowledge is a set of interacting mindsets about data activated by an event. Hence, in most circumstances the word 'agent' means a human being or a group of people. Information is the set of data filtered by the agent within the bounds of the knowledge held by the agent. It establishes a link between the agent and the data.

Hence, the foundations for 'information education' lie in these new definitions of information and information superiority.

## 2. THE PRESENT SITUATION

The definitions given above imply three major things:

- In a modern organisation all functions (including the Information Security function) should be dynamically assisting the organisation to achieve information superiority

- The information security function is about human and data management (and their associated communication, storage and processing technologies), and

- The definition of 'information' used above is more akin to the conventional meaning of 'intelligence'.

However, the present practice of information security education concentrates more on the passive defence of data. Humans are included in topics such as 'vetting' but are generally excluded. Information security is lumped in with the general security functions and with physical and building security. It is often confused with computer or network security. Hence, in many organisations, it becomes within the province of the technician. It is an 'add on' the real business of the organisation. Thus, it becomes marginalised from what are regarded as the core business activities much as information technology (IT) was in the 1970's and 1980's when IT and its staff were regarded and as a necessary evil, but not a true **business** function. In the Information Age, this can be a fatal mistake not only for the organisation but for security professionals as well.

The ideas above are encompassed in the recent acceptance of the notion of 'information warfare'. This has both in its offensive and defensive (security) modes and is closely aligned with information superiority. This is has been well documented by authors such as Schwartau (1996), Knetch (1996), Denning (1999), Waltz (1998), Hutchinson and Warren (2001), and Jones *et al* (2002). Thus, information security professionals should recognise the information warfare paradigm and become an integral part of the organisation's business and not peripheral to it. If this accepted then training for Information Security courses should be revamped to give professional a grasp of the overall **use** and **protection** of information within an organisation. Information security has links with other forms of security but is fundamentally different in that it should be associated with information and general management rather than the more technical areas of IT and physical security.

If the flow of information within an organisation is examined (see figure 1) then the enormity of the information security task can be seen. Information is derived and disseminated both internally between operational units and management, as well as the external environment by environmental scanning and releasing data to the environment by perception management. An integrated information process is needed to manage the integrity of data/information flow both to and from the external world as well as the internal realm. This substantially broadens the perception of information security into the realm of intelligence. One cannot be fully understood without the other. The reactive security world merges now with the proactive intelligence domain. The author argues that this concept should be the basis of general Information Security (as well as Intelligence) education. From the ideas of offensive and defensive modes of operation, the topics that need to be considered can be included (see figure 2) in the curriculum. Thus, the course will enable the student to develop skills necessary for the dynamic 21$^{st}$ century organisations, rather than the passive, *Maginot Line* paradigm of conventional security practice.

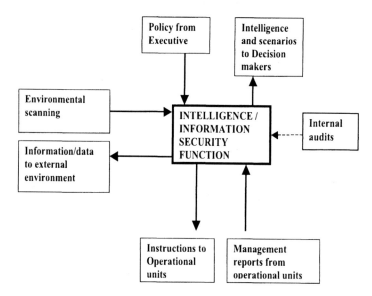

*Figure 1*: A simplification of data/information flow in an organisation (based loosely on a model developed by Beer, 1984. 1985)

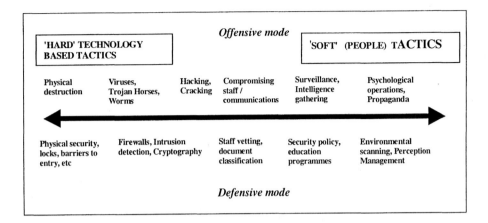

*Figure 2:* Examples of the range of topics involved in the concept of information security (author)

# 3.  AN EXAMPLE OF AN IMPLEMENTED POST GRADUATE CURRICULUM

As these ideas were being developed, it was decided that the courses at Edith Cowan University in Western Australia would be redesigned. At the undergraduate level, there are a number units within a computer security minor covering computer, information, database and network security. Until 2002, this was the case with postgraduate offerings. It was decided that a course embracing the ideas above was need as well as the more technically oriented computer security courses. A coursework Masters level course was created to cope with that market need. It specialises in network and computer security plus more specific topics such as wireless security and forensic computing. A new Masters course focusing on information security and intelligence was created to develop skills in the 'information warfare' paradigm. The underlying thoughts behind this were based on the assumption that organisations would need people who understood the true nature of information and its roles as a 'weapon' and a 'target'.

This initiative was taken by the School of Computer and Information Science within the university, but was intended to be a multi-school, interdisciplinary course.

The course had to include all the elements included in the Boisot based model: data, knowledge/context, and information.

In order, these mapped into:

- Data: conventional computer/network, information security
- Knowledge/context: perception management
- Information: intelligence

These elements had to be held together with a 'general' unit on information warfare that brought them all together. The Boisot model was emphasised in each of the units especially the first introductory subjects. The initial Information Warfare unit introduced the unity of all these elements in an organisational sense. The advanced Information Security unit also integrated the subjects. (This unit should really have been named Advanced Information Warfare). Treating 'information security' as a proactive and dynamic activity was thought to make it more relevant to organisations and bring it more into the mainstream business, rather than a marginalised function regarded as a cost. Information Security became a value added business role.

The course developed is a postgraduate offering in Information Security and Intelligence and is available in on-campus mode or fully on-line. It consists of three stages: Graduate Certificate, Graduate Diploma, and Professional Masters. Entry requirements are an undergraduate degree or five years appropriate work experience. Table 1 shows the composition of the units for each stage.

The compulsory content gives the student the range of technical skills required in a technological environment as the softer management and psychological aspects of information security. The elective content gives the participant the ability to either take a range of units in the area, or concentrate on a specialist area such as computer/network security. As it was originally designed as a course work Masters, Stage 3 originally consisted of three, advanced specialist units. However, a number of prospective students expressed a desire to either complete work-based projects or research. The option was then added to allow students to complete a work or research related project instead of the final three advanced units

In stage 1, the compulsory units cover both the defensive ('Information Security') and offensive ('Introduction to Information Warfare') aspects of the area. The two elective units allow the student to complete two specialist units from the hard and soft spectrum of topics. Stage 2 covers the range of topics within the intelligence function. The units cover advance Information Security (from both defensive and offensive perspective), the psychological impacts of information usage ('Perception Management'), and the principles of intelligence and counter-intelligence ('Contemporary Intelligence'). Stage 3 then allows a student to further research a topic of interest, or take advanced subject units.

The main, desired graduate attributes from this course (apart from content knowledge and computing skills) are based in the cognitive realm. Each unit has its own stated objectives but overall the student should develop skills in observation, analytic and forensic skills, inductive and deductive reasoning, and lateral thinking.

*Table 1:* The break up of units for Information Security and Intelligence awards

| Compulsory units | Elective units |
|---|---|
| **Stage 1: Graduate Certificate**<br>Information Security<br>*(a conventional information security unit*<br>*covering the defensive function of security)*<br>Introduction to Information Warfare<br>(a general unit integrating all the elements in<br>the Boisot model) | *Take any 2 units from:*<br>*Technology based units*<br>Database Security<br>Computer Security<br>Introduction to Knowledge Management<br>The Information Society<br>Fundamentals of Cyber-crime<br>Physical Security<br>*Social/human related units*<br>Media and Advertising<br>Media and Nation<br>Global Communications Introduction to<br>Media and Communication |
| **Stage 2 - Graduate Diploma**<br>Contemporary Intelligence<br>(covering the information/intelligence<br>aspects of the Boisot model)<br>Perception Management<br>(covering the knowledge/context aspects of<br>the Boisot model)<br>Information Security<br>(covering a continuation of the both the<br>lower level Information Security and<br>Information Warfare units, integrating them<br>both) | |
| **Stage 3 - Masters project (3 units)**<br>**OR**<br>*any three Advanced from:*<br>*Technically oriented units*<br>Computer Security<br>Network Security<br>Database Security<br>*Social/human oriented units*<br>Media and Social Issues Ethics, Values and<br>Moral Decision Making<br>Current Issues in Security<br>Advanced Security Risk Management<br>Advances in Security Technology | |

Also, there is a requirement to set information security in a social, ethical, political, and organisational context. Basically, the student will have to have the skills to think both like an attacker and a defender, and make decisions whilst considering the social, ethical, organisational, and legal context of the problem.

## 4.    CONCLUSION

The development of the information warfare paradigm is still in its early stages. The overall success of this venture has yet to be determined as there have been no graduates; the course starting in mid-2002. There has been much interest from industry, intelligence related government departments, the military, law enforcement, and even local government. The present student cohort comes from the finance industry, law enforcement, military related private industry, and local government. The course's effectiveness will be monitored and be fine-tuned to accommodate any shortcomings.

The approach described above takes a different approach to information security making it a part of the overall intelligence role within an organisation rather than the closely related security role. It is based on the assumption that the exploitation and protection of information. (hence, knowledge and data) cannot be separated.

# REFERENCES

Alberts, D.S. and Garstka, J. (2000) Information Superiority and Network Centric Warfare, talk given at *InfoWarCon2000*, Washington, September, 2000.

Alberts, D.S., Garstka, J.J., Stein, F.P. (1999) *Network Centric Warfare*, CCRP, Washington.

Arquilla, J., Ronfeldt, D. (1996) *The Advent of Netwar,* RAND, Santa Monica.

Beer, S. (1984) The Viable System Model: its provenance, development, methodology and pathology. In, Espejo R, Harnden R.(eds.), *The Viable System Model,* John Wiley & Sons, Chichester. pp.211-270.

Beer, S. (1985) *Diagnosing the System for Organisations.* Wiley, Chichester.

Boisot, M.H. (1998) *Knowledge Assets.* Oxford University Press, Oxford.

Campen, A.D. (ed) (1992) *The First Information War*, AFCEA International Press, Fairfax.

Denning, D.E. (1999) *Information Warfare and Security*, Addison Wesley, Reading: Mass.

Hutchinson, W.E., Warren, M.J. (2001a) *Information Warfare: Corporate Attack and Defence in the Digital Age*, Butterworth-Heineman, Oxford.

Hutchinson, W., Warren, M. (2001b) Principles of Information Warfare, *Journal of Information Warfare*, **1**,1: 1-6.

Ignatieff, M. (2000) *Virtual war*, Chatto and Windus, London.

Jones, A., Kovacich, G. L., Luzwick, P.G. (2002) *Global Information Warfare*, Auerbach, Washington

Knecht, R.J. (1996) Thoughts About Information Warfare, in: Campen, A.D., Dearth, D.H., Thomas Godden, R (eds) Cyberwar: Security, Strategy, and Conflict in the Information Age, AFCEA International Press, Fairfax.

Owens, B (2000) Lifting the Fog of War, FSG, New York.

Schwartau, W. (1996). Information Warfare – second edition, Thunder's Mouth Press, New York.

Waltz, E. (1998) Information Warfare – Principles and Operations, Artech House, Norwood.

# INTERNET SECURITY MANAGEMENT
## A Challenging Joint Postgraduate Curriculum Design

Helen L. Armstrong
*School of Information Systems, Curtin University of Technology, GPO Box UI987, Perth, Western Australia 6845, Australia  Tel:  61  8  9266  7017  Fax:  61  8  9266  3076 email: armstroh@cbs.curtin.edu.au*

**Abstract:**      This paper describes the design of a joint program in Internet Security Management between the Schools of Information Systems and Computer Science. An overview of the curriculum is given, and the roles played by each School in the teaching of the courses described. The advantages and hurdles of designing offerings across independent Schools are also discussed.

**Key words:**   Internet Security, Internet Security Management, Curriculum Design, Postgraduate Studies

## 1.      INTRODUCTION

With the growth in cybercrime comes a realization that organizations need to address the security of their information and associated information systems networks. The call for more educational programs in information security has emerged from both the private and public sectors, government agencies promoting specialist education and business organizations with a professional need for information security expertise.

A media release in February 2001 by Senator the Hon Richard Alston, Minister for Communications, Information Technology and the Arts (NOIE, 2001a), states that Information Security is a major national priority in Australia. In addition, the draft Report on E-Security R&D in Australia released by the National Office for the Information Economy states that "The [Australian] Government has a clear role to protect information infrastructure, which is critical to national security, and protect the public from criminal or malicious activity occurring through electronic mediums, primarily the Internet." (NOIE, 2001b).

In response to these national priorities and the needs of industry and government, Curtin University has designed a postgraduate program in Internet Security Management. The program is run jointly by the School of Computing and the School of Information Systems, and attempts to balance the technical, conceptual and human skills required to meet the above challenge.

In order to meet these growing demands, two Schools within Curtin University of Technology in Perth, Western Australia, joined forces to offer postgraduate studies specializing in Internet Security Management. The curriculum aims to produce graduates with generic, technical and management skills in the field of Internet security.

The aim of this paper is to discuss the design of the postgraduate curriculum in Internet security management across two academic schools in differing faculties within a university. The advantages of a joint program are discussed along with the problems encountered in the design process.

## 2.    OVERVIEW OF THE INTERNET SECURITY MANAGEMENT PROGRAMS

The new programs are designed for students who have completed a Bachelor degree in a computing related discipline. Students embarking on the programs require an understanding of computer programming, operating systems, networks and computer architecture.

The programs incorporate studies designed to develop students' conceptual and practical skills. Students are encouraged to think 'outside the box' in problem solving and applying security solutions. Numerous educational theories supporting learning by experience, action and reflection (eg Bloom et al., 1956; Kolb, 1984; Argyris, 1982) form the basis of the program design.

The units of study within the new programs are designed to meet the needs of students not only in the technical network and security aspects but also management skills. In particular graduates from the computer science discipline have requested more problem solving and management skills, whereas graduates from the information systems discipline have requested more network and security technical skills.

The new programs are offered at three levels:

- Postgraduate Diploma in Internet Security Management

- Master of Internet Security Management - professional masters degree

- Master of Commerce (Internet Security Management) – masters degree by coursework

The structure of the programs is illustrated in Table 1.

The programs include management units of study in problem solving, organizational behavior and change management, information security management and project and risk management. Technical areas covered relating to the security of Internet and electronic commerce include network and communications security, database security, distributed computing security, computer forensics, encryption and software security, web programming languages and tools, web site management and engineering, business intelligence and cyberwarfare, electronic commerce security, and Internet law. Two additional advanced units listed as options are machine perception and artificial intelligence – these two units of study encompass the application of advanced technology to the security industry, particularly pattern recognition, neural networks and speech recognition. For example, two of the areas students can apply this knowledge is the design of intrusion detection systems and biometrics. These two units also run as part of the computer science programs and are very popular with the students.

The new programs have been designed to meet a demand for both technical and management skills in a business environment where organizations are becoming more reliant upon global networks and electronic business environments. The numerous optional units ensure the programs are flexible and allow students to choose the most beneficial content for their needs.

## 2.1    Postgraduate Diploma in Internet Security Management

This program is designed for students who wish to enhance skills and knowledge in the design and management of Internet security and electronic commerce in business organizations. The program comprises eight units of study each carrying 25 credit points, totaling 200 credit points. The postgraduate diploma course can be completed in one year (two semesters) of full-time study or two years of part-time study.

*Table 1:* Structure of the Internet Security Management Programs

| Study Plan Full-time | Postgraduate Diploma in Internet Security Management | Master of Internet Security Management | Master of Commerce (Internet Security Management) |
|---|---|---|---|
| Year 1 Sem 1 | - Network & Communications Security<br>- Information Security Management<br>- Problem Solving<br>- Organizational Behavior<br>Or<br>- JAVA Programming | - Network & Communications Security<br>- Information Security Management<br>- Problem Solving<br>- Organizational Behavior<br>Or<br>- JAVA Programming | - Network & Communications Security<br>- Information Security Management<br>- Problem Solving<br>- Organizational Behavior<br>Or<br>- JAVA Programming |
| Year 1 Sem 2 | - Project & Risk Management<br>- Database Design & Security<br>- Distributed Computing Security<br>- Research Methods | - Project & Risk Management<br>- Database Design & Security<br>- Distributed Computing Security<br>- Research Methods | - Project & Risk Management<br>- Database Design & Security<br>- Distributed Computing Security<br>- Research Methods |
| Year 2 Sem 1 | | Computer Forensics<br>1 Optional Unit<br>Plus Either:<br>Security Project<br>(50 credits = 2 units) or<br>2 Optional Units | Computer Forensics<br>3 Optional Units |
| Year 2 Sem 2 | | | Security Project & Dissertation<br>(100 credits = 4 units) |
| Sem = Semester | | Optional Units:<br>Encryption & Software Security<br>Networking & Mobile Communications<br>Advanced JAVA Programming<br>XML Programming<br>Business Intelligence & Cyberwarfare<br>Electronic Commerce Security<br>Web Site Management<br>Web Site Engineering<br>Internet Law<br>Machine Perception<br>Artificial & Machine Intelligence | |

The units of study cover information security management, problem-solving, computer networks and communications, organizational behavior, JAVA programming, research methods, project management, distributed computing and database design and security.

The postgraduate diploma articulates to either the Master of Internet Security Management or the Master of Commerce (Internet Security Management).

## 2.2 Master of Internet Security Management

This course is a professional masters degree containing a total of twelve units of study. It is designed for computing professionals who wish to take leadership roles in the management of Internet security. Students need a computing-related degree plus a minimum of two years' relevant industry experience to enter this program. This course can be completed in eighteen months (three semesters) of full-time study or three years of part-time study.

The first eight units of the Master of Internet Security Management are the same as the Postgraduate Diploma course, with four additional units required to complete the degree. Computer forensics is a core unit of study in the masters program, and students may choose three optional units or undertake a research project. Optional study units include encryption and software security, business intelligence and cyberwarfare, web site management, electronic commerce security, XML programming, JAVA programming, Internet law, networking and mobile communications, machine perception and artificial intelligence.

There is no direct articulation from this professional masters to other masters degrees or doctorates. Students wishing to progress to doctoral studies are advised to enroll in the masters by coursework program in section 2.3, or a masters by research, in preference to this program.

## 2.3 Master of Commerce (Internet Security Management)

This course is designed for students who wish to continue their studies in Internet security management to gain further knowledge and skills in managing Internet security and electronic commerce environments. Unlike the professional masters degree students do not need relevant industry experience to undertake this course. The total program is 200 credit points containing a mix of eight coursework and research units. The Master of Commerce (ISM) consists of two stages, the first stage is the Postgraduate Diploma in ISM, the second stage is the Masters component. The Masters component has a duration of one year (two semesters) of full-time study or two years of part-time study.

The first eight units of study in stage one are the same as the Postgraduate Diploma in ISM above. The Masters stage comprises a unit of study on computer forensics and a choose of three other units of study from software security and encryption, business intelligence and cyberwarfare, web site management, electronic commerce security, XML programming, JAVA programming, Internet law, networking and mobile communications, machine perception and artificial intelligence.

The final component is a substantial research project in a security related area, resulting in a dissertation. The size of the research project must be equivalent to four units, or one full-time semester of study. This project is written up as a research dissertation, assessed by two examiners, and published by the university, thus satisfying the entrance requirements for doctoral studies.

## 3.  COLLABORATION ON THE JOINT PROGRAM DESIGN

There are many advantages and challenges in a joint program of this nature. This project has required the commitment of both schools to the time and resources required to design, develop and run these programs. The content has been based upon a shared understanding that an Internet Security Management professional needs to be holistic in approach, requiring generic, technical and practical skills. In addition, the joint offerings have provided students the opportunity to gain a much broader set of skills and knowledge. Computer Science students are exposed to computing in a business and organizational context, while Information Systems students acquire a greater depth of technical knowledge and expertise. The need for a graduate with a more rounded skill-set is thus met.

Recognition of each other's strengths and expertise has emerged from the curriculum design process. Agreement on the technical and management content has proven to be a challenge, particularly with regard to pre-requisite knowledge for the technical areas and sequencing of the courses. Difficulties arose where students with an IT undergraduate degree were considered to have insufficient technical knowledge to undertake some of the Computer Science owned units. Some of the advanced Computer Science units required a number of pre-requisite units only offered by that School. In addition, units are usually offered in either semester 1 or semester 2, not both. This added complexity to the sequencing of units to be studied, juggling units containing pre-requisite knowledge with the semesters offered. Fortunately, the two schools currently work closely together, recognizing duplications in units of study, and allowing students to undertake optional units in the other school.

Funding of staff and teaching resources within a university is a complicated matter. Sharing staff and resources across two different schools in different faculties is quite complex. The larger the body, the slower it moves, and the university is a unique organism. In order to work within the restricted University systems, the two Schools have agreed to share the teaching equally. Units offered by each school utilize resources from that school – for example, a unit owned by the School of Information Systems is taught by staff within that school using classrooms and laboratories under the control of that school. This is not the desired approach, however, as team teaching involving staff from both schools would have been the preferred teaching mode.

The new program has raised the requirement within both schools for isolated laboratories to carry out practical work and it has been necessary to hire appropriate laboratories from other schools within Curtin University for the initial running of some of the new units. New laboratories are currently being fitted to meet the requirements of the new programs. Administration of joint programs across more than one school is best handled by only one of the stakeholders. The School of Information Systems will administer the new program as the infrastructure and systems to handle the required administration are already in place within that school.

The university requires the overall program design to be approved by both Schools before being presented to the University Senate for final approval. The two schools have held numerous meetings to design the structure of the three programs, define the required content, develop a logical sequence, plan semester offerings and resolve problems relating to overlapping content and prerequisite knowledge. Industry partners common to both Schools were also part of the curriculum design team.

*Table 2:* Sample of Security Management Programs at other Universities

| University | Degree Name | Duration | Security Contents |
|---|---|---|---|
| University of Glamorgan (GLAM, 2002) | MSc in Information Security & Computer Crime | 1 year full-time | Security Management, Project Management & Research Methods, Network & Distributed Systems Security, Cryptography & E-commerce, Computer Law & Criminology, Computer Forensics |
| Royal Holloway University of London (RHUL, 2000) | MSc in Information Security | 1 year full-time | Security Management, Cryptography, Network Security, Computer Security (O/S), Secure E-Commerce, Standards & Evaluation Criteria, Advanced Cryptography, Database Security, Computer Crime, Project |
| London School of Economics University of | MSc in Information Systems Security | 2 years part-time | Security of Information, Secure Electronic commerce, Modeling Secure Business Systems, |

| | | | |
|---|---|---|---|
| London<br>(LSE, 2002) | & Access | | Global Consequence of IT,<br>Issues in Information Systems Security,<br>Information Security and the Law,<br>Models for Open Access |
| University of<br>Westminster<br>(WMIN, 2002) | MSc in<br>Information<br>Technology<br>Security | 1 year<br>full-time<br>2 years<br>part-time | Security Awareness,<br>Threats, Countermeasures, Standards &<br>Procedures,<br>Legal & Ethical Aspects,<br>Risk Analysis,<br>Business Needs, Policy & Planning,<br>Security Analysis, Post-incident<br>Reviews,<br>Security Management,<br>Computer Forensics,<br>Security,<br>Project Module |
| University of<br>Leicester<br>(LE, 2002) | MSc in Security<br>Management | 1 year<br>full-time<br>2 years<br>part-time | Intro to Security Management,<br>Crime and the Workplace,<br>Research Methods in Security<br>Management,<br>Managing Risk and Security,<br>Law, Procedures & Security<br>Management,<br>Management, Organizations & Security,<br>Dissertation |
| Edith Cowan<br>University<br>(ECU, 2002) | MSc in Computer<br>Security | 2 years<br>full-time | Information Security,<br>Computer Security,<br>Database Security,<br>Network Security,<br>Research Preparation,<br>Thesis (5th Year),<br>Computer Security Thesis (6th Year) |

## 4.    SIMILAR PROGRAMS

In the design of the new programs a search was conducted on similar programs run at other universities. The content of the programs investigated was quite diverse. Table 2 illustrates a small sample of the programs at other institutions that were studied.

Programs generally focused upon one of the following areas - security management, risk management, law and crime, cryptography, network security, electronic commerce security, computer forensics or information warfare. Many of the programs concentrated solely on the technical aspects and these appeared to be offered by computer science and engineering-related faculties. It was interesting to note, however, that studies in network security, cryptography, electronic commerce security and security management were common inclusions.

Only a few institutions offered courses in risk analysis or computer forensics. Several included project or research courses but no research methodology or project preparation courses. None of the courses investigated appeared to offer studies in conceptual skills, problem solving or change management. Programs specializing in electronic commerce security appeared to have the closest match in content to the proposed programs at Curtin University.

The growing number of programs offered at universities around the globe indicates that this is an area of growth in education. The reliance upon computer networks, global communications and the Internet (for engaging in electronic commerce in particular) together with the rising rate of crime associated with these mechanisms provide a demand for education and training in the Internet security area.

## 5. CONCLUSION

The design of the new programs and their formal approval by the university has taken eighteen months. The new programs will be running in 2003/4 provided the university's final seal of approval is granted. The effective life of the three programs is estimated at 3-4 years, provided the unit content is regularly updated. Although the design and approval process has been time-consuming the resultant programs are promising to be in high demand.

## REFERENCES

Argyris, C. [1982], *Reasoning, Learning and Action*, Jossey-Bass, USA

Bloom B, M. Englehard, E. Frost, W. Hill & D. Krathwohl [1956], *Taxonomy of Educational Objectives: The classification of Educational Goals:* Handbook 1, Cognitive Domain, Longmans, New York

ECU [2002], *Masters of Computer Security*, Edith Cowan University, http://www.ecu.edu.au/acserv/hb2002/pg/chs/

GLAM [2000] *MSc Information Security and Computer Crime*, Glamorgan University http://www3.glam.ac.uk/Prospectus/view.php3?ID=849&sfrom=easy&dosommat=string& year=2002

Kolb, D.A. [1984], *Experiential Learning: Experiences as a Source of Learning and Development*, Prentice-Hall Inc, Englewood Cliffs, New Jersey

LE [2002] Postgraduate *Prospectus, MSc in Security Management*, Leicester University, http://www.le.ac.uk/cgi-bin/tab_int/usr/netscape/suitespot/docs/ua/ hd/pgprospectus/courses/courses.txt?operation=retrieve&primary=m900d4

LSE [2002] *MSc Information Systems Security and Access*, London School of Economics University of London, http://www.lse.ac.uk/graduate/courses/msc_ information_systems_security.html

NOIE [2201a] *Information Security – A Major Priority*, Media release from the National Office for the Information Economy, Available WWW http://www.noie.gov.au/publications/media_releases/feb2001/infosecurity.htm

NOIE [2001b] *Report on E-Security R&D in Australia: An Initial Assessment*, National Office for the Information Economy, Canberra, Australia, June

RHUL [2000] *MSc in Information Security*, Royal Holloway University of London, http://www.isg.rhul.ac.uk/msc/info.shtml

WMIN [2002] *MSc in Information Technology Security*, Westminster University, http://www.wmin.ac.uk/solape/item.asp?ID=3888&

# INFORMATION SECURITY FUNDAMENTALS
*Graphical Conceptualisations for Understanding*

Per Oscarson
*Research Group VITS, Department of Business Administration, Economics, Statistics and Informatics, Örebro University, Sweden*

Abstract: This paper deals with some fundamental concepts within the area of information security, both their definitions and their relationships. The included concepts are information asset, confidentiality, integrity, availability, threat, incident, damage, security mechanism, vulnerability and risk. The concepts and their relations are modeled graphically in order to increase the understanding of conceptual fundamentals within the area of information security.

Key words: Information security, security concepts, information asset, threat, incident, damage, security mechanism, risk

## 1. INTRODUCTION

As a university lecturer and researcher in the topic of information security, I have identified a lack of material that supplies conceptual fundamentals as a whole. Authors often stipulate definitions without any discussion regarding their semantic meaning, and I claim that the relationships between these concepts seldom are explicit discussed or defined. An increased understanding of relationships between concepts may lead to an increased understanding of the concepts themselves, and inversely. Hence, I argue that these two types of understanding may contribute to a conceptual understanding as a whole. The aim of this paper is to increase the understanding of information security fundamentals. This is done by graphical representations of the concepts mentioned above and their relationships.

This paper is based on a licentiate thesis (Oscarson, 2001) that was built upon theoretical as well as empirical studies. However, the conceptual work has been continued during the year 2002, and the fundamental concepts and their relationships have therefore been further developed. One important part of this work is interaction with students; the graphs have been used when tutoring students' final theses in bachelor and master programs. The experiences of that work are good, even if no systematic empirical research has been done. During the spring 2003, the graphical conceptualisations are used in a basic distance course in information security. An evaluation of the usefulness of the graphs in that course is currently under design.

## 2.    INFORMATION ASSETS

The foundation for security is assets that need to be protected (see e.g. Gollman, 1999). Assets may be people, things created by people or parts of nature. In the area of information security, the assets are often labelled as information assets, and enclose not only the information itself but also resources that are in use to facilitate the management of information (e.g. Björck, 2001; ISO/IEC 17799, 2001), as depicted in Figure 1.

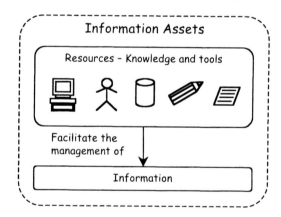

Figure 1. Information assets consist of information as well as resources to facilitate the management of information

I claim that it is the information that is the primary asset, and IT and other resources are tools to facilitate information management. Resources have hence an instrumental value in relation to the information (of course, information may be highly integrated with resources that manage the information, e.g. in a database). The term information security expresses therefore a more holistic view than IT-security, which manifests a more technical view since technical resources are focused (Oscarson, 2001). As it will be seen in Figure 2, I define IT as *digital* tools for managing information. A more exhaustive definition of IT is (translated from Oscarson, 2001, p 56):

> Information technology (IT) is a concept that refers to digital technology, i.e. hard- and software for creating, collecting, processing, storing, transmitting, presenting and duplicating information. The information may be in the shape of e.g. sound, text, image or video, and IT mean hence a merging of the traditional areas of computers, telecom and media.

IT artefacts in the shape of e.g. personal computers, networks, operative systems and applications constitute thus one of several types of supporting resources for manage information. It is not only IT artefacts to be counted as resources when managing information. Information may be managed manually, which make humans an important resource. People are also indirectly an important resource because that is always people that handle tools that manage information. Tools that help humans to manage information may be electronic or non-electronic. Moreover, electronic tools may be divided into digital and analogue tools. Figure 2 shows a simple classification of information-managing resources.

Non-electronic tools may be for example pens, papers, staplers and notice boards while analogue tools are for example over-head devices, paper-shredders and telephones (which also can be digital). Security mechanisms (safeguards) may also be counted as resources for managing information. Security mechanisms may belong to all of the categories illustrated in Figure 2 (more about security mechanisms in section 4).

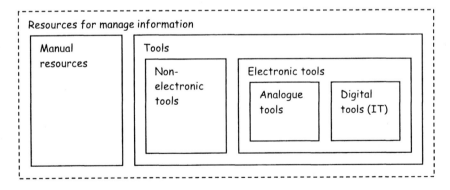

Figure 2. A classification of resources for information management

Information as an asset in organizations is a wide domain of knowledge, and is not only about information (represented by data) stored in IT-based information systems. A great amount of an organization's information is non-formalized and is not digitalized or even on print. Information that seems to be unimportant for one organization may be important to other actors, e.g. competitors. Some information, e.g. negative publicity, may arise at the same moment when an incident occurs. For example, the information that an information system has been hacked may become very sensitive information at the same moment the incident occurs. Moreover, information as an asset is not only about information that exists in an organization – it is also important that an organization can obtain relevant and reliable information when necessary.

## 2.1    Confidentially, Integrity and Availability

Security concerning IT and information is normally defined by three aspects, or goals; confidentiality, integrity and availability (see e.g. Gollman, 1999; Harris, 2002; Jonsson, 1995). The concepts can be seen as the *objectives* with security regarding IT and information and are often referred to as the 'CIA triad' (Harris, 2002). Definitions of the CIA triad may differ depending on what kind of assets that are focused, e.g. a specific computer/IT system, information system or information assets as defined above. Regarding information assets, the three concepts can be defined as follows:
- Confidentiality: Prevention of unauthorized disclosure or use of information assets
- Integrity: Prevention of unauthorized modification of information assets
- Availability: Ensuring of authorized access of information assets when required

The definitions are influenced by Gollman (1999) and Harris (2002), but are revised in the following way: Gollman and Harris use 'information' and/or 'systems' for the three concepts, while I claim that all three concepts should concern both information and resources for managing information, i.e. information assets. The objective is that both information and resources will stay confidential, unmodified and available. For example, weaknesses in confidentiality may be caused both by disclosure of sensitive information *and* by unauthorized use of a computer system. Integrity can be seen as a quality characteristic of information assets, while confidentiality and availability are characteristics of the relations between information assets and an authorized user (availability) and an unauthorized user (confidentiality), as depicted in Figure 3.

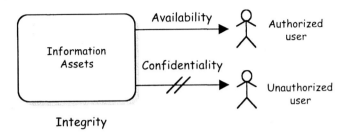

Figure 3. A graphical description of the CIA triad – Confidentiality, Integrity and Availability (influenced by Jonsson, 1995; Olovsson, 1992)

For simplifying reasons, the CIA triad will henceforth in the paper be treated as characteristics of information assets, even if correct definitions in two cases are characteristics between information assets and users (which may be authorized or unauthorized).

## 2.2 Threats against Information Assets

Information assets may be exposed for threats. There are a number of definitions of threat in the field of computers, IT and information. Here are a few examples:

'...an indication that an undesirable event may occur' (Parker, 1981),
'...any potential danger to information or systems' (Harris, 2002),
'...circumstances that have the potential to cause loss or harm' (Pfleeger, 1996).

If the objective of information security is to reach and maintain the CIA triad of information assets at a required level, threat is something that potentially can impair the CIA triad in the future. Parker (1981) mentions 'undesirable events' above (which I label as incident, see next section below), which I interpret as if confidentiality, integrity or availability will be impaired. That means that a threat consists of a potential action or occurrence that may affect the information asset's CIA triad negatively. Actions and occurrences do not happen by themselves, there must be causes lying behind. Harris (2002) calls such underlying causes for threat agents, and it may be actors (humans or organizations), by human made artefacts or natural phenomena (cf. e.g. Pfleeger, 1996). In my definition of threat I hence include both actions/occurrences and underlying causes:

Threats are potential undesirable actions or occurrences, that performs or causes by actors, by human created artifacts or natural phenomena and which are supposed to impair the CIA triad of current information assets.

Using the definitions discussed so far, we can define the relations between threat agent, threat, the CIA triad and information asset as well (see Figure 4).

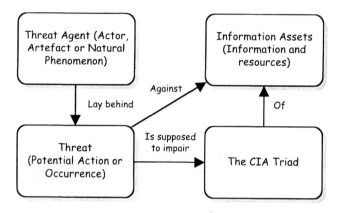

Figure 4. The relations between threat agent, threat, the CIA triad and information assets

Human threat agents may be intentional or accidental (see e.g. Harris, 2002). Terrorism, information warfare, sabotages and intrusions are examples of intentional threats, while carelessness, mistakes and ignorance are unintentional threats. Non-human threats, i.e. artefacts and natural phenomena, may be floods, fires, earthquakes and thunderstorms. Artefacts may function in undesirable ways, and since humans create artefacts, threats often have a combination of underlying threat agents. That is, humans may construct, implement, configure or handle artefacts in inappropriate or destructive ways, for example people who creates destructive IT-artefacts as viruses and worms.

Physical threats are threats that appear in a physical manner, like floods, thefts and fires. Non-physical threats, or logical threats, are often connected to software as viruses, computer intrusion and user's software mistakes. Such threats will mostly affect non-physical assets, but may affect physical assets as well.

Sometimes there are reasons to expect that actors, artefacts or natural phenomena that are not yet existing, or not for the moment performing actions or causing occurrences may do so in the future. They can be apprehended as potential threats.

## 3. INCIDENTS AND DAMAGES

While a threat is an assumption that an undesirable event may occur in a future, the term *incident* refers to the actual occurrence of such event. In other words, a threat may be realized as one or several incidents. A threat may still exist after a realization, since underlying causes still may have capabilities to realize the threat several times. The probability for realization will however often decrease since people often increase the protection against realized threats. Like threats, an occurred incident may be unknown. Such incidents may be discovered after a while or remain unknown. Incidents that are realized by unknown threats are unexpected incidents.

Incidents may lead to consequences. If a consequence affects the CIA triad of information assets uncontrolled and negatively, it is labelled as *damage*. There may be incidents that not impair the CIA triad, for example a virus that infects an information system without causing any damage. The infection is still an undesired event that probably happens out of the control of the system managers.

Figure 5 shows the relationships between threat agent, threat, information asset, the CIA triad, incident and damage (the definitions of threat and assets have been removed from the illustration to make the graph more simple).

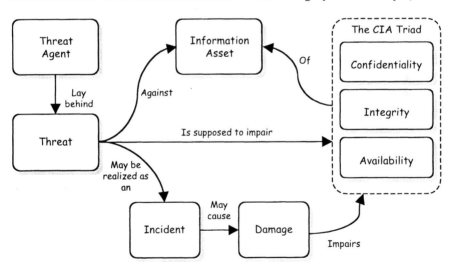

Figure 5. The concepts incident and damage are added to the growing graph

A definition of damage may be extracted from the objectives of information security:

Damages are uncontrolled impairs of the CIA triad of information assets.

Practically, there may be many kinds of damages. Information can be changed in an uncontrolled and undesirable way, information may disappear or be read by unauthorized persons and information and IT artefacts may be unavailable for authorized persons.

## 4.    SECURITY MECHANISMS

*Security mechanisms* are something that will improve the CIA triad of information assets, i.e. increase the information security (Oscarson, 2001). The terms protections, countermeasures, controls and safeguards may be used as synonyms to security mechanisms. Security mechanisms can be categorized in several ways. Bases for categorizations may be for example their relation to the CIA triad (Jonsson, 1995; Oscarson, 2001) or what they consists of – e.g. hardware, software and policies – (e.g. Pfleeger, 1996). One way is to categorize them based on their functionality in relation to the time of an incident; security mechanisms can be preventing, averting or recovering (SIG Security, 1999). Preventing security mechanisms are highly directed to the threat; to affect threat agents in purpose to reduce the danger of a threat, or the probability that a threat will be realized to incidents. Examples of preventing security mechanisms are security awareness and laws. Averting security mechanisms intend to obstruct incidents, e.g. in the shape of firewalls or encryption programs. Recovering (or restoring) security mechanisms recover already damaged information assets. An example of a security mechanism is anti-virus software that repairs infected files.

In accordance to the four objects threat, incident, damage and the CIA triad, there is one link missing in the chain. There are security mechanisms that reduce damages, as for example fire extinguisher, that either avert incidents nor recover an already damaged information asset; such security mechanisms are *damage reducing*. Summing up, a categorization of security based on time of an incident consists of four categories: preventing, averting, damage reducing and recovering security mechanisms (see Figure 6).

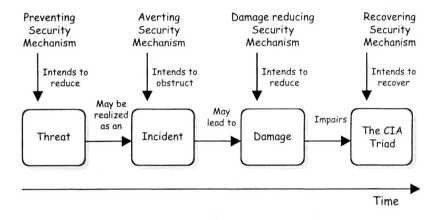

Figure 6. Four categories of security mechanisms based on their relation in time to incidents

Two other categories that closely fit in to this categorization are detective (e.g. Gollman, 1999; Olovsson, 1992) and reporting security mechanisms (Statskontoret, 1997). The reason why they do not can be used in this type of categorization is that they may be used in any time in relation to an incident; before, during or after the realization of a threat. Detecting security mechanisms may be used for discovering/reporting new kinds of threats, detecting/reporting intrusions or intrusion attempts, as well as detecting/reporting already damaged information assets. Detective security mechanisms are almost always also reporting; when some threat, incident or damage has been detected, it may also be reported. That means that preventing, averting or recovering security mechanisms may be detecting and/or reporting as well. Additionally, it is important to understand that specific security *products* may have several functionalities, i.e. preventing, averting, damage reducing, recovering, detecting and reporting.

The four categories of security mechanisms that are presented in this section can be connected to the growing conceptual graph and is shown in Figure 7; preventing security mechanisms may affect threat agents, averting security mechanisms may obstruct incidents, and damage reducing mechanisms may reduce damages. Finally, recovering security mechanisms may completely or partially restore impaired confidentiality, integrity or availability of information assets.

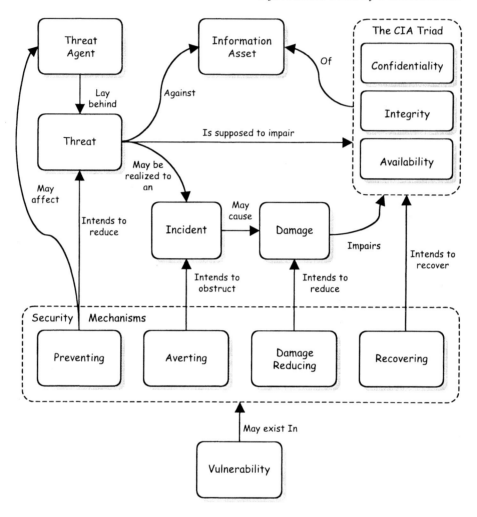

Figure 7. A graphical representation of fundamental concepts and their relationships

## 4.1    Vulnerability

*Vulnerability* is absence of security mechanisms, or weaknesses in existing security mechanisms (see e.g. Harris, 2002; Ozier, 2000). Vulnerability may exist in all of the categories of security mechanisms that are mentioned in the previous section (see Figure 7), and may be known or unknown.

# 5.    RISK

Risk is another fundamental concept in the area of security. However, the risk concept is difficult to range in the graph presented above, since risk is a concept that concerns assessed future conditions; some of the objects in the graph are changing when it comes to risk assessment, e.g. 'potential damage' instead of 'damage'. Moreover, the graph tends to be too complex if it includes a large number of concepts and relations. This section presents hence another conceptual graph concerning risk assessment.

Risk is someone's estimation concerning the occurrences of incidents and potential damages caused by incidents (e.g. Parker, 1981 and Ozier, 2000). Consequently, the concept of risk consists of two parts; the *probability* or the *expected frequency* of that an incident will occur and the *potential damages* an incident may cause. This can be expressed in the following equation:

$R = L * P$

R stands for risk, L is potential loss, and P is probability or expected frequency of loss (Parker, 1981). Even if an incident leads to a serious damage, there is no risk if the probability or expected frequency is zero, and reverse. This means that $R = 0$ require $L = 0$ and/or $P = 0$. In accordance to the discussion about damages above, the terms damages and loss are used synonymously. In the standard ISO/IEC 17799 (2001, p 8), risk (assessment) is defined in a similar way, i.e. it consists of the likelihood of an incident as well as the potential negative consequences.

The risk concept including probability, expected frequency and potential damage may be connected graphically to threat, incident, information asset and the CIA triad (see Figure 8). As shown in Figure 8, the risk concept is closely related to threats, incidents and the CIA triad of information assets. That means that risk assessment must deal with estimation of those phenomena. However, the risk concept is not connected to security mechanisms and vulnerabilities in this graph. As discussed previously in this paper, security mechanisms may intend to affect threat agents, reduce threats, obstruct incident, reduce damages or recover impairs of the CIA triad of information assets. This means that security mechanisms may decrease risks by decreasing the probability or the expected frequency of the occurrences of incidents, or by decreasing damages of occurred incidents. Vulnerabilities in security mechanisms will increase risks.

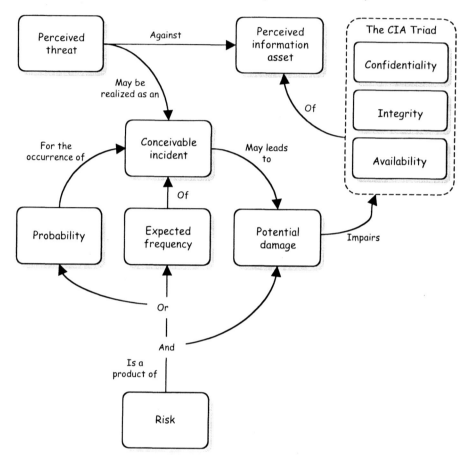

Figure 8. The risk concept in relation to threat, incident, the CIA triad and information assets

## 6.    SUMMARY

This paper has introduced some graphical conceptualisations of fundamental concepts within the information security area. Conceptual modelling is based upon linguistic and philosophical perceptions and standpoints, and is hence heavily dependent on underlying perspectives. That means that linguistic definitions of concepts, or relations between concepts, never can be regarded as a "universal truth", but may represent a way to study a phenomenon or an area. With that in mind, the graphs may be useful in future research as well as for educational purposes. As mentioned in the introduction section, an empirical study in form of a course evaluation is planned. Such study may work as a further grounding, and/or a refining of the graphs presented in this paper.

Even if my own perspective is business oriented, I believe this conceptual work is quite generic in the sense that it may be valid even for more technical areas of security, and therefore may be useful in more technical oriented education. However, I believe that the business-oriented perspective has some impact on the result, especially the concept of information asset. In more technical oriented perspectives, assets often consist of data and system rather than information and resources for information management (cf. e.g. Jonsson, 1995). My intention is to continue this work in purpose to create a framework regarding actual and perceived information security. This work will among other things include modelling of concepts in different conditions of time and if they are referring to actual conditions or subjective perceptions. For this work, this paper may serve as one part of a conceptual base.

## REFERENCES

Björck F (2001). Security Scandinavian Style – Interpreting the Practice of Managing Information Security in Organisations. Licentiate Thesis, Department of Computer and Systems Sciences, Stockholm University/Royal Institute of Technology, Stockholm

Gollman D (1999). Computer Security. Wiley

Harris S (2002). CISSP Certification Exam Guide. McGraw-Hill/Osbourne,

Jonsson E (1995). A Quantitative Approach to Computer Security from a Dependability Perspective. Doctoral Dissertation, Department of Computer Engineering, Chalmers University of Technology, Göteborg

Olovsson T (1992). A Structured Approach to Computer Security. Technical Report No 122, Department of Computer Engineering, Chalmers University of Technology, Göteborg

Oscarson P (2001). Informationssäkerhet i verksamheter. (Information Security in Organizations – in Swedish). Licentiate Thesis, Department of Computer and Information Science, Linköping University

Ozier W (2000) Risk Analysis and Assessment, in Information Security Handbook, Tipton H F & Krause M, Auerbach publications

Parker D B (1981). Computer Security Management, Prentice Hall

Pfleeger C P (1996). Security in Computing. Prentice-Hall,

SIG Security (1999). Säkerhetsarkitekturer (Security Architectures, in Swedish). SIG Security, Studentlitteratur

ISO/IEC 17799 (2001). Information Technology – Code of Practice for Information Security Management. International Organization for Standardization

Statskontoret (1997). Handbok i IT-säkerhet (IT Security Handbook, in Swedish), The Swedish Agency for Public Management

# AUSTRALIA'S AGENDA FOR E-SECURITY EDUCATION AND RESEARCH

M.J. Warren
*School of Information Technology, Deakin University,G eelong, Victoria, Australia, 3217*

**Abstract**: The paper describes the development of a national E-security strategy for Australia. The paper discusses the rationale behind its development and the issues that relate to the policy and its possible implementation and its impact upon E-security teaching and E-security research. The paper also discusses how current situations are having an impact on the development of a national education and research initiative.

**Key words**: Australia, National Policy, E-security, Security education and Security research.

## 1. INTRODUCTION

The widespread use of computer systems has resulted in a new dependence upon computers and the data they contain. Computer systems now contain millions of records relating to commerce, healthcare, banking, defence and personal information. All this information is at risk of either being mis-used for fraudulent purposes or modified for malicious reasons. This description describes the situation in most Western countries including Australia. The problem that all developed countries face is how to define a policy for E-security at a national level. In order for this policy to be effective it must also cover key issues such as security education and security research.

This paper describes the steps that Australia has taken and some of the issues that Australia faces in development of a national policy.

In terms of the paper the term E-security will be used, this is the term used by the Australian federal government to represent what is known as IT Security, Information Security, etc.

## 2.    THE AUSTRALIAN SECURITY PROBLEM

A recent AusCERT Survey (Auscert, 2002) has focused upon the state of E-security within Australia, the following is a summary of the main results:

- 67% of all organizations surveyed have been attacked in 2002 - twice the 1999 level and 35 per cent of these organizations experienced six or more incidents;

- 98% of companies had experience either computer Security incidents / crime or other forms of computer abuse (such as network scanning, theft of laptops, employee abuse);

- Of Australian organisation who were victims of computer incidents, 65% of these attacks were from internally parties within the organisation and 89% came from external sources;

- 43% of Australian organizations were willing to hire ex-hackers to deal with security issues, three times more than in the US.

The survey showed that E-security and computer misuse are a major problem within Australia. The survey showed that external attacks were the source of the majority of attacks. An Australian Federal Government department NOIE (National Office of the Information Economy) sponsored project tried to determine the risks associated with the Information Economy. They determined that 43% of survey respondents were concerned with privacy issue and 42% of survey respondents were concerned about fraud (Allen Consultancy Group & NOIE, 2002).

These studies indicated that Australia has a major problem in regards to E-security and that people are concerned about the associated E-security risks. This also points to the importance of E-security education and E-security R&D in helping to reduce this problem.

## 3.    DEVELOPMENT OF A NATIONAL POLICY

NOIE has been looking at the Australian E-security situation by undertaking a number of projects. The aim of the first project was to determine what the situation was within Australia in regards to E-security education. The project found that the main issues were (Aeuckens, 2001):

- Demand for people with E-security skills is expected to be strong over the few years;

- Recruitment of personnel with E-security skills is difficult compared to other IT&T skills.

This project also identified some key issues that related to Australian organisations and the impact of E-security, these key issues were (Aeuckens, 2001):

- *Demand is rising.* As E-security becomes an integral business issue, demand for skilled personnel is growing within Australia;

- *Recruitment of people with the right skill sets is difficult.* The greatest difficulty is in recruiting people with well-rounded security and risk management skills (likely to include technical and business skills);

- *E-Security is not just an issue for security personnel.* All IT personnel should have an awareness of E-security issues and its place in a business environment;

- *Limited Graduate programs.* Many organisations recruited new IT graduates. Graduates did not generally have any specific understanding of security, therefore it was necessary for them to undergo further training;

- *Education and training opportunities in E-security are not widely available.* The minimum qualification demanded by employers is generally at the Bachelor level but these lack security content.

A further NOIE investigation was into E-security research and its development within Australia. This NOIE project found it was essential to ensure the long-term future of Australia's E-security research for a number of reasons (King, 2001):

- Dependence on foreign E-security providers limits the input that Australia has into the type and character of products and services developed. Australia should not be reliant upon other countries dictating appropriate levels of security;

- A commercial imperative also exists. A secure and trusted electronic environment is a necessary condition enabling electronic commerce;

- The E-security industry is experiencing substantial growth. R&D is an important link in the innovation chain driving developments in this industry sector. The Government has an important role to play ensuring that Australia is a global supplier as well as a consumer of E-security products and services. Eventually, some kind of security technology, be it hardware or software, will be resident in every networked device. Maintaining a critical mass of E-security R&D in Australia is essential to achieving this aim;

- A robust E-security R&D environment can also play a key role in attracting skilled E-security workers to Australia, and keep homegrown talent from moving overseas;

- E-security R&D will assist in providing the Government with the tools to perform its role in law enforcement activities to protect information infrastructure and the public.

These projects showed the importance of E-security teaching and E-security R&D in an Australia context. The outcome of the NOIEs projects was the need to develop a National E-security strategy. The objectives and aims of the draft policy were defined as (Aeuckens, 2001):

- That Àustralian Defence Signals Directorate (DSD) to scope the feasibility of new schemes, e.g. a Scholarships for Service program to provide scholarships to students in exchange for a period of service with DSD upon graduation, etc;

- That NOIE canvass the interest of other major government IT employers in participating in a scholarships and/or internship/vacation employment program;

- That key academics and government and industry representatives work towards a security core body of knowledge reflecting the latest developments in security technologies and policies;

- That a comprehensive survey of industry and government be conducted to obtain views on a wide range of security skills-related issues in order to inform the design and implementation of future initiatives;

- That NOIE undertake further work to scope the establishment of a National E-security Education Centre (NESEC), in conjunction with universities (Australian and overseas), DSD and other government and industry representatives. NESEC would be a central repository of E-security course information, which institutions could build into their existing IT/Computer Science courses;

- The feasibility of an industry-backed E-security professional certification scheme should be further investigated, including the potential applicability of the internationally available schemes to Australian industry and government needs.

NOIE had defined within its National E-security strategy two major key areas that were important for the future of Australia, these were:

- E-security Teaching – ensuring that E-security skills are taught at Australian Universities to all students. Ensuring there is co-operation between Australian Universities and industry to teach and develop courses;

- E-security R&D – ensuring that E-security R&D is considered important area for Australia's future R&D national strategy.

Then events outside Australia caused a major impact, the bombing of the World Trade Center (September, 11th, 2001) and the Bali bombing (October, 12th, 2002) had a direct impact upon Australian national policy. In the Australian Federal budget (2001-02) the government announcement that A$400 million would be allocated over four years for defence purposes (Scott, 2001. This had an impact that budgets of other government departments were reduced.

In 2002 the structure and role of NOIE was changed, the area of IT industry policy and its development was removed from its portfolio, this has in impact upon the role of NOIE (Cant, 2002). Following the budget, the role of NOIE's strategy was refocused upon the following areas (Western Australia Government, 2002):

- developing strategic advice on the demand drivers for Broadband, and provide the secretariat for the Australian Broadband Advisory Group;

- mapping the long term strategic environment for the ICT industry, as a contribution to the ICT industry 'Framework for the Future' study;

- accelerating the uptake of E-business and E-procurement by small to medium business enterprises; and

- promoting E-security, facilitating implementation of a coordinated national E-security agenda.

An important policy refocus during this time was the fact that NOIE was more involved with "Protecting National Infrastructure: E-security". NOIE became more involved with a number of projects aimed at protecting Australian Critical Infrastructure such as e.g. National Security Australia, (http://nationalsecurity.ag.gov.au), and Business-Government Task Force on Critical Infrastructure (http://www.cript.gov.au/). This was a major shift away from general E-security and a move towards National Security Protection.

The author went to Canberra in 2002 to talk to key stake holders of NOIE to find out about the current state of the National E-security strategy. The outcomes of the meetings were:

- Key staff had left NOIE, this had a direct impact upon the project as there was no one left to 'champion' it;

- Budgets cuts and realignment of strategic aims had a major impact upon NOIE with a refocus of its goals and objectives.

The amended National E-security strategy was cut back to only **one area** of the initial National E-security strategy, which was:

- The feasibility of an industry-backed E-security professional certification scheme should be further investigated, including the potential applicability of the internationally available schemes to Australian industry and government needs.

Currently NOIE is working with AusCERT to develop a strategy for this objective. This means that all the key issues put forward by the National E-security strategy in relation to E-security teaching and E-security R&D have been abandoned including the need to develop an Australian common body of knowledge and surveys of industry to determine needed security skills with Australia.

## 4.     CONCLUSION

The aims of the draft National E-security strategy was to define key areas for Australia's development, which were E-security teaching and E-security R&D. But because of world events the focus of NOIE and National E-security strategy has moved towards critical infrastructure protection. This change in strategic direction could cause long-term damage for Australia's development as E-security teaching and E-security R&D is abandoned.

## REFERENCES

Aeuckens D (2001) E-Security Skills, Education and Training in Australia: A Policy Scoping Paper, NOIE Report. Canberra, Australia.

Allen Consultancy Group & NOIE (2002) Report: Australia Information Economy – the Big Picture, Sydney, Australia.

AusCert (2002) 2002 Australian Computer Crime and Security Survey, University of Queensland, Australia.

Cant, S (2002) Confusion reigns as NOIE role shifts, The Age, June 24th, Melbourne, Australia.

King G. (2001) Report on E-security R&D in Australia: an initial assessment, NOIE Report. Canberra, Australia.

NOIE (2001) Protection of Australia's National Information Infrastructure & E-security Policy (Administrative and Operational Arrangements), Canberra, Australia.

Scott B (2001) Media Release: Budget 2001-02 - Defence People Win, MIN 144/2001, Department of Defence, May, Canberra, Australia.

Western Australia Government (2002) NOIE focus on economic transformation, improving government information.

URL: http://www.ecommercecentre.online.wa.gov.au/government/noie.htm

Accessed 12/12/02

# IS SECURITY A GREAT PRINCIPLE OF COMPUTING?
*Invited Talk*

Peter J. Denning
*Naval Postgraduate School, Monterey, California, USA*

In the 1960s, when computing was still a young discipline, the core courses were automata theory, logic design, numerical analysis, programming, and language translation. These courses represented the core technologies in which a basis of math and science existed. Today there are 20 core technologies and their representatives compete fiercely for slots in the stable of required courses.

Security made its first formal appearance in operating systems around 1960. Today it is a field of its own, competing for slots in core curricula, for tracks and certificates in CS degree programs, and even for status as a Masters Degree program in many schools. Does security deserve this status? Is it a transient response in a time of uncertainty about war? Is it based on deep and enduring principles that merit a place in every computing professional's education?

The approach of aligning the core curriculum with core technologies was good during the early days when the key technologies were few. But today learning the inner workings of 20 technologies and their 400 possible direct interactions is a daunting challenge. A new approach is needed.

A good model comes from the old sciences such as astronomy, life sciences, chemistry, and physics. Each identifies a small set of invariant principles and builds rich structures from the base principles. The newcomer finds this to be a much more rewarding approach because it promotes understanding from the beginning and shows how the science transcends particular technologies. We can adopt this model in computing.

The principles of computing are in five main categories:

- Computation -- what can be computed and at what cost?

- Communication -- how are data represented and transferred?

- Coordination -- how are computing and work processes coordinated?

- Storage -- how are data named, stored, retrieved, and shared?

- Automation -- what can be automated and at what cost?

But the field cannot be understood by its principles alone. The practices of computing are in four main categories:

- Programming   -- using programming languages to write programs that solve problems.

- Systems   -- organizing software and hardware components into large, reliable, and dependable systems.

- Modeling -- formulating models of systems in their operating contexts which guide design and configuration.

- Innovation   -- designing systems that produce sufficient new value and are adopted into standard practice.

Security is a pervasive concern in all categories of principles and practices.

## SPEAKER

PETER J. DENNING is Professor and Chairman of the Computer Science Department at the Naval Postgraduate School in Monterey, California. He was the founding director of the Research Institute for Advanced Computer Science at the NASA Ames Research Center, was co-founder of CSNET, and was head of the computer science department at Purdue. He received a PhD from MIT and BEE from Manhattan College. He invented the working set model for program behavior and made seminal contributions to performance evaluation. He has published 7 books and 290 articles on computers, networks, and their operating systems, and is working on 3 more books. He was named one of Mason's 5 best teachers in 2002, the best teacher in the School of Information Technology and Engineering, and one of Virginia's 10 Best Teachers. He holds three honorary degrees, three professional society fellowships, two best-paper awards, three distinguished service awards, the ACM Outstanding Contribution Award, the ACM SIGCSE Outstanding CS Educator Award, and the prestigious ACM Karl Karlstrom Outstanding Educator Award.

# IT SECURITY READINESS IN DEVELOPING COUNTRIES
*Tanzania Case Study*

Respickius Casmir and Louise Yngström
*Department of Computer and Systems Science (DSV), Stockholm University / Royal Institute of Technology, Forum 100, 164 40 Kista, Sweden, Fax:46 8 703 90 25, si-rc@dsv.su.se and louise@dsv.su.se*

**Abstract**: Much as computer and network security is increasingly becoming a global concern for enterprises, government agencies, academia and even for individuals' home use, still there are some people in some parts of the world who are not even informed of the existence of such a problem. Specifically, of these people are in developing countries. Tanzania is a typical example of the countries in which IT security issues have not been addressed adequately. This was revealed during the course and seminars on IT security conducted in Tanzania in the fall of year 2001. In this paper we shall start by describing the background and current situations of IT and connectivity in the country, followed by a summary discussion of evaluations of the course and seminars. Then we shall cite some of the fatal few reported computer security breach incidents in the country. Finally, we shall discuss what is our next step towards an attempt to deal with the problem.

**Key words**: IT Security, Developing Countries, Security Education and Training

## 1. INTRODUCTION

This paper is part of an ongoing research work by the authors in order to establish typical IT security needs for developing countries upon which we can develop security education program(s) for these countries. The research commenced early in January 2001. In the course of this study, we managed to conduct a short course on IT security to the University of Dar es Salaam students from different academic disciplines. We, also, conducted a seminar on IT security to the IT practitioners from the industries, government agencies, and legal firms. We, finally, organised a separate seminar to the University of Dar es Salaam academic and non-academic staff to discuss IT security issues.

## 2.      BACKGROUND

In the course of ten years back, Tanzania has experienced a dramatic change in the field of Information and Communications Technology (ICT) [1], [6]. Precisely, we can put it, as it is a cut-off from nothing to something. Before 1994, Tanzania had no Internet connectivity, no cellular phone operations, no Automatic Teller Machines (ATM) bank services, and no even television broadcast (except TV-Zanzibar, which was covering the Isles part of Tanzania only). The only way an ordinary citizen could get news and information both local and International was through radio broadcast and newspapers.

Early in 1994, the first television station was inaugurated in the country. In the mid to end of the same year another TV station came into operation making the count of the TV stations in the country to two. Both TV stations were privately owned. Year 1994, can be termed as the year of "Information and Communication Technology (ICT) Revolution" since it is in the same year the first Cellular phone Company opened its business for the first time in the history of the country. The following year 1995, witnessed the establishment a second cellular phone operator, and two more private Television stations.

It was not until 1996 when for the first time Tanzania became part of the global information network, this is the Internet. The University of Dar es Salaam (www.ucc.co.tz) Computing Centre made it. The Internet link was through VSAT link through Transtel in South Africa, which is a subsidiary of TRANSNET (www.tnet.co.za). This was the first Internet Service Provider (ISP) in the country. A few months later in the same year, a local private Company, in the name of CyberTwiga, established another Internet connection over X.25 packet switched network. Standard Chartered Bank was the first bank in Tanzania to introduce the Automatic Teller Machines (ATM) services in Tanzania in 1996.

## 3.      CURRENT SITUATION

Today, there are at least seven Internet Service Providers in Tanzania [11], [7]. The number of TV stations is now seven including one cable TV. Cellular phones operators have increased in number from a single operator in

1994 to five operators in year 2002 [7]. Banks that are offering ATM services have increased to three in February 2002 when NBC bank inaugurated this kind of service. The other bank offering ATM services in the country is Barclays. A number of banking and financial institutions, Government institutions, private companies and other business organisations have been computerised, and some are in the process of computerizing their Information Systems. The systems that are being computerised include payrolls, library systems, banking and insurance systems, hospital systems, accounting systems, academic registration systems and many more [6].

In a report issued by Accenture, the Markle Foundation, and the United Nations Development Programme (UNDP) public-private partnership (the Digital Opportunity Initiative (DOI)) in July 2001 [1], Tanzania was commended for its effort and progress to towards exploiting the benefits of Information and Communication Technology (ICT). DOI was formed at the G8 Okinawa Summit in July 2000. The report further added that, despite having very low per capita income, Tanzania is preparing to reposition itself in the global network economy. Bold steps are being taken to leverage the benefits of ICT for its national priorities of growth and poverty reduction [13]. Key actions include: the creation of an e-secretariat [6], including key stakeholders to create supportive leadership for ICT development; communications infrastructure improvements, both in the capital city and in secondary towns; and restructuring of the financial sector to sustain a more market-driven economy [8]. As it prepares for the shocks associated with the transition from an agriculture-based economy to a knowledge-based economy, Tanzania hopes to illustrate that starting off on the right foot is the key to leapfrogging or "antelope-jumping" many stages of ICT development [1].

## 3.1    International Connectivity

At the moment, all public data communication providers in the country reach the Internet Backbone via Very Small Aperture Terminal (VSAT) [7]. However, there are prospects that soon or later Tanzania will access the Internet via a high capacity optical fibre backbone network following the completion and inauguration of SAT-3 project [10]. The government of Tanzania through the Ministry Transport and Communications is working to see if Tanzania can get connected to SAT-3 in the near future.

## 3.2    SAT-3/WASC/SAFE Project in a Nutshell

Commissioned in May 2002, SAT-3/WASC/SAFE cable is co-owned by a 36-member consortium formed for construction of the submarine optic fibre cable system [10]. This state-of-the art cable system connects Europe with Africa and Asia. Going around Western Africa, South Africa and India from Portugal in Europe before terminating in Malaysia in the Far East, this cable provides enhanced capacity, diversity and connectivity to all the consortium members. The recently commissioned SAT-3/WASC/SAFE submarine cable has been operational since May 27, 2002. The cable system has an ultimate capacity of 120 Gbps that will enable it to convey a total of 5.8 million simultaneous telephone channels. The world's first undersea optic fibre cable system around Africa to Europe and Asia was, officially inaugurated by the Senegalese Head of State Mr Abdoulaye WADE. See Figure 1 for the map of SAT-3.

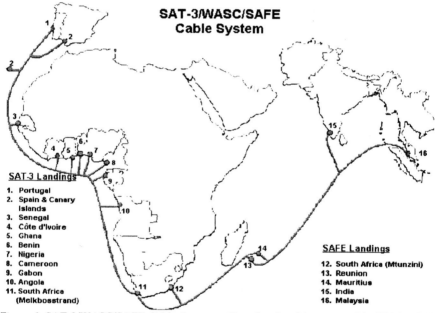

*Figure 1.* SAT-3/WASC/SAFE Cable System – Completed and inaugurated in 27 May 2002 (Source: http://www.safe-sat3.co.za/configuration.htm [10])

Although Tanzania is not part of this phase, the opportunity to connect to the system exists [7]. There is already a project backed by Transnet, Telekom South Africa, the rail group Africa East Coast and others to lay 2500 KM of optic fibre from Dar es Salaam along the existing railway line to Livingstone in Zambia. The plan is then to link this with a fibre optic cable laid by Namibia Telecommunications from Windhoek to Livingstone, with connections to other east and central African countries planned (Kenya, Uganda, Burundi and Rwanda) [7]. Windhoek already has a high capacity fibre optic link to South Africa that can then connect to SAT-3.

## 4. EVALUATION OF THE COURSE AND SEMINARS

In the fall of year 2001, we organised a short course on IT security for the University of Dar es Salaam students in Tanzania. The course offering was a result of a collaborative effort between the authors and the department of computer science at the University of Dar es Salaam. All interested students were invited to attend the course from different disciplines at the University. Besides the course, we organised a seminar on IT security for the practitioners from the industry, government agencies, and any interested individuals. We, also, conducted another seminar for academic and non-academic staff at the University of Dar es Salaam. In both the course and seminars we discussed about general security including security objectives, threats, vulnerabilities, and security services and mechanisms.

These seminars and a course were aimed at giving us an insight of the current scenario, especially, in terms of the level security awareness and IT security readiness for the IT practitioners and academia in the country. Both the seminars and a course were purposely made interactive in that they were dominated by discussions between presenters and the audiences. In all sessions we dedicated an ample time for participants to ask questions and give their comments and suggestions. This enabled us to get the feedback on the feeling and thinking of the people on the subject matter. We, also, distributed questionnaires to the students during the course to get their feedbacks.

### 4.1 Course Evaluations

About 200 students attended a course. This was really beyond our expectations as the course had coincided with the exams period at the University. The course was about IT security overview including the security objectives. Security risks, threats and vulnerabilities were also discussed. On going through the questionnaires, the following were observed:
- Students were very much impressed by the course, and they indicated their appreciation and satisfaction of the material taught and the way they were presented to them
- More than 78% had no idea about IT security concept
- About 11% of students said they thought IT security was all about using strong passwords to prevent unauthorised access to data
- More than 85% proposed IT security to be taught as part of their academic programmes

- About 58% of the students wanted to know more about hacking techniques; some said they wanted to become "white hat hackers" in future
- Some students wanted to have hands on training in the implementation of different security mechanisms, especially firewall implementation
- Some wanted to learn more on cryptology in relation to IT security
- Almost all students requested for the course material to be made available, and if possible in electronic form. In response to this, we uploaded both the course material and seminar material into a web server on the net (www.teil.udsm.ac.tz) for them to access. We grated them access to the material through Blackboard application software, an online software for e-learning.
- Almost all students who participated to the course expressed their interests and enthusiasm in learning more on IT security.

## 4.2     Seminar Evaluations

A total of 64 participants attended a seminar on IT security. Initially, we expected to have 50 participants. We made an advert in one of the local newspapers about the seminar one week prior to the event. The response was far beyond our expectations because within two days of the advert, 44 participants had already registered. On the third day all the 50 vacancies were full booked and still more requests for registration were coming in. We had to accept 14 more requests in favour of those who appealed that they couldn't afford to miss such a seminar. Following discussions and comments during the seminar, and the after communications with the seminar participants the following were commented as, there is a need to:
- Conduct regular seminars of the kind in order to raise public awareness on IT security issues
- Introduce IT security to employees at their working places
- Integrate IT security into formal academic programmes in the country
- Educate top managements on the importance of IT security to their organizations
- Incorporate IT security policy into corporate policies
- To develop independent IT security policies for their organizations

## 4.3     Further Observations

- Most of the people who are administering/managing IT/IS systems had different academic backgrounds. While some had a computer science background, others were from engineering, electronics, statistics, economics, physics, commerce and management, mathematics and business administration.

- Most of the systems administrators/managers each possesses at least a bachelor degree
- Most of systems administrators have not had formal security education. Their security knowledge is based on security features of specific IT products as specified in the products' manuals. They do not go beyond the scope of a given product.
- Some of the participants complained that it is still too difficult to have top management concern and commitment on security issues, particularly, budgeting for security
- Some of participants thought it were secure enough to install a particular security mechanism such as firewall
- While some of the participants were not much worried about attacks from within their organisations, others were not even aware of such a threat
- Almost all supported an idea from one of the participants to think of forming an association or a society of IT professionals in the country, through which all IT related matters could be discussed on regular basis including IT security issues.
- Participants suggested creating a mailing list, to start with, through which we can exchanges ideas.
- Participants exchanged contacts so that we can keep in touch, and keep posted on security issues.

## 4.4    Sense of Insecurity

To the contrary of our expectations, the seminar had some negative effects to some of the participants. Some people expressed their feelings after the seminar that they felt even more insecure than they thought they were before the seminar. Others wanted to know about some training institutions elsewhere where they could send their systems administrators/managers for some hands on training in IT security. At least two important government institutions requested for some guidelines in developing their own IT security policies.

## 4.5     Summary of Evaluations

From the discussions, comments and suggestions made during and after the course and seminars, the following were deduced:

1. No single institution is offering IT security skills at any level in the country so far
2. People sees the need for training/education and awareness in IT security
3. People are ready and willing to invest in IT security training
4. The level of security awareness to most of the people is considerably low
5. Since most of the systems administrators/managers are undergraduates, there is a need to develop security curricula at undergraduate level
6. Since there are vast majority of the people out there in the industry interacting with IT/IS systems in their day to day operations without proper training in IT security, this suggests for a need to develop a separate approach to raise their security awareness.

We tried to take each and every comment/opinion from the participants at face value. We did not ignore any because we assumed that every opinion was representing, at least implicitly, a feeling and thinking of a certain group of people in a society, however small that group may be.


## 5.     REPORTED SECURITY BREACH INCIDENTS

We managed to get at least two fatal security breach incidents that have been reported to the general public by the high ranked Tanzania government officials.

1. In one incident, at least 1Billion Tanzania Shilling (about 1 Million US$) was reported to have disappeared or stolen through computer fraud [4]. This was revealed during the Tanzania Parliament sitting in June 2002. The Parliamentary Public Accounts Committee (PAC) says it has uncovered security holes in the government's accounting system through which hundreds of millions of shillings are being quietly stolen using high-tech computer methods. The report of the PAC on government accounts submitted to the Parliament said a staggering Tsh700m (about US$ 7m) was stolen from the Ministry of Community Developments, Women Affairs and Children in year 2001 through computer-assisted fraud while another Tsh300m (about US$3m) disappeared from the Prime Minister's Office through similar holes. This was made publicly know by the PAC chairman, adding that in recent days there has been a surge of

thefts of public funds through the use of computers. The PAC chairman warned in his report that the traditional method of auditing by going through various financial documents was obsolete, and that computer fraud was too loosely regulated because most of the government's auditors lacked the necessary computer security skills to trail suspects. The report finally cautioned that auditors would continue having a hard time trying to detect fraud if the government does not equip them with the necessary IT security skills. And recommended that the government needed to urgently address the computer security issues following fears that the high-tech fraud could now be widespread.

2. In another incident, it was reported that the lone Tanzania electric utility firm, Tanzania Electricity Supply Company (TANESCO) suffered a severe loss due to poor information systems (IS) management. This made publicly known by the President of the United Republic of Tanzania, Benjamin William Mkapa, when addressing the nation in April 2002 [12]. The president noted that in audit reports carried out by two different and independent International Auditing Companies all showed that there was money loss through computer systems. The Auditing Companies that were involved in auditing TANESCO's financial reports at different times are Deloitte Touche Tohmatsu and KPMG, both are Swiss based International consulting and auditing firms. For instance, the President cited out that KPMG revealed in its report that 36 percent of revenue from the pre-paid (LUKU) computer system did not feature in any of the company reports since 1995. The head of state noted in his speech that in the period covering 1995 to 2000, the company recorded an aggregate loss amounting to more than Tsh125b (about US$125m). Information management systems security problems contributed significantly to this loss. Following this huge loss of money, the government had to dismiss the entire Company's management and replace it with a hired South African based NETGroup solutions management to run the company and rectify the problems.

3. In October 2001, KPMG Forensic consulting firm, conducted a fraud survey to 400 public and private companies in East African countries, Kenya, Tanzania, and Uganda. In its final report, East Africa Fraud Survey 2002 [5], it is indicated that 82 percent of respondents considered their computer and information systems to be a potential security risk. The report cited measures used by these companies against computer risks as including access logs, firewalls, passwords and others. Figure 2 shows the typical responses on the use of these security measures. The report further indicated that ownership of intellectual property was, also, considered to be at risk for fraud as shown in Figure 3. The respondents in the report cited Tanzania as one of the four major countries that have experienced

international fraud. Others include United States of America, United Kingdom, and South Africa.

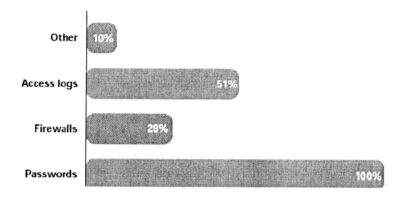

*Figure 2.* Measures used against computer risks [5, pp.18]

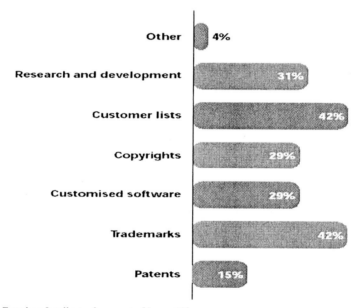

*Figure 3.* Fraud on Intellectual property [5, pp. 19]

## 6.    OUR NEXT STEP

Having observed and learned from the current situation, we are developing an IT security curricula-based approach not only for Tanzania, but also that can be adapted by any other developing country with similar environment as that of Tanzania. We understand, however, that one cannot devise a universal approach that can suite all the varying security needs of different computer systems users in every country. In view of this, we have narrowed our research work to focus on security education at an undergraduate level. One of the reasons behind this choice is that most of the practicing computer systems administrators/managers in Tanzania are, at least, holders of bachelors' degrees in various disciplines (see course and seminar evaluations). Second, it is at this level of education where students get minimum qualifications and skills required to enter into the real world security practices.

In collaboration with the Department of Computer Science and the Department of Computer Engineering and Information Technology at the University of Dar es Salaam, Tanzania, we plan to launch a new Degree Program in IT Security at the University. Plans are underway to launch the Program in the 2004/2005 academic year. The Program will attract mainly students coming direct from advanced secondary education with a sound background in science subjects, especially, physics and mathematics. In-service students from the industry with adequate experience with IT/IS systems shall be encouraged to apply.

This approach is likely to produce IT security professionals who can manage IT systems securely, do research and development projects on IT security, and routinely teach others on security awareness at their respective working places.

## 7. CONCLUSION

We came to learn during our field work in Tanzania, and this is supported by Miller's report to Sida [7] that, one of the differences between Tanzania and other Southern Africa Development Community (SADC) countries is the proliferation of Internet cafés, particularly in Dar es Salaam but also elsewhere. It is very difficult to give the exact figure for the number of Internet cafés in Tanzania because they are mushrooming on a tremendous scale. However, the number was estimated to 1000 plus as of November 2001 [7] most of them in Dar es Salaam, which is the business capital of Tanzania. Retail Internet surfing charges in most cafes in Dar Es Salaam recently dropped from roughly US$1 to US $ 0.5, that is equivalent to Tsh1000.00 and Tsh500.00 respectively per hour, but this is still enough to meet the operating costs and also make a little profit. The bulk of clients in most cafés are young people, business people, office workers, students and academics. E-mail services are the most popular at Internet cafés, followed by general website surfing. While a number of people go to make telephone calls abroad which is cheap via the net, others go to the cafes on e-business missions but the proportion in this category is relatively small.

Again all these sorts of statistics bring security concerns on how to approach issues of security education to the kids and teenagers in this region. We suggest that a separate study be carried out to see how this can best be dealt with. We have, also, noticed that there is a category of other professionals out there such as lawyers, accountants, nurses and doctors, journalists, schoolteachers, and even politicians who are working with computers and computer systems everyday without proper security awareness training. To this end, we plan to have frequent IT security training and awareness programmes and seminars to discuss security issues for improved awareness.

Should Tanzania get connected to SAT-3 network backbone [10], chances are that many more companies, business organisations, colleges and schools, government agencies and individuals at home will subscribe to the Internet and get reliable access to the world wide web. On the one hand this shall be a blessing to the country since citizens shall be able to share networked information resources with the rest of the networked world. On the other hand, this shall create a big challenge to the country on how to best safeguard the critical information systems infrastructures they are putting in place now against various threats, especially, Internet-based threats. To this end we are of the opinion of the old adage that "Prevention is better than Cure", and that it is high time for Tanzania and similar countries do something in advance as far as IT security is concerned. This stands to reason for our approach to introduce IT security education programs in developing countries such as Tanzania.

Serious security breach incidents like ones cited in this paper are indication that security education is needed in this region. We strongly believe that Universities in developing countries have a role to play to prepare a cadre of IT security workforce, and in raise security awareness in their respective countries.

## REFERENCES

1.  Accenture, Markle Foundation, & United Nations Development Programme (UNDP). Creating a Development Dynamic – Final Report of the Digital Opportunity Initiative: A Global Call to Action, 2001. Also, available at http://www.opt-init.org/framework/pages/contents.html
2.  Alec Yasinsac; Information Security Curricula in Computer Science Departments: Theory and Practice, Department of Computer Science Florida State University, Journal of Computer Security, January 2002.

3. Cynthia Irvine, Shiu-Kai Chin, and Deborah Frincke, "Integrating Security into the curriculum", IEEE Computer, December 98, Vol. 31, Num 12.

4. Daily News Tanzania Newspaper, "1bn/- Stolen through computer fraud, Says PAC", of Thursday, June 13, 2002. Available at http://www.dailynews.co.tz/full.asp?ID=120&PubID=1

5. KPMG, "East Africa Fraud Survey 2002". At http://www.kpmg.co.ke/

6. Lamtrac AB, Survey of the Need for a Vocational Training Programme for ICT Professionals in Tanzania Final Report, January 2001. Also available at http://www.ethinktanktz.org/esecretariat/DocArchive/Final%20report%20IT-Survey.pdf

7. Miller Esselaar and Associates; A Country ICT Survey for Tanzania Final Report for Sida, November 2001. Also available at http://www.sida.se/Sida/articles/9400-9499/9481/tanrep.pdf

8. National ICT Policy of Tanzania (First order draft [v3.2e]), Ministry of Communications and Transport, The United Republic of Tanzania. Also available at http://www.moct.go.tz/ict/zerothorder.pdf

9. NIST Special Publication 800-16: Information Technology Security Training Requirements: A Role- and Performance-Based Model. April 1998.

10. SAT-3/WASC/SAFE Project. Also available at http://www.safe-sat3.co.za/

11. Tanzania Communications Commission (TCC), http://www.tcc.go.tz/

12. The Guardian Newspaper, "TANESCO mismanaged, funds misused – Mkapa", of Tuesday, April 30, 2002. Available at http://www.ippmedia.com/guardian/2002/04/30/guardian1.asp

13. The Tanzania Development Vision 2025: Planning Commission, The United Republic of Tanzania, 1999. At http://www.tanzania.go.tz/vission_2025f.html

# A PROGRAM FOR EDUCATION IN CERTIFICATION AND ACCREDITATION

Craig W. Rasmussen, Cynthia E. Irvine, George W. Dinolt,
Timothy E. Levin, Karen L. Burke
*Naval Postgraduate School, Monterey, California, USA*

Abstract:     Large complex systems need to be analyzed prior to operation so that those
              depending upon them for the protection of their information have a well-
              defined understanding of the measures that have been taken to achieve security
              and the residual risk the system owner assumes during its operation. The U.S.
              military calls this analysis and vetting process *certification and accreditation.*
              Today there is a large, unsatisfied need for personnel qualified to conduct
              system certifications. An educational program to address those needs is
              described.

Key words:    Information Assurance, Certification and Accreditation, Graduate Education

## 1. INTRODUCTION

Computer and network systems process information critical to enterprise security. Should these information systems be vulnerable to security failures or attacks, the consequences could be grave. Although individual components may provide security features and assurance of correct policy enforcement, their encompassing systems and subsystems are frequently large and complex. How can a system owner assess the suitability of a system to operate in a particular environment? Factors that will affect this determination include the sensitivity and criticality of the information to be processed; the physical and cyber context in which the system is expected to operate; the personnel who will administer and use the system; as well as a wide variety of technical factors that affect security.

The process used to assess networks and systems and to then officially authorize their use is known as *certification and accreditation.* As an example, an avionics system might be the subject of a certification and accreditation. *Accreditation* is a formal declaration by a designated approving authority that an AIS is approved to operate in a particular security mode using a prescribed set of safeguards.

In general, accreditation will result in the approval for the system to be operated with defined physical conditions, interconnections, personnel security attributes, and system assurances, in combination with procedural and technical countermeasures to security threats. The accreditation describes the operational objectives of the system, defines the threats to the system and the countermeasures taken to mitigate those threats, and the resulting residual risks. As part of the process it is recognized that a reassessment of system security is required periodically, so the accreditation will have a limited lifetime.

*Certification* supports the accreditation process by providing analysis of the technical and non-technical aspects of the system. As the system moves through its lifecycle, the certifier works with component designers and integrators to ensure that a specified set of security requirements are met. Certification supports the accreditation process.

System Certification and Accreditation [7] can help to identify and mitigate risk in a wide variety of systems. Consequently, the U.S. Department of Defense (DoD) has stated that all information systems will be certified and accredited to operate at an acceptable level of risk. Given the sheer numbers of systems in operation, from business systems to weapons system, this is a daunting task.

It is clear that a highly skilled cadre of system certifiers is needed, not only to address the current demands of the government but also to provide similar support for the complex systems being fielded in the private sector. Yet, there are relatively few analysts with the background, training and education that would qualify to senior leadership for system certifications. To address the gap between requirements and available qualified personnel, we are establishing an educational program for system certifiers.

Herein, we provide a high-level overview of the certification and accreditation process using the U.S. DoD certification and accreditation model as our example. We will then describe the program we are developing to provide certifiers with the education and experience needed to progress from a beginner to an intermediate level.

## 2.      CERTIFICATION AND ACCREDITATION

To ensure that all services perform accreditations to some standard level, the DoD has published an instruction called The DoD Information

Technology Security Certification and Accreditation Process (DITSCAP) [2]. This instruction process provides a degree of confidence that all accredited systems have undergone an equal and adequate level of analysis and testing. Realistically, however, the outcome of certification and accreditation is dependent on the education and experience of the personnel conducting the exercise. Qualified personnel are in short supply, and the need for individuals to provide technology support for Certification and Accreditation will continue to grow.

The following sections provide a brief summary of the information system certification and accreditation (C&A) process defined in relevant instructions and publications [1, 2, 3, 4, 5, 6]. We have chosen to focus on Navy requirements and our overview is intended to illustrate the complexity of the C&A task, and the fact that the transition from apprentice to journeyman certifier requires training, formal education, and field experience.

## 2.1    Who is Involved?

There are four principal participants in the C&A process:

*Program Manager (PM)*. According to the DITSCAP, "program manager" might refer to three distinct roles over the life of a system. During system acquisition, the program manager is the individual responsible for system procurement and development. During the operation of the system, the role belongs to the system manager, who is responsible for system operations. When the system undergoes a major change, the role belongs to the maintenance organization's program manager.

*Designated Approving Authority (DAA)*. It is the DAA who is ultimately in the position of accepting an inevitable compromise between the desire for perfect security, the minimum set of security features required by applicable legal or regulatory constraints, and the needs of the user community to have a functional system that meets its needs. It is the DAA who assumes the risk; only upon accreditation by the DAA does the system become operational and able to run with "live" data.

*System Certifier*. Either alone or as a member of a team, the system certifier provides a comprehensive evaluation of the security features, limitations, and vulnerabilities of a target information system. It is the certifier's responsibility to document for the DAA the target system's level of compliance with security requirements and the level of residual risk present in putting the system in operation

*User Representative*. This individual requires that the system in question achieve a specified level of functionality.

## 2.2    'Functional Components of Certification & Accreditation Process

This section provides an overview the functional components of the Certification and Accreditation process. By appreciating this process, the role and contribution of the System Certifier can be understood in context. Appendix A provides a glossary of terms.

The DITSCAP process is divided into four major phases: Definition, Certification, Validation, and Post-Accreditation. Table 1 provides a synopsis of the steps that must be accomplished during each phase. The DITSCAP process may be iterative and for large, complex systems it is sometimes necessary to conduct several iterations.

*Table 1.* Functional Components in the Certification and Accreditation Process

| Phase | Step | Description |
|-------|------|-------------|
| Definition | | |
| | 1 | Document Mission Need |
| | 2 | Conduct Registration |
| | 3 | Perform Negotiation |
| | 4 | Prepare System Security Authorization Agreement |
| Certification | | |
| | 5 | Support System Development |
| | 6 | Perform Certification Analysis |
| Validation | | |
| | 7 | Certification Evaluation |
| | 8 | Develop Recommendation to Designated Approval Authority |
| Maintenance | | |
| | 9 | Compliance Validation |
| | 10 | Maintenance of System Security Authorization Agreement |

### 2.2.1    Definition

This phase comprises the first four steps discussed in this document: documentation of mission need, registration, negotiation, and preparation of the System Security Authorization Agreement (SSAA) (this step is often incorporated into the negotiation step).

### Document Mission Need

This preliminary phase occurs whenever development of a new information system or modification of an existing system is initiated. Planning the certification begins with acquiring a thorough understanding of the system to be certified, the functions that the system must fulfill, and the mission served by the system. This planning also requires a comprehensive understanding of the steps required in all C&A processes. The certifier keeps all concerned personnel fully informed even at this early stage in the process. Of particular importance are the following:

- Proposed system mission.

- Proposed system functions.

- Proposed system interfaces.

- Category and classification of information to be processed.

- Anticipated system lifecycle.

- Characteristics of system users.

- Operating environment.

### System Registration

The registration phase is the beginning of the dialogue among the key players in the C&A process. The steps vary, depending on whether the subject system has been fielded previously or is under development. The first step in the registration phase is a review of the materials from either a new Document Mission Need phase or from previous life cycle iteration. The final step in the registration phase is the development of a draft (or draft update) of the System Security Authorization Agreement (SSAA). In either case, the draft SSAA represents an agreement among the Program Manager, the DAA, the CA, and the user representative, and describes the goals that must be achieved in support of certification as well as the strategy by which those goals are to be met. The following list describes key steps in the process.

- Register the system: Inform key participants (DAA, Certifier, User representative) that the C&A process must be undertaken.

- Prepare mission description and system identification. In the case of a new system, this step relies on the documentation developed in the previous step. In the case of a system that has already been in operation, this step relies on the body of documentation, including the existing SSAA that should accompany the system throughout its life cycle.

- Describe the system environment and threat description. The system environment has both physical and logical components. For example, a locked cage in a guarded room presents a much different picture from the standpoint of vulnerability than does a desktop in a busy office. Similarly, a stand-alone system presents a much more difficult target than, for example, a networked system with an Internet connection.

- Describe the system architecture and C&A boundary. This boundary describes precisely which equipment and systems within the domain of the DAA are to be subjected to the C&A process under development.

- Determine the IT security system class and system security requirements. The precise C&A tasks from the DITSCAP are sensitive to this evaluation, in that they must be performed at one of four certification levels, ranging from Level 1 (basic security review) to Level 4 (comprehensive analysis). Minimum security requirements are mandated by the DoD level, and can be strengthened (but not weakened) by the constituent military services.

- Prepare a DITSCAP plan based on the assembled documentation. Based upon the preceding steps, this step tailors the DITSCAP tasks to the system under consideration. For example, execution details of each of the DITSCAP tasks are dependent upon the IT security class determined in the previous step.

- Identify organizations and additional resources required for the C&A process; this step facilitates measurement of the level of effort that will be required.

- Develop the draft SSAA. This document constitutes the basis for the negotiation phase, which follows.

### Perform Negotiation

In the negotiation phase all parties have an opportunity to express their needs and agree on their respective responsibilities. The Certifier must exercise skills whose relevance to the C&A process might be surprising. These include listening skills, written and oral communication skills, and the power to persuade. In principle, the idea is not that the key players lock themselves in a room until they agree on what must be done, in that compliance with statutory constraints is mandatory. Instead the principals agree on strategy, resources, roles, timeline, etc. In reality, the certifier might have to, for example, convince a user representative that allowing users to hold administrative privileges is unacceptable, or persuade a DAA the level of residual risk claimed by the certifier. The draft System Security Authorization Agreement (SSAA) resulting from the registration phase provides a framework for the negotiations. The DITSCAP identifies three key negotiation tasks:

- Review the draft SSAA for accuracy and completeness, updating as necessary.

- Conduct a review of the certification requirements, modifying the SSAA as necessary.

- Approve the final SSAA, which constitutes the blueprint for the balance of the certification process. Here "final" is a relative term, in that the SSAA is under perpetual scrutiny and, as a living document, is subject to update as required.

### Prepare the System Security Authorization Agreement (SSAA)

The SSAA encompasses in a single document all essential security-related information about a system. The "final" SSAA is the product of the activities performed in the first three steps, i.e., documentation, registration, and negotiation. As a living document, the SSAA is still subject to updates at every subsequent step prior to accreditation. The principal components of the SSAA are:

- Mission Description and System Identification. Much of this can come from the mission needs statement. Of interest are the system name and identification, the physical and functional descriptions of the system, and a summary of the system concept of operations.

- Description of System Operating Environment. This encompasses technical and non-technical context in which the system will be operated, software, and maintenance environments, as well as a threat description.

- Description of System Architecture. This comprises hardware, software, firmware, interfaces, information flow, and accreditation boundary.

- IT Security System Class. There are four levels of certification effort specified in the DITSCAP. Level 1 consists of a basic review of security features. Level 2 adds to the Level 1 effort some minimal analysis. Level 3 requires detailed analysis, and Level 4 requires comprehensive analysis. Determination of system class is simplified by a checklist-based scoring system applied to a profile of the target system. There are overlaps between adjacent levels, so the Certifier plays a role in ensuring that the appropriate level of effort is adopted.

- System Security Requirements. These, including national and DoD/DoN requirements, data security requirements, security concept of operations, network connection rules, configuration and change management requirements, and re-accreditation requirements.

- Organizations and Resources Required for the C&A Effort. This item identifies the principals (PM, DAA, Certifier, User Representative) and sponsoring organization, enumerates staffing and funding requirements, certification team training requirements, describes roles and responsibilities, and identifies any additional organizations or groups whose participation is required.

- The DITSCAP Plan (tailored as necessary). This includes tailoring specifics, tasks/milestones, the schedule of work, level of effort, and specification of roles and responsibilities.

- Appendices containing supporting and/or amplifying documentation are also prepared.

### 2.2.2   Certification

This phase comprises the next two steps: support of system development and certification analysis.

**Supporting Systems Development**

This is the first step in the Certification Phase of the DITSCAP, concerned with verification that a system that is in development system remains compliant with the security specifications of the SSAA. This requires more or less continuous oversight on the part of the Certifier as system development and/or integration progresses. The precise details are determined by a number of factors, including the certification level specified in the SSAA and the position of the system in its lifecycle, e.g., new system development or system maintenance. Education in the area of computer and network security is essential in this part of the certification process. The NSTISSI certifier training document (#4015) identifies the following performance items associated with this step:

- Coordination with Related Disciplines. This involves coordination with various security disciplines for expert assistance. For example, it might be necessary to call in experts on physical security, or emanation security, or cryptography. The certifier needs to justify to the DAA the need for such coordination, and to ensure that the coordinated effort is successfully accomplished.

- Configuration Control. The certifier must evaluate configuration and change control with regard to consistency with requirements, recommending changes and/or reporting deficiencies as necessary. Included in this step is verification of associated activities, such as audits, component inventories, etc.

- Information Security Policy. The certifier must identify all applicable information systems security policies, keeping the development team fully informed in order to enable system compliance. The certifier must also monitor development to ensure compliance.

- Life-Cycle System Security Planning. The certifier must evaluate the life-cycle security plan adopted by the development team. If the plan is deficient, the certifier must become an active participant in life-cycle security planning to ensure the desired outcome.

- Principles and Practices of Information Security. The certifier must understand the principles and practices of information security and the way in which those principles apply to the certification effort in question. The certifier must also adhere to these principles and, if necessary, explain these principles to the development team.

- Network Vulnerabilities. The certifier must perform system analysis to identify potential network vulnerabilities for the development team, evaluate the potential impact of such vulnerabilities, and suggest corrective measures.

### Perform Certification Analysis

The certification analysis step determines whether the system in question is ready to advance to the evaluation and testing that precede a recommendation to accredit. The DITSCAP specifies the following component tasks:

- System Architecture Analysis. This task provides documented assurance that

- The system architecture is consistent with the architecture specified in the SSAA.

- Security architecture is consistent with specified security policy and requirements.

- Interfaces between the subject system and other systems are identified and evaluated in terms of supporting the required system security posture.

- Software Design Analysis. The output of this step documents that security features required of the Trusted Computing Base (TCB), such as authentication, access control, and auditing, are implemented as specified.

- Network Connection Rule Compliance Analysis. This step provides assurance that neither the network nor the subject system will have undesired effects on the other's security posture.

- Integrity Analysis of Integrated Products. The subject system might integrate software, hardware, and firmware from a number of sources, e.g. commercial-off-the-shelf, government-off-the-shelf, specialized, etc. This step provides assurance that:

- Interaction of integrated components does not result in degradation of the integrity of individual components.

- The result of this integration is compliant with the specified system security architecture.

- Application of components must be consistent with their intended use.

The complexity of this step can be considerable, depending upon the level of certification required. For example, it might be necessary to verify the security features of individual components.

- Life Cycle Management Analysis. This step provides documented assurance that the security posture of the system will be preserved by the implemented change control and configuration management practices.

Vulnerability Assessment. This step verifies satisfactory progress in implementation of the security requirements of the SSAA, by evaluating vulnerabilities and recommending countermeasures. Any vulnerability identified during certification analysis must be analyzed in terms of susceptibility to (and likelihood of) exploitation, and of the associated threat. The output of this process is a statement enumerating and evaluating residual risks and estimating the operational impact of accepting or rejecting them. Residual risk cannot exceed the level of acceptable risk determined by the DAA.

### 2.2.3 Validation Phase

Like the Certification Phase, the Validation Phase also comprises two steps: certification evaluation and development of the recommendation to the DAA culminating in accreditation.

### Certification Evaluation

The objective of this step is to ensure that the system, configured for deployment, complies with the security specifications as given in the SSAA. Certification evaluation is applied to hardware, software, firmware, and additionally includes site inspection. Main functional items are listed below and definitions, where definitions of terms may be found in the glossary:

- Security Test and Evaluation

- Penetration Testing

- TEMPEST and Red-Black verification

- Validation of COMSEC compliance

- System management analysis

- Site accreditation survey

- Contingency plan evaluation

- Risk-based management review

### Develop Recommendation to DAA

In this activity the Certification Authority (i.e., the manger of the certification process) submits to the Designated Approving Authority a report detailing all findings from the certification process. If the process has been successful, the DAA formally accepts the (positive) recommendation and the outcome is accreditation. If change is required, an Interim Approval to Operate may be granted and, all or part of the certification effort is revisited. The following elements are identified:

- Access Control Policies. Access control policies implemented in the system to be certified must be explained to the DAA. Included in this explanation are descriptions of who makes authorization decisions and on what basis as well as the effectiveness of the implementation from the standpoint of the requirements. The certifier recommends changes, if necessary.

- Administrative Security Policies and Procedures. The certifier must consider not only those policies and procedures required by law, but also those additional policies and procedures that might be required by agency instruction or other organizational mechanism. The certifier must document to the DAA all applicable policies and procedures and the degree to which the system is in compliance, recommending countermeasures as needed to address any deficiencies.

- Certification. This is a conditional recommendation, outlining (if necessary) conditions that must be met before a decision to accredit is recommended.

- Presentation of Security Test and Evaluation Results. This might require translation, depending on the audience; however, the objective is to communicate the results to management and technical personnel.

- Identification of Potential Corrective Approaches
- Determination of Residual Risk

### 2.2.4    Post-Accreditation

Finally, the Post-Accreditation Phase corresponds to ongoing maintenance of the SSAA.

#### Compliance Validation
At intervals specified in the SSAA, the system and its operational environment are subject to review to verify compliance with the SSAA in terms of security specifications and concept of operations, and to verify that the threat assessment described in the SSAA remains accurate. The principal functional components are:

- Physical security analysis
- Review of SSAA with an update to the SSAA as needed
- Risk-based management review
- Procedural analysis
- Compliance re-verification

## 2.3    Maintenance of the SSAA

While the SSAA is subjected to continuous review and update during system development, the maintenance step outlined here occurs post-accreditation to ensure that the SSAA is not allowed to become stale with respect to the operational system. The principal players are the same as they have been throughout the process. As the operational system undergoes incremental change, the certifier evaluates the impact of these changes on system security features, updating the SSAA, if necessary. Similarly, updates to the SSAA must themselves be evaluated in order to determine whether the Certification process must be repeated. If so, the process reverts to the appropriate DITSCAP phase. The certifier ensures that the DAA has up to date information, and the DAA will determine whether continued operation of the system is approved. Key components in this step are:

- Control of Configuration Changes
- Maintenance of Configuration Documents
- Periodic Review of System Life-Cycle
- Contingency Planning

- Compliance Validation
- Physical Security
- SSAA Review
- Risk-based Management Review
- Compliance Re-verification

## 3.        CERTIFIER EDUCATION

A considerable amount of technical and non-technical analysis is required to support an accreditation. This process of system certification provides a way by which the technical and non-technical aspects of a system's security can be assessed from inception through retirement. The factors that must be addressed include the sensitivity and criticality of data to be processes, the system's environment, its users, its location, its applications, interconnections, configuration, etc. To achieve these objectives, such activities as security test and evaluation, risk analysis, and a variety of other analyses and evaluations are conducted. The level of technical expertise required for individuals involved in certification is high. Even while focussing on a single security component of the system, the certifier must keep the larger system context in mind and be able to understand the impact and side effects of that component on overall system security. Thus the certifier cannot address his or her task using a check list, and focus on individual pieces, while neglecting the whole.

As is the case with many other aspects of computer science and system development, e.g. construction of operating systems or construction of physical databases, one does not learn everything in books or in a standard classroom. Even laboratory activities can be inadequate unless they are specifically designed to foster the development of both implicit as well as explicit knowledge. In the case of system certifiers, it has been found that a combination of knowledge and experience are essential for achieving mastery of the profession.

The U.S. Department of Defense has imposed requirements for the certification and accreditation of all information systems to ensure that they are operated at an acceptable level of risk. Given the sheer numbers of systems in operation, from business systems to weapons system, this is a daunting task. The certification and accreditation problem is further compounded by the lack of experienced certifiers able to conduct the required fieldwork. While concentrating on a particular detail, less experienced certifiers may overlook security weaknesses of the system that would be found by their more seasoned colleagues.

To address this problem, we have developed an educational program for certifiers. It is intended to compress the time it takes an apprentice certifier to achieve the experience and expertise to become a journeyman certifier. We believe that master certifiers are those individuals who have considerable experience and have the education, knowledge and fully internalized skills to assess the security properties of highly complex systems. In a sense the activities of the certifier parallel those of a systems integrator. Just as there is no expectation that a highly experienced systems integrator can be created through a set of classroom activities, there is no expectation that a master certifier can be manufactured.

Students in the program will be of two types: short course students and resident graduate students. Short course students will typically be personnel who may already be working in the area of certification and accreditation or who are moving into this field. The resident students will be active-duty officers, or civilians employed either by the DoD or by DoD contractors. In all likelihood, graduates of the short program will eventually report to graduates of the resident program. The short-program students will spend approximately eight weeks in formal courses over a period of from eighteen months to two years. The courses will be of short duration (typically two weeks) and high intensity, with eight hours devoted to class and laboratory exercises each day. The intervening periods between visits to school will be spent in the field, where students acquire essential experience. Resident students will include certifier courses as electives as part of their Computer Science graduate program. Depending upon student background, validation of prerequisites, and other factors, this program can last between 12 and 24 months. The certifier courses taken by the resident students will differ from those taken by the short-program students. The courses taken by the resident students will be taught in the usual way, meeting four hours per week over an entire academic quarter. Course content might also differ somewhat in reflection of the different educational and career paths taken by the two populations of students.

A prerequisite for all resident students is an undergraduate degree in computer science or a closely related engineering field.

*Table 2.* Courses of the Certifier Education Program

| Title | Catalog Description |
|---|---|
| Introduction to Information Assurance: Computer Security | Provides a comprehensive overview of the terminology, concepts, issues, policies, and technologies associated with the field of Information Assurance. It covers the notions of threats, vulnerabilities, risks and safeguards as they pertain to the desired information security properties of confidentiality, integrity, |

| Title | Catalog Description |
|-------|---------------------|
| | authenticity and availability for all information that is processed, stored, or transmitted in information systems. |
| Information Assurance: Secure Management of Systems | Provides students with a security manager's view of the diverse management concerns associated with administering and operating an automated information system facility with minimized risk. Students will examine both the technical and non-technical security issues associated with managing a computer facility, with emphasis on DoD systems and policies. Students will earn CNSS (formerly NSTISSI) certification for: INFOSEC professional, Systems Administrator, and ISSO. |
| Network Security Threat Analysis | This course is designed to give the student exposure to Internet security threats in a lab environment. Lectures and labs provide the student with a "hands on" experience with current network attacks and vulnerabilities. Foot-printing, scanning, enumeration and escalation are addressed from an attack prospective. Emphasis on detection and protection of critical data and nodes is addressed. A final project that demonstrates skills and knowledge is required. |
| Introduction to Certification and Accreditation | This course provides an introduction to the Certification and Accreditation (C&A) process as applied to procurement and lifecycle management of DoD and Federal information systems. Topics include: principal roles, functional components, and output documents of the C&A process; and a comparison of the government C&A process specification currently in use (DITSCAP/NIACAP, FIPS, DCID 6/3) with the emerging effort to produce a unified specification. |
| System Certification Case Studies | This course is part two of the two-course (CS4680 and CS4685) Certification and Accreditation course sequence. Students will investigate 2-3 case studies of systems that have been evaluated, and then apply the lessons of CS4680 to make final accreditation decisions. Successful completion of this two-course sequence leads to NSTISSI DAA and Certifier certification. |

Our educational program is based on courses already in use as well as two new courses specific to the Certification and Accreditation Process. The courses are briefly described in Table 2. The first three courses are intended to provide students with an understanding of the problem domain for system certification. Introduction to Information Assurance is a survey course and provides students with a broad overview of the many aspects of the certification domain. The second course, Secure Management of Systems, leads to and understanding of the administrative, procedural, and personnel issues that might affect the ongoing security of a system. Finally, Network Security Threat Analysis provides students with an appreciation of the techniques and skills that will be brought to bear by adversaries attacking their systems. When combined with their background in computer science the three-course sequence described above prepares students for the two courses specific to certification.

Introduction to Certification and Accreditation is intended to teach students about all aspects of the certification and accreditation process. They are introduced to procedural aspects of the process as well as to the variety of technical issues that might be addressed. A considerable amount of social skill and team building is required for a successful certification, and students learn about the give-and-take required to achieve success. Students must understand when certain security requirements must be adhered to at all cost and when some flexibility may be appropriate.[2]

The capstone course in the sequence centers on a group of case studies. These are taken from real systems and allow students to understand how a certifier can help ensure that the security requirements are met. The cases include not only technical and procedural aspects of the certification, but discussion of the social process required to accomplish the certification.

An unusual aspect of the program is its mentoring process. Students in the program will have the opportunity to interact with instructors and staff who have experience in DITSCAP certification. This mentoring experience will help speed their mastery of the certification process. A member of our educational team with significant experience in certification keeps in touch with short course students while they are in the field gaining on-the-job experience. Students can communicate and commiserate with each other about their challenges and experiences. Because the certifier community is relatively small, it is expected that students will get to know senior certifiers and be able to ask them questions as they progress.

Program assessment will be a feedback mechanism that should benefit from the involvement of the sponsoring organization. It is one of the principal Navy commands involved in certification and accreditation of IT systems and components. Student assessment will be to some extent program-dependent. The performance of resident students will be assessed in the usual ways, by examination scores, performance on laboratory exercises, quality of written work, etc. The performance of the nonresident students will be based not only on their classroom and laboratory performance while here at NPS but also on their performance on the job between visits to NPS. Both populations will be assessed on their abilities to apply the regulatory framework (e.g., DITSCAP) to systems that vary widely in their makeup. Students in both populations will benefit from success factors that are built into the program. For example, the students will arrive on board with appropriate backgrounds, the material covered will be chosen with the

---

[2] Long ago, a flag-level officer complained to one of the authors about the inability of a command to deploy a system because, from his perspective, the certifier appeared to be unusually inflexible regarding a particular point. A certifier's communications and interpersonal skills might prevent possible misunderstandings and resulting frustration.

assistance of experienced professionals from the field, and case studies will include both system-level and component-level case studies.

Two surveys will be used for requesting feedback from the nonresident graduates and their "on-the-job" mentors. When the nonresident students graduate from the course, they will go to certification organizations as certifiers. In most certification organizations, the new certifiers are teamed with experienced certifiers for their initial certifications. These experienced certifiers act as their mentors. Generally these initial certifications are on the less complex systems that require a lower level of certification. As the new certifiers gains experience, they undertake increasingly more complex or secure systems. These progressions occur with the approval of the experienced certifier/mentor, until eventually the certifier is considered experienced enough to certify alone.

The senior mentors will be asked to complete a survey, giving us feedback on whether or not the mentor feels the certifier had enough classroom training and what areas need to be modified or added. The school will ask the new certifiers to evaluate how well the certifiers' course prepared them for their certification experiences. Again, we would welcome suggestions for improvement. Also, the school will maintain a continuing relationship with its graduates, offering them continued mentoring. Not only will this feedback loop assist the school in assessing the certifiers' course, it will assist us in ensuring that the course material reflects current systems.

## 4.     SUMMARY

Large complex systems should be analyzed prior to operation so that those depending upon them for the protection of their information will have a well-defined understanding of the measures that have been taken to achieve security and the residual risk the system owner assumes during its operation. The U.S. military calls this analysis and vetting process certification and accreditation. Today there is a large, unsatisfied need for personnel qualified to conduct system certifications. We have described an educational program designed to address those needs.

## ACKNOWLEDGEMENTS

The authors wish to thank the United States Navy, in particular CNO, N6 and the Space and Naval Warfare Systems Command, for support that has made this work possible.

## DISCLAIMER

The views expressed in this article are those of the authors and do not reflect the official policy or position of the Naval Postgraduate School, the Department of the Navy, or the Department of Defense or the U.S. Government.

## REFERENCES

National Training Standard for System Certifiers, NSTISSI Document #4015, December 2000

DoD Instruction 5200.40, December 1997 (This instruction established the DITSCAP.)

DoN IA Publication 5239-13, Volume I: Introduction to Certification and Accreditation, December 2000.

DITSCAP Application Manual, DoD Manual Number 8510-1-M, July 2000

DoN IA Publication 5239-13, Volume III: Program of Record Information Systems, June 2000

DoN IA Publication 5239-13, Volume II: Site, Installed Program of Record, and Locally Acquired Systems, December 2000

DoD, Introduction to Certification and Accreditation, NCSG-TG-029, January 1994.

## APPENDIX A: GLOSSARY

**Accreditation:** Accreditation is the statement granting approval to operate to a particular information system, with specified security safeguards and at a level of residual risk deemed acceptable. Accreditation is issued by the DAA in the form of the System Security Authorization Agreement (SSAA).

**Certification:** Certification is the process of evaluating the security features of a given system and the assurance levels achieved. Certification also refers to the documentation that results, specifying the extent to which the system complies with identified security requirements and the level of residual risk inherent in placing the system in operation at that level of compliance.

**Certification Authority (CA):** The individual with responsibility for managing the certification process. The CA determines whether the complexity of a system requires that the System Certifier be an individual or a team, by identifying the types of expertise required for the certification.

**Communications Security (COMSEC):** The steps taken to ensure security and integrity of information during telecommunications, especially encryption, electromagnetic emissions security, and physical security steps.

**Designated Approving Authority (DAA):** The DAA is the individual, typically a senior officer, who ultimately accepts the risk inherent in making a system operational. The decision is based on the evaluation of residual risk provided by the Certification Authority, Information System Security Manager, or equivalent. This evaluation is in turn likely to be assisted by the Certification Agent, or ISSO, and the Program Manager. The DoN uses the term DAA to describe two distinct roles. First is the Developmental DAA, who is in the DAA seat during program development. The Developmental DAA issues a type accreditation statement for the system in question prior to deployment. At the time of deployment, control passes to the Operational DAA, who is ultimately responsible for the risk incurred at system startup. The type accreditation statement generated during development is part of the system documentation and is thus available to the Operational DAA.

**DITSCAP:** The DoD Information Security Certification and Accreditation Process established by DoD Instruction 5200.40. The process formalized by the DITSCAP is fundamentally identical to the process described in this document, although there are superficial differences. The DITSCAP breaks the C&A process into four phases. Phase 1 (Definition) comprises the first four steps discussed in this document: documentation of mission need, registration, and negotiation, and final preparation of the SSAA (this step is incorporated into the negotiation step). Phase 2 (Verification) comprises the next two steps: support of system development and certification analysis. Phase 3 (Validation) also comprises two steps: certification evaluation and development of the recommendation to the DAA culminating in accreditation. Phase 4 (Post-Accreditation) corresponds to the final step in this document, which is maintenance of the SSAA. The DITSCAP was designed to be a flexible standard, readily tailored to support C&A efforts on a variety of systems including program-of-record, legacy, site, installed program-of-record, and locally-obtained systems.

**Information System Security Manager (ISSM):** The ISSM advises the DAA on Information Assurance issues.

**Information System Security Officer (ISSO):** The individual responsible for ensuring that the security safeguards of a system are maintained as specified in the accreditation, throughout the system lifecycle.

**Interim Approval to Operate (IATO):** An IATO can be issued for a number of reasons. For example, it might be that (a) ST&E has not been completed in the operational setting, thereby preventing completion of the C&A process, or (b) the DAA is unwilling to accept the identified level of risk except on a provisional basis.

**Program Manager (PM):** The individual responsible for system procurement and development, operations, or maintenance, depending upon life cycle stage.

**Residual Risk:** Amount of risk remaining after security measures have been applied.

**Risk:** A combination of the likelihood that a threat will occur, the likelihood that a threat occurrence will result in an adverse impact, and the severity of the resulting impact.

**Software Support Activity, System Support Activity (SSA):** Individual or organization responsible for life cycle support.

**Security Test and Evaluation (ST&E):** Testing and evaluation of the security features of a system as applied in an operational setting, to determine compliance with the specifications in the final SSAA.

**System Certifier:** An individual or member of a team, responsible for conducting a comprehensive analysis of the security features in a given system, and for evaluating the risks inherent in operating the system in question.

**System Security Authorization Agreement (SSAA):** The SSAA represents an agreement among the principals (PM, DAA, CA, User Representative), and documents the DITSCAP process. The final SSAA documents acceptance by the DAA of the level of risk inherent in making the system operational.

**TEMPEST:** The DITSCAP describes TEMPEST as the "short name referring to investigation, study, and control of compromising emanation from IS equipment.

**Threat:** Any circumstance or event with the potential to harm an IS through unauthorized access, destruction, disclosure, modification of data, and/or denial of service

**Trusted Computing Base (TCB):** The TCB is the suite of security features interacting within a given information system to enforce a specified security posture.

# MASTERING COMPUTER FORENSICS

Colin J. Armstrong
*Curtin University of Technology, School of Information Systems, Perth, Western Australia,
email ArmstrongC@cbs.curtin.edu.au*

**Abstract**: This paper discusses the importance of computer forensics to both business and law enforcement environments and describes the passage along the path from act of crime to the court. It highlights the need for computer forensic training and education and gives an overview of the computer forensic course taught in a Masters degree at Curtin University.

**Key words**: Computer forensics, Masters Program, security education, system administrators, law enforcement, crime investigation.

## 1. INTRODUCTION

Police are responsible for upholding the law and investigating, apprehending and prosecuting breaches of the law. The successful prosecution of computer based crime is reliant upon the investigator being able to prove beyond a reasonable doubt who, what, how and when a criminal event occurred within the stringent principles of forensic examination of evidence. Computer crime is of such a nature that it is often difficult for the general public to perceive or to understand that a crime has actually occurred. Criminals are using computers to store records regarding drug deals, money laundering, embezzlement, mail fraud, telemarketing fraud, prostitution, gambling matters, extortion, and a myriad of other criminal activities (Icove et al, 1995). The victim may be a large corporation, may be far away, or may be considered an unfriendly nation, competitor or even an enemy.

The nature of the Internet provides a borderless environment, easy anonymity, concealment of activities and new low cost tools with which to perpetrate crime (Vatis, 2000). Evidence that computer and Internet crime incidences continue to in increase is confirmed in publications such as the annual Computer Security Institute report. (Powers, 2002) Computer crime is on the increase but there are indications that some public perception of malicious abuse may be inflated. Furnell, (2002) discusses how some figures relate to reported incidents from one particular set of surveys and that the true level of computer crime may be much higher because much is not reported due to risk of undesirable consequences; bad publicity, legal liability, loss of custom. Also financial loss is only one type of impact. Others include; disruption of service, loss of data, damage of reputation and these are difficult to quantify and could be more significant (Furnell, 2002).

An investigation of computer crime may use tools, procedures and methods not readily be available to the public and therefore not be readily understood and accepted. For these investigative findings to be accepted they must be recognised by other experts within the field and conform to national and international standards of practice. The risks facing a computer forensic investigator include loss of credibility if another expert witness can demonstrate that proper or appropriate courses of action were mismanaged. It is the role of the independent expert to explain technical issues in layman's terms so that the judge, jury, accused, barrister and solicitor alike can understand the evidence put before them (Armstrong, 2002).

This paper discusses the needs of law enforcement and IT professional in computer forensic training and education. An overview of a course in Computer Forensics in a Masters program at Curtin University is also presented.


## 2.       THE CRIME TO COURT PATH

Kruse and Heiser (2002) suggest that cyber lawyers are constantly facing a changing legal environment and need to be flexible and learning continually. There are two particular participants in the battle against computer crime that would benefit from education and training in computer forensics. They are the systems administrators of corporate computer systems and the law enforcement investigators. Both may be required to present prosecution evidence in a court of law either as an expert witness or a prosecuting officer of the law. If the representatives for the defence can reduce the credibility of the prosecution case the prosecution may fail.

Law enforcement offices investigating computer related crime are often introduced to the case well after a criminal act has been discovered. The offices carrying out computer forensic investigators most frequently commence their activities part way along the crime to court path. The path shown in Figure 1 commences when the criminal act is committed and continues through to prosecuting the case in court. Figure 1 also shows the points along the path where the involvement of systems administration and law enforcement personnel start, overlap and fade into the background.

After a computer related criminal act is committed, it may be some time before anyone notices. The act may be first noticed by friends or family at home but as many acts are committed on networked computer systems in the work place, educational institutes, or public facilities such as Internet cafes, it is the systems administration staff that will probably have their curiosity attracted when they notice unusual activity. To satisfy this curiosity a period of observation would clarify whether further action is justified. Assuming that an act justifies further action it is reasonable to expect evidence to be sought to confirm something untoward is in progress. This leads to the suspicion being confirmed and at this point one could state that the criminal act has been discovered. It is at this point that someone will decide to either ignore and forget the matter, or to continue along the path and to collect evidence to support a response to the situation.

This is another critical point along the path because now the decision required is to either deal with the matter privately or to advise law enforcement authorities. Until this stage the responsibility for action resides with computer systems administration personnel and no law enforcement office is involved. Once a law enforcement agency is advised of the situation and they commence a crime investigation the situation changes dramatically. It is now imperative that activities comply with accepted practices and nothing is done to jeopardise a successful prosecution. Law enforcement offices may now seize digital data and identify and preserve evidence. From about this point along the path the systems administration staff fade into the background and law enforcement offices take control and responsibility for the case. They will copy, analyse, and interpret the data before presenting the prosecution report in court.

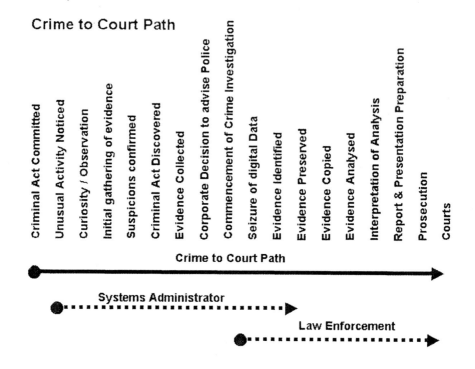

*Figure 1.* Crime to Court Path

Figure 1 shows that the systems administrator may be critical to the success of a prosecution case because their early recognition of a situation and their subsequent actions may either greatly assist or hinder the work done by law enforcement offices. Although they have distinctly separate and vastly different roles and responsibilities, by working in concert they may dramatically improve the chances of bringing about a successful result to a prosecution case.

The danger of criminal activity not being successfully prosecuted due to the failing of a computer forensic process is very real. This is further exasperated by the provision of advice that works against the objectives of computer forensic investigators. Advice given by Bologna and Lindquist (1995) discusses how to use a computer, modem, communication software, procomm, tymnet and databases such as TRW and D&B. They then state that, "You are now ready to dig into files. The procedure is to (1) turn on the PC; (2) insert the communications software diskette in the A: drive; (3) when the program is loaded, dial up the database provider; (4) when connection is made, sign on with your user ID and then your code name; (5) when the menu is displayed, select an area of interest and follow instructions." (Bologna and Lindquist, 1995). Further, in discussions on forensic accounting of large computerised account systems Bologna fails to acknowledge computer forensic science in any way (Bologna and Lindquist, 1995). Anyone following this advice will seriously compromise any prospective computer forensic investigation because the very search for evidence will intrude and alter critical files. A primary principle of computer forensic investigation is to conduct any analysis of digital evidence on a replication of the original data after it has been gathered in such a manner that the original data is not contaminated or altered.

While an investigation may be considered successful because a conviction was gained many convictions result from the suspected criminal confessing to an accusation and the need to prepare and present conclusive evidence is not demanded. In some cases the computer evidence is collaborating or circumstantial evidence that supports, but is not essential to, a case. In a recent Perth murder case, the female suspect admitted killing her husband after evidence showed that she had visited two Web sites. One site was on how to hire a hit man and the other on how to dispose of a body. In other situations the perpetrator of the crime may be a professional and much respected computing expert familiar with how evidence may be obtained and too clever to be easily incriminated. In this type of case a more in-depth investigation may be required to produce evidence for prosecution and the evidence presented may include very technical concepts relating to sophisticated tools and systems that requires to be explained in non-technical terms so that members of the court will comprehend the issues.

The credibility of an expert witness may be crucial to the outcome of a case and where the volume of work and the increasing number of investigations demand quick results there may be a tendency to select new automated examination and analysis tools. Government agencies within the USA have approximately 1400 active cases of cyber crime being investigated and this number does not include the myriad of cases where computers have been seized and evidence gathered and analysed to support other crime cases (Hatcher, 2001). Under these circumstances there is a potential to discredit expert witnesses because as "point & click" wizards they may be perceived to have little or no expertise and not understand what they have done, nor why (Barbin and Patzakis, 2002).

## 3. THE ROLE OF ACADEMIA

Academia has an important role in meeting the needs raised by this increase in computer related crime and the subsequent investigations.

The aim of teaching computer forensics is primarily to meet industry demands by addressing the needs of law enforcement personnel and those that manage and operate computer systems. Academic research, teaching and training to support industry and law enforcement should improve confidence and credibility of investigators that result in better success rates of litigation which in turn may lead to crime reduction.

By comparing law enforcement requirements with existing solutions, the gaps in existing technology can be determined. By working together, researchers in academia, industry, and government can give our public servants the tools they need to address one of the critical public security and national security issues of the $21^{st}$ century." (Vatis, 2002). This statement promotes the need by both law enforcement personnel and corporate system administrators to undertake training and education programs. Training in individual tools to improve competency skills and further education to enhance a broad understanding of concepts and processes related to subject that leads to gaining an academically recognised qualification. Together these help to improve the perception of being a creditable expert.

## 4.    CONTENT OF A COMPUTER FORENSICS COURSE

In order to meet this demand from industry a computer forensic course has been designed to suit both law enforcement offices and IT professionals. The objectives of the course include developing an understanding of the principles and practices of computer forensics. By the end of the course students are expected to be able to understand and to practically demonstrate how to correctly access digital data equipment, obtain an exact working image, analyse the image and recognise evidence, then report their finding in an adversarial environment. The students are expected to maintain and document investigation notes, follow chain of evidence practices and have a thorough overview of computer forensic tools and the appropriateness of their use.

This computer forensics course is a core unit in the Masters of Internet Security Management. It is undertaken in the final semester of full-time study. This is to ensure that students have a knowledge base of Masters level units that includes network and communication security, operating systems and software security, business intelligence and cyberwarfare, encryption, and Internet security.

The course addresses the points along the crime to court path. Students from law enforcement agencies backgrounds will be able to extend their skills by engaging in the concepts on which the practices they apply in the field are based. Students employed in systems administration areas will gain a perspective of law enforcement issues and the practical application of policing investigation practices. Students from these backgrounds would normally be expected to share their work place and field experiences for the benefit of the other students.

The content of the computer forensic course offered at Curtin University assumes a prior knowledge and understanding of network and communications security. Areas to be covered in the course include;

- computer forensic technology tools and concepts

- computer and Internet architecture

- isolation and seizing of equipment and files

- computer image verification and authentication

- data recovery

- investigation processes

- discovery of evidence

- chain of evidence

- national and international legal issues, rights and responsibilities

The course will be conducted over 12 weeks with each week consisting of three hours split between lectures and laboratory exercises. Students engage in practical exercises where computer forensic tools are used to capture, copy and analyses digital data so that the students gain an appreciation of the physical requirements of undertaking a computer forensic investigation. This is seen as a vital ingredient to the course. Currently, Curtin University academic staff are working closely with a number of law enforcement agencies on joint research projects and teaching programs. Students will investigate criminal cases taken from the public domain supported by evidence from enforcement agencies. Students are expected to take digital media and progress along the crime to court path to the extent where they will be expected to present their findings in a simulated adversarial environment.

The course will run for the first time in the second semester of 2003.

## 5. CONCLUSION

Law enforcement agencies are responsible for investigating and prosecuting breaches of the law. Computer related crime is increasing and the workload of investigators is growing.

New automated examination and analysis tools assist investigations but there is an established need to provide additional training and education programs plus a need for University research to support computer forensic education.

The crime to court path shows points along the way from the time that an act of crime is committed through to when it is dealt with by the courts. It shows where IT professionals may assist law enforcement offices and at which point crime investigators take up a case.

An explanation of the Curtin University Master of Internet Security program put into perspective how the computer forensic course relates to and addresses the needs of industry and law enforcement officers.

The computer forensic course offered at Curtin University is designed to meet industry needs by adopting a practical application of knowledge approach.


## REFERENCES

Armstrong, I. (August 2002) *Now in Session. The Judiciary and the Digital World,* SC Info Security Magazine. p19.

Barbin, D. and Patzakis, J. (2002) Computer Forensics Emerges as an Integral Component of an Enterprise Information Assurance Program, Information Systems Control Journal, Volume 3, p25.

Bologna, G. J. and Lindquist, R. J. (1995) *Fraud Auditing and Forensic Accounting (Second Edition),* John Wiley & Sons, Inc., New York.

Furnell, S. (2002).. *Cybercrime : Vandalizing the Information Society,* Addison-Wesley, London

Hatcher, T. (2001). *Survey: Costs of Computer Security Breaches Soar* . CNN.com, . Available on-line at : http://www.cnn.com/2001/TECH/internet/-3/12/csi.fbi.hacking.report/index.html . (12 March 2001)

Icove, D., Seger, K. and VonStorch, W. (1995) *Computer Crime. A Crimefighter's Handbook,* O'Reilly & Associates, Inc, Sebastopol CA.

Kruse, W. G. and Heiser, J. G. (2001) *Computer Forensics. Incident Response Essentials,* Addison-Wesley, Boston.

Powers, R. (2002) Computer Security Issues & Trends : *2002 CSI/FBI Computer Crime and Security Survey,* Computer Security Institute. Available on-line at : http://www.gocsi.com . (9 November 2002)

Vatis. (2000) . Statement of the Director, National Infrastructure Protection Center, Federal Bureau of Investigation on Cybercrime before the Senate Judiciary Committee Criminal Justice Oversight subcommittee and House Judiciary Committee, Crime Subcommittee, Washington, D.C. February 29, 2000 . Available on-line at : http://www.usdoj.gov/criminal/cybercrime/vatis.htm . (14 December 2001)

Vatis, Michael. A. (June 2002). *Law Enforcement Tools and Technologies for Investigating Cyber Attacks. A National Needs Assessment.* Institute for Security Technology Studies, at Dartmouth College, Hanover, NH.

# ASSEMBLING COMPETITIVE INTELLIGENCE USING CLASSROOM SCENARIOS

Helen L. Armstrong and John Davey
*School of Information Systems, Curtin University of Technology, Perth, Australia, email: armstroh@cbs.curtin.edu.au*

*Defence Security Authority, Department of Defence, Canberra, Australia, Adjunct Research Fellow, Edith Cowan University, Perth Australia, email: jack.davey@defence.gov.edu*

Abstract:     This paper describes a scenario carried out in an intensive course in competitive intelligence and cyberwarfare. The scenario features two business organizations in tight competition and is designed to run over two days. The paper provides details of the scenario and discusses its application as part of a Master of Internet Security Management at Curtin University.

Key words:    competitive intelligence, business intelligence, postgraduate education, and educational scenarios

## 1. INTRODUCTION

Competitive intelligence is not a new concept; numerous high-profile corporations have used it for decades. In order to survive, excel and outstrip rivals an organization must have an intricate knowledge of their own business, the industry and their competitors. The growth in awareness of competitive intelligence is evidenced by the growing number of publications describing how to establish a competitive intelligence department within an organization and how to carry out such a department's functions.

Competitive intelligence is undertaken in many different forms in both public and private organizations. Miller (2000) suggests that government agencies conduct intelligence focused more on threats than on opportunities, but in corporations this situation is reversed, with emphasis more on opportunities than threats. Shake and Gembicki (1999) suggest modern business executives are equipped with tools of combat with well appointed fortresses where information warfare in a business context involves achieving and maintaining an information advantage over competitors.

Competitive intelligence is seen as an essential part of the modern organization just as Sun-Tsu considered it an essential part of warfare strategy in 400BC. It incorporates both intelligence (analyzing gathered data about rivals) and counterintelligence (protecting ones own information sources). Intelligence is not confined to the military domain, and Kanaher (1998) suggests it is imperative to corporate organizations due to the rapid pace of business, information overload, increased global competition from new competitors, more aggressive competition, rapid technological change and forceful global changes in international trade agreements. The race to survive in a cutthroat global marketplace is on. Jones recommends every morning you ask 'what can I do to beat Company Z today' as neither your competition nor technology will wait for you (Jones et al., 2002). Competitive intelligence is as important as a good marketing department and has emerged as a 'must-have tactical tool' in the corporate world (Thomas, 1998).

The heightened awareness of competitive intelligence has been spirited by increased global competitiveness characterized by increased industry consolidation and fragmentation (Fleisher & Blenkhorn, 2001). The Internet provides both the data and tools for competitive intelligence, offering a wealth of information and search bots for those wishing to gather information about corporations and individuals.

Although competitive intelligence is not a recent phenomenon in the business community and awareness of the benefits of competitive intelligence to organizations is evident, the tertiary education industry has been chided for lack of response to this need. Fleisher and Blenkhorn (2001) state that competitive intelligence is rarely included in MBA programs, and Shaker and Gembicki (1999) believe competitive intelligence is an essential ingredient to effective management and state a manager's knowledge is derived from both formal and information education. They go on to suggest that the IT culture at large and education programs, at the Masters level in particular, neglect the area of competitive intelligence.

## 2.        BACKGROUND

The unit of study presented is titled Business Intelligence and Cyberwarfare and is primarily a unit covering intelligence, competitive intelligence and corporate information warfare strategy formulation and response. The unit is included in several Masters programs within the School of Information Systems at Curtin University, but is primarily undertaken by students enrolled in the Masters of Internet Security Management. Students require pre-requisite knowledge in Internet security and network architecture to enroll in the business intelligence unit.

The overall objective of the unit relating to competitive intelligence is to develop in students an understanding of the nature of business intelligence and its purpose in contemporary business environments. The unit encompasses both competitive intelligence and cyberwarfare and the topics covered include the competitive business environment, asset evaluation and identification, information systems and networking, intelligence and counterintelligence, information collection and analysis methods, counterintelligence by deception and denial of service, conflict in cyberspace, information systems protective security, insider system attacks, external system attacks, intrusion detection, incident reporting and situational awareness, reaction to attack, damage control and business continuity, national infrastructure issues and practical use of hacking and intrusion detection software tools.

The unit is conducted as an intensive course over two consecutive weekends. The unit is very practical in nature with the classes conducted in laboratories and small tutorial rooms. Students use the Internet to collect intelligence about organizations and then form groups to devise business strategies based upon given information and questions. Students are given a warm-up exercise, an actual case of sabotage in industry, to investigate. The students work in pairs and are required to answer a number of questions relating to the incident. The final part of the exercise is to take on the mindset of the saboteur and identify ways the perpetrator could have caused more damage. Their ideas are then shared with the class. In summing up salient points of the exercise, a number of questions are asked of the group, including "What does your partner now know about the way you think?", "How much information are you now willing to share with your partner?", and "How well could your partner or the rest of the group predict your action or reaction to a given situation based upon the knowledge they now have about the way you think?". The main objectives of this exercise are not only to use some tools for gathering intelligence, but also to raise students' awareness of the confidential nature of information and the way information can be used.

One of the most effective tools used in the teaching of this unit was a scenario carried out over two of the four days. The scenario featured two organizations competing for government funding and contracts in a high-tech industry. Each student was assigned either a management or technical role in one of the two organizations. In an effort to encourage all students to fully participate the senior management roles were assigned by the lecturer to specific students. Experience has shown that the majority of classes contain a few natural leaders who dominate and take control rather than capitalizing on talents hidden in the more reserved students.

## 3.     THE SCENARIO

Two organizations are competing for a government contract to build the rockets to launch communications satellites. Each organization is to build a prototype and the government will decide the successful product. Immense government funding has been made available to both organizations for the development of their prototypes. The two organizations are in a highly competitive situation and in order to survive, need to develop a leading edge over their rival. This requires gathering information regarding the activities of the other, turning it into intelligence, and devising strategies to gain a leading edge.

The overall aim of running the scenario is to allow students to apply methods of intelligence gathering, design competitive intelligence strategies and learn from the human interaction.

## 3.1     Phase 1

The aim of this phase is for students to devise strategies for gathering information about their rival and determine not only the short and long-term impact of their actions, but also the ethical considerations. They must also devise appropriate counterintelligence measures to ensure their competitor does not gather information about them.

Students are assigned to one of the two organizations. Management roles are allocated to members of the group, with about half the group assigned engineer and technician roles. Management roles assigned should include (as a minimum) the Managing Director, the CEO, Engineering Director and Financial Director for each organization. In both organizations the CEO is the driving force within the organization with power over resources and decision-making. The CEO advises the Managing Director who puts the stamp of approval on decisions following advice from the CEO. Before making decisions, the CEO consults the other Directors for information and advice.

Students are advised that the level of competition between the two organizations is very high as both are competing for the same government contract. Each organization needs to gather intelligence about the other, and implement counterintelligence measures to ensure their competitor does not gather information about them.

Prior to commencement of the scenario activity, two appropriate students are separately approached to take on the roles of spies for the competition. The first spy works for Organization A but is having a secret affair with the CEO of Organization B and passing on confidential information. The second spy is an engineer employed within Organization B and is passing on selected information and data directly to the CEO of Organization A for a handsome fee. The CEOs are aware of the spy working for them, but not aware of the spy within their own organization.

The main activity in this phase is for each group to meet and decide what intelligence and counterintelligence measures they will implement. An opportunity for the spies to transfer information must be included at this stage, either a coffee break or end of the day's proceedings.

## 3.2    Phase 2

This phase covers a change in government funding for the project and the effect this has upon the two organizations. With cuts in funding both organizations must devise and produce a plan to reduce costs while still remaining the leader in the research and development.

After an election, the opposition political party takes power. The CEOs of the two organizations are called to separate meetings with the Chief of the Government agency handling the research and development grants (one of the academic staff) and are advised that the new government has decided to cut back on funding for the project. The CEOs are informed that their prototype should no longer require the same amount of initial funding as the majority of the research and development work should be close to completed, leaving only the testing to carry out. In effect, the funding available for engineering and technical research has been more than halved. Leaked information from the government agency regarding the proposed reduction in funding and proposed massive job losses reaches the media and hits headlines of the major financial newspaper.

The Financial Directors are given information showing that salaries are by far the greatest cost to the organization, particularly salaries for the engineers and technicians. Raw materials and overheads are insignificant in comparison to the salary costs. In order to complete the prototype they must use the available funds to purchase the remaining required raw materials, complete assembling the product and carry out launching tests. The CEOs are advised to gather information and opinions from their respective Directors and devise a course of action. As it is now the beginning of June, the new government funding arrangements come into effect in July, one month's time. While the Directors are meeting, the engineers and technicians are given the newspaper article to read.

A plan of action must be decided upon by the management of both organizations, however, before this plan can be communicated to employees, the scenario moves to phase 3.

## 3.3     Phase 3

The aim of this phase is to highlight the use of perception management and its effect on a competitive situation, and the role uncertainty plays in the actions of individuals. Given the information contained in the press article, engineers and technicians are now uncertain of the status of their jobs. An opportunity is given to employees to mix with their rivals and colleagues at an industry function. This presents the staff with an opportunity to solicit information about the competitor, transfer confidential information by informants, or to develop potential employment opportunities in case they are retrenched.

The new government has redesigned the government portfolios and established a new agency to handle ITC (information technology and communications). To market this event the government has sent invitations to attend a promotional seminar to all employees in the industry, including all employees of the two organizations involved. Coffee and cake is provided and open networking between professionals in the industry is encouraged.

After completing their action plan in phase 2, the CEOs must now meet with their staff and inform them of the government funding decision and the management's resultant action plan. The obvious course of action is to retrench a sizeable number of engineers and technicians. After considering the plan of action presented by the respective CEOs, the engineers and technicians in each organization meet and decide their course of action, and report back to their management.

## 3.4     Phase 4

The aim of the final phase is to share information, strategies, and to develop a big picture of the situation. The two groups join in the classroom and present their intelligence and counterintelligence strategies, and their action plans for the funding cuts. The engineers and technicians discuss their reactions to the management plans. In concluding the exercise, the spy employed by Organization A makes a confession, stating they regret the affair and trust it will not effect their respective marriages. The informant employed by Organization B also confesses.

As a final exercise, students are requested to reflect upon the exercise, and write a report on what they learned about themselves, the situation, and the methods they used in the scenario. This final exercise supports an action learning approach where reflection consolidates the learning process by evaluating strategies and tools. In addition, it allows the student to reflect upon their own thinking and the impact of their actions as well as that of others involved.

## 4.       APPLYING THE SCENARIO

The aim of the scenario was to apply some of the information on intelligence and counterintelligence the students had read from books and articles or covered in lectures and to give the students some insight into the complexity of their application, by people, in an organizational setting.

The scenario was run for the first time in the second semester of 2002. The phases of the scenario were carried out over two days, allowing the students to make notes, consider strategies and develop ideas away from the classroom. There were 26 students enrolled in the unit, from a variety of backgrounds and nationalities. Many of the students, particularly those from Asian countries studying full-time in Perth, had little or no IT business experience. It was noted that those with business experience tended to be more outspoken.

The intelligence and counterintelligence strategies developed by the two groups contained not only the usual intelligence gathering techniques, but also a few 'off-the-wall' suggestions bordering on the unethical. Some examples included causing physical harm to key employees of the rival organization, infiltrating the rival organization (cleaning staff, maintenance technicians, etc), hacking into the opposition's computer networks and not only copying information but also modifying engineering formulae and counterfeiting data in order to sabotage the product development.

The reactions of students to given situations as the scenario unfolded would have been an interesting study in culture and ethics. For example, after a few of the engineers employed by Organization A became aware of the funding cuts and threats to their jobs they approached management employees of Organization B at the ITC industry seminar, offering services and confidential information about intelligence and counterintelligence activities. Engineers employed by Organization B approached a few of the directors and engineers of Organization A and proposed a merger.

The engineers from Organization B offered to work for little or no pay until the contract was awarded by the government agency in the hope that they would retain their jobs in the long term. When the CEO of Organization

B was asked if she would give up her BMW corporate vehicle to assist payment of the engineers' salaries, she adamantly refused and became quite upset. She admitted she would rather leave the organization than give up her status symbol.

As is often the case in group exercises, one or two members of the group become dominant with opinions and suggestions. The group of directors for Organization A contained two such students, who regularly tried to coerce other members of the group, or take control and implement actions without due consideration of consequences. As the exercise progressed the proposed actions became more radical and unethical, and the reserved members of the group gradually became more outspoken in their opposition to these suggestions.

The feedback from the students was very positive, with all students stating they learned significantly from the scenario, particularly regarding intelligence, counterintelligence, strategy, security and many lessons in human relationships. The university carries out a student evaluation of units conducted, seeking feedback on the learning and academic value of the unit, instructor enthusiasm, individual rapport, grading, comparison with other classes, lecturer rating, organization and clarity, breadth of coverage, and group interaction. The ratings for all these factors exceeded the university norms.

## 5.     CONCLUSION

The scenario described above proved to be an interesting and effective means of applying much of the intelligence and counterintelligence theory taught in the lectures and textbook. Students were able to apply this theory in an interesting and challenging situation, being supported by the learning environment.

The scenario enabled the teaching objectives for the competitive intelligence elements of the course to be met, and students found the exercise to be of great academic value. Students also valued and learned from the group interaction. Not only were they able to devise strategies and partially apply them, but were also made aware of the complexities and constraints of a real-world environment. Other than those who had been told prior to commencement of the scenario, none of the students were aware of the informants in either group, and no procedures for internal checking were included in the intelligence and counterintelligence strategies.

In addition, the scenario prompted students to consider the impact and the ethics of their actions. The building of the big picture by sharing information and feelings at the end of the exercise allowed students to see the holistic view and how their actions affected others. The final activity involving reflecting upon what had been learned, not only in the application of theoretical concepts but also in human thinking and interaction.

## REFERENCES

Fleisher, C.S. & Blenkhorn, D.L., 2001, *Managing Frontiers in Competitive Intelligence*, Quorum Books, Connecticut, USA

Jones, A., Kovacich, G.L. & Luzwick, P.G., 2002, *Global Information Warfare: How Businesses, Governments and Others Achieve Objectives and Attain Competitive Advantages*, Auerbach Publications, Washington DC, USA

Kahaner, L., 1998, *Competitive Intelligence*, Touchstone Books, New York, USA

Miller, J.P., 2000, *Millennium Intelligence: Understanding and Conducting Competitive Intelligence in the Digital Age*, Cyberage Books, New Jersey, USA

Shaker, S.M. and Gembicki, M.P., 1999, *The WarRoom Guide to Competitive Intelligence*, McGraw-Hill, New York, USA

Thomas, J., 1998, Intelligent Intelligence, *The Wall Street Journal*, December 7, No. 29

# PANEL: TEACHING UNDERGRADUATE INFORMATION ASSURANCE

Matt Bishop
*Department of Computer Science, University of California, Davic, bishop@cs.ucdavis.edu*

As the importance of information assurance and computer security has become recognized, the number of institutions teaching these subjects in their undergraduate curriculum has grown. But methods of integrating this material into the undergraduate program are varied, as are the methods used to teach the material itself. Two key issues highlight the differences in instructional methods and techniques.

There is no commonly accepted body of knowledge in information assurance that an undergraduate should know. The first question is whether an undergraduate should be taught about information assurance, and if so, in what courses. Specifically, should undergraduates take a course in information assurance, or should the contents of such a course be distributed over existing courses such as networks, operating systems, software engineering, and theory? The importance of this question lies in the structure of the undergraduate programs. Many, particularly those in engineering, require a large number of courses. In some cases, there is enough room for electives that a student can take a course in information security (possibly at the loss of taking another course). In other cases, there is little room for electives, and adding a course in information security may not be feasible. If a course on information assurance provides a better education in that subject than integrating the material into other courses, then the undergraduate program will need to be revised to allow such a course. Otherwise, the material in each course must be revised to include information assurance aspects of the subject.

When teaching information assurance (either in its own course or as part of other courses), many instructors assign projects. Often, these projects take the form of penetration testing (or "ethical hacking") projects. The second question is whether these penetration testing projects are effective and appropriate vehicles to supplement classroom education? The importance of this question lies in the way a project relates to the material being taught. Survey papers and projects cover lots of material, but rarely in depth. More focused projects provide the depth but not the breadth. Some projects present unique problems. Penetration testing in particular is a popular project, but is it useful pedagogically? If so, why, and how should the exercise be conducted and evaluated? How can the exercise be contained to minimize the effects of errors? If not, what other types of projects would be useful?

## PANELISTS

*Mr. Colin Armstrong* is the Overseas Program Manager for the School of Information Systems in the Curtin Business School, Western Australia. He administers off shore undergraduate and postgraduate courses for the School. He also established a Center for Information Warfare. He currently teaches classes in computer and Internet security, and computer forensics.

*Dr. Natalia Miloslavskaia* is an associate professor of Information Security of Banking Systems at Moscow Engineering Physics Institute (State University). She has taught undergraduate and graduate classes in network security and has supervised post-graduate students in computer security. Her Information Security Faculty is a Head educational and scientific center on information security of the Russian Ministry of Education.

*Dr. Daniel Ragsdale* is a lieutenant colonel in the US Army, and a professor in the Department of Electrical Engineering and Computer Science at the United States Military Academy, West Point. He teaches undergraduate computer security and information warfare courses, and has supervised information warfare exercises involving both students and other military personnel. His program has been designated a Center for Academic Excellence in Information Assurance Education.

*Dr. Rayford Vaughn* is currently a professor of computer science at Mississippi State University where he teaches and conducts research in the areas of Software Engineering and Information Security. He established the MSU Center of Computer Security Research and led the effort at MSU to obtain a National Security Agency designation of Center of Academic Excellence in Information Assurance Education – one of only thirty-six in the United States.

## MODERATOR

*Dr. Matt Bishop* is an associate professor in the Department of Computer Science (a Center of Academic Excellence in Information Assurance Education) at the University of California at Davis. He has taught undergraduate and graduate courses in computer security there and at Dartmouth College. He has been active in information assurance education for many years, and gave the academic keynote addresses to the first and fourth Colloquia on Information System Security Education. His textbook, *Computer Security: Art and Science*, was published by Addison-Wesley-Longman in December 2002.

# PANEL: TEACHING UNDERGRADUATE INFORMATION ASSURANCE

Rayford Vaughn
*Mississippi State University, vaughn@cs.msstate.edu*

It is rare to find computer security course offerings at most academic institutions today. There are exceptions, of course, and some institutions are offering concentrations in this area of study. Such courses are found at NSA Centers of Academic Excellence and in some cases, degree programs in IA topics are being implemented or proposed. While NSA certifies COE/IAE's based on published criteria – there is no established program of study and each institution approaches the topic in their own way. At Mississippi State University, we believe that IA is properly placed within our Software Engineering research area and that it is best taught by integrating it into existing courses in our Software Engineering degree and our Computer Science degree programs. We also believe that by doing so, it better prepares the student for a dedicated IA course during their senior year of study.

The practice of security engineering requires a foundation of study in operating systems, database systems, networks, architectures, and, to some extent, artificial intelligence. It would appear that including computer security course offerings toward the end of a computer science or software engineering undergraduate program as a required course is an effective way of providing graduates with an emphasis in security engineering. One would expect that a comprehensive pedagogical approach would suggest that current CS or SE course content be modified to include course specific discussion related to security in networks, database, operating systems, architectures, and software engineering followed by a capstone course toward the end of the program that is specific to information security issues. The prerequisites for the capstone course should likely include, as a minimum, operating systems, database, and software engineering.

When teaching the senior level capstone course in IA, it seems critical to have a series of lab exercises that some might consider the "teaching of hacking". This panel member has sixteen labs over a sixteen week period that involve the cracking of passwords, spoofing of web sites, sniffing of networks, and other such activities that acquaint the student with risk and vulnerabilities in a way that lecture cannot. Having taught the IA course with and without a lab, this panel member believes strongly that the lab exercises are a necessary part of learning in this area.

# PANEL: TEACHING UNDERGRADUATE INFORMATION ASSURANCE IN RUSSIA

Anatoli Maljuk, Natalia Miloslavskaia, and Alexander Tolstoi
*Moscow Engineering Physics Institute (State University) milmur@mephi.edu, ait@mephi.edu*

According to the Russian educational system first two years at the higher educational institutions are destined for basic education when the students are taught humanities and science. Only after that they begin to study disciplines of their speciality. There are seven specialities on information security (IS) in Russia because this area is very complicated and includes not only technical but also legal, organizational and other aspects.

Teaching IS at undergraduate level is divided into three main streams.

1. For future specialists on IS that means teaching of introduction to their speciality. Duration of that educational course at the Moscow Engineering Physics Institute (State University) (MEPhI) is 32 hours (1 term). Some years ago we have tried to teach it on the 5<sup>th</sup> term (3<sup>rd</sup> year). But the practice have shown that it is too late. The reason is the absence of links with their basic education. Now we teach "Introduction to IS" at the 1<sup>st</sup> term. Duration of the course is 68 hours including 34 hours of lectures. The other 34 hours are intended for self-work of the students ending with writing and protecting of an essay on the topic given by a Professor. The main parts of the course are the following: IS threats in computer-based systems; main tasks and categories of information protection systems (IPS); problems of user identification and protection against information leakage via electromagnetic radiation; cryptology; computer viruses and protection against them; organizational and legal maintenance of IS; principles of IPS design. Every part of the course is logically connected with the educational courses taught on the following terms. A Professor points out what prerequisites from mathematics, computer science, cybernetics and electronics are needed for successful

learning of those courses. "Introduction to IS" have become basic course for the Russian universities preparing expert on IS.

2. The "ISB" course has been taught for specialists on information technologies for the last ten years. At present the course is an integral component in expert training for any field. Information exists at any area of knowledge and of our lives (for example, medical data, privacy, copyright, etc). It should be protected against different threats. Our experience have shown that it is more effective to teach IS for that category of students not as one separate course, but elements of IS maintenance should be described every time at every educational course when it is needed. Besides at the beginning of the education on the $1^{st}$ year we should teach one introductory ISB course, discussing both IS problems for information technologies and methods and tools of information protection. The course should prepare the students for perception of the following specialized courses on information technologies. There is no one standard course on that theme in Russia. Every educational institution decides how to teach ISB and in what courses itself.

3. The "ISB" course is needed for non-professional on information technologies as well. That is why we taught it for all MEPhI's faculties – for mathematicians, physicians and so on. There are some specifics that should be stressed specially. The best period for its teaching is the $5^{th}$ term. There is such a basis course in Russia. But our society is not ready enough for teaching it at present because it is very difficult to approve that IS affects all spheres of human live including art, culture, literature etc.

What are the prerequisites for IS classes? The knowledge gained at school is sufficient. We clearly understand that it should be a separate course discussing different aspects of IS problematics at school. Unfortunately we have not it at present. The potential students know about IS problems from mass media mainly. The Russian universities as a rule have several basic secondary schools where it is necessary to begin teaching "ISB". "School – higher education" joint efforts are the best solution of expert training on IS.

The main form of teaching IS at the undergraduate level is lectures. That is why the number of students of one faculty (at MEPhI 100-120 trainees) determines the size of classes. The total amount of the $3^{rd}$ year students is about 1000. All of them should pass progress testing in the middle and at the end of the term. It is a great problem for a Professor to talk with all of them. We have found a very effective solution – to use new educational technologies in the form of distance progress testing via the MEPhI Intranet.

We have no practical laboratory works for undergraduates. They are designed only for graduates for specialized courses on different IS aspects.

While teaching IS ethics problems are discussed. But only graduates work at "Network Security" Scientific and Research Laboratory. They are old enough to understand responsibility for all their activities at the Laboratory.

# OUTCOMES-BASED ASSESSMENT AS AN ASSURANCE EDUCATION TOOL

Susan Older and Shiu-Kai Chin
*Department of Electrical Engineering and Computer Science, Systems Assurance Institute, Syracuse University, Syracuse, NY 13244*

Abstract:     The goal of Syracuse University's Certificate of Advanced Study in Systems Assurance (CASSA) program is to develop students who (1) comprehend the concepts underlying security and system assurance; (2) can apply those concepts to construct assured systems; and (3) can critically analyze and evaluate systems' conformance to their requirements. Because of this third requirement, a key component of the CASSA program is an emphasis on using formal mathematics and logic to provide a rigorous basis for the assurance of information and information systems.

Our purpose in writing this paper is twofold. The first is to report on our progress in delivering an assurance curriculum with a strong emphasis on logic and formal methods. Specifically, we describe what we are teaching in two of our foundational courses, as well as what our students are learning. The second and broader purpose is to advocate the use of an outcome-based approach when developing IA courses and curricula. We have found that focusing on the desired educational outcomes from the outset has made it easier to identify what is working and what is not, and we wish to share our experiences.

Key words:    Formal methods, educational outcomes, assessment of student learning, assurance.

## 1.     INTRODUCTION

Systems Assurance focuses on the correctness, integrity, reliability and security of the systems upon which our society is constructed and thus depends. The multi-disciplinary Systems Assurance Institute (SAI) at Syracuse University has been established to promote improvement in systems assurance through research, education, and technology transfer. The

SAI comprises faculty from four distinct colleges: the College of Engineering and Computer Science, the School of Information Studies, the Maxwell School of Citizenship and Public Affairs, and the Newhouse School of Public Communications. The model that we have adopted for educational programs allows each academic unit to define its own discipline-specific foundation, while taking advantage of other units' offerings for electives to produce well-rounded students.

The most mature of these individual programs is the Master's-level Certificate of Advanced Study in Systems Assurance (CASSA), which has been approved by the New York State Department of Education. The CASSA program exists within the framework of the Computer Science and Computer Engineering Master's programs: students must satisfy all requirements of their home Master's program, as well as satisfying CASSA-specific requirements. A key—and, we believe, unique—component of the CASSA program is its emphasis on using formal mathematics and logic to provide a rigorous basis for the assurance of information and information systems. All students must take a combination of courses that provides hands-on experience not only in systems building but also in using formal methods to analyze and evaluate system behavior.

Our purpose in writing this paper is twofold. The first is to report on our progress in delivering an IA curriculum with a strong emphasis on logic and formal methods. In [OC02], we described our experiences in developing the CASSA program, as well as the challenges inherent in incorporating mathematical and logical rigor into an IA curriculum. In this paper, we provide more specific information about what we are doing in our courses, as well as our ongoing attempts to answer the following questions:

*To what degree are we being successful? What are our students learning?*

We discuss two specific courses that serve as elective courses in the CASSA program: *Modeling Concurrent Systems (CIS 632)* and *Principles of Network Security (CSE 774)*. For each course, we describe the educational objectives, what we have done to realize those objectives, our observations of student achievement (both subjective and objective), and the changes we have made or intend to make as a result of these observations. We hope that our experiences are informative for others interested in introducing formal methods and logical rigor into an IA curriculum.

The second and broader purpose is to advocate the use of an outcome-based approach when developing IA courses and curricula. To be explicit, we do not wish to promote additional bureaucracy or the complex instrumentation of courses. Rather, we have found that focusing on the desired educational outcomes from the outset has made it easier to identify what is working and what is not, and we wish to share our experiences. In our opinion, this approach is especially useful for developing IA curricula. IA is such a broad field that no individual program can cover everything. Emphasis on desired outcomes helps identify which topics to include and in what depth. Furthermore, the greater specificity of desired outcomes allows for more detailed and precise discussions across disciplines.

The rest of this paper proceeds as follows. In Section 2, we describe the high-level educational outcomes of our CASSA program and how the requirements relate to these outcomes. The next two sections then illustrate how one of the high-level CASSA outcomes is addressed through two separate courses. Section 3 presents the course *Modeling Concurrent Systems*, an applied concurrency-theory course in which IA applications are an integral component. Section 4 focuses on *Principles of Network Security*: this course uses a variety of logical systems to describe, verify, and analyze properties related to network security. We conclude in Section 5 with some final observations.

## 2. CASSA EDUCATIONAL OUTCOMES

In 1998, the EECS Department adopted an *outcome-based* curricula design approach [Syr98], in which we first formulate the outcomes we desire of our graduates and then use those outcomes to guide the development of rational curricula. This approach represents a distinct shift from the traditional faculty-centered viewpoint of "what do we *teach?*" to a student-centered viewpoint of "what do our students *learn?*"

We made use of this approach in developing the CASSA program, focusing on our expectations for those students who successfully complete our program. No single curriculum can possibly address all of Information Assurance: concentrating on the desired educational outcomes helped us determine how to structure our program. In our case, the goal was to develop a coherent collection of courses to ensure the following educational outcomes:

1. Students comprehend the concepts underlying security and systems assurance.
2. Students can apply those concepts to construct assured systems.
3. Students can critically analyze and evaluate systems' conformance to their requirements.

Not surprisingly, these outcomes reflect EECS department's long-standing emphasis on the use of mathematical and logical methods in engineering, computer science, and security.

The CASSA educational outcomes are broadly addressed by the program requirements. For example, students must successfully complete both the Systems Assurance Seminar and a non-technical IA elective course (such as telecommunications policy, Internet law, or e-commerce). The seminar course serves as a gateway to more advanced assurance courses, introducing basic terminology and many of the nonmathematical issues related to information assurance. Together, these two courses are intended to address Outcome 1. Furthermore, students must successfully complete a total of five courses from the *Foundations for Assurance* and *Assurance Applications* tracks, including at least two courses from each track. The *Foundations* track includes courses in cryptography, concurrency theory, and logical principles of network security. The *Applications* track includes courses such as Internet security, computer security, and security of wireless networks. Via this requirement, students are assured to receive hands-on experience both in building systems and in using formal methods, thus addressing Outcomes 2 and 3.

This setup raises an obvious question: what *specifically* can students do in the areas of constructing assured systems and critically analyzing and evaluating systems' conformance to their requirements? In this paper, we focus on the formal-methods aspect and describe our experiences assessing our students' learning in two separate *Foundations for Assurance* courses. We realize that, when the topics of outcomes and assessment are initially brought up, the typical reaction is resistance, due to a belief that it will be cumbersome, bureaucratic, and of little practical use. This has not been our experience. We have found that a good way to start is to follow Diamond's suggestion ([Dia98], page 134):

> As an alternative to writing objectives in the abstract, ... [one can] develop strong, clear objectives by playing the role of the student and asking, "If I'm your student, what do I have to do to convince you that I'm where you want me to be at the end of this lesson, unit, or course?"

This approach is exemplified by the description of *Modeling Concurrent Systems* in Section 3. One can also take a more structured approach suggested by Diamond and write objectives that include "a verb that describes an observable action" and "a description of the conditions under which the action takes place: 'when given $x$, you will be able to ...' " ([Dia98], page 132). This approach is used in *Principles of Network Security*, which is described in Section 4.

# 3.        CIS 632: MODELING CONCURRENT SYSTEMS

The purpose of this course is to provide students with an in-depth understanding of the process-algebraic approach for specifying, modeling, and analyzing system behavior. Process algebras such as CSP [Hoa85, Ros98] and CCS [Mil80] provide a way to describe system behavior in terms of the *events* (i.e., abstract actions deemed "observable") that can occur. The underlying theory also includes several useful notions of program equivalence and refinement, which are useful for compositional reasoning and analysis. There are automated and semi-automated tools available that allow one to apply the theory in practice to verify properties of nontrivial applications.

In the last two offerings, this course has been taught as a 400/600-level split: undergraduate and graduate students attend the same lectures, but they have different assignments, exams, and grading criteria. In Fall 2002, thirteen students (all undergraduate computer-science majors) took the CIS 400 version, while eleven graduate students (from both computer science and computer engineering) took CIS 632. The following discussion and statistics refer only to the graduate version of the course, except for where undergraduates are explicitly mentioned.

## 3.1      Educational Outcomes and Course Content

In Fall 2002, we focused on the use of CSP to specify and verify concurrent systems and to understand the emergent behavior of such systems. The educational outcomes appear in Table 1.

*Table 1.* CIS 632 Educational Outcomes

| **After completing this course, you should be able to:** |
| --- |
| Use CSP or related calculi to write process descriptions and behavioral specifications. |
| Use traces and failures refinement to analyze and relate system behaviors at multiple abstraction levels. |
| Distinguish between the traces and failures models, and explain when each is appropriate to use. |
| Use the model checker FDR to verify valid refinements or debug invalid refinements. |
| Apply these techniques to specify and analyze nontrivial applications |

We used Steve Schneider's CSP textbook [Sch00], supplemented with several exercises and examples from Bill Roscoe's textbook [Ros98]. In the first portion of the semester, we introduce the basic operators of CSP, their operational semantics, and the trace and failures models, both of which induce notions of refinement. The trace model, for example, formally describes a process's behavior in terms of the set of traces—that is, sequences of events—that it can perform. These trace sets provide a basis for comparing, equating, and refining processes. Two processes are trace-equivalent when they have precisely the same sets of traces. A process $Q$ refines $P$ in the trace model (written $P \leq_T Q$) if every trace of $Q$ is also a trace of $P$. Intuitively, if $P$ corresponds to a specification of permissible behavior and $Q$ refines $P$, then $Q$ is guaranteed to exhibit only permissible behaviors.

Similarly, the failures model supports a notion of refinement based on a process's set of failures, which pair traces with sets of events. A process has the failure $(t,X)$ if it can perform the trace $t$ and then reach a state where its only possible actions involve events not in the set $X$. The failures model provides a finer notion of equivalence and refinement than the trace model does: it distinguishes processes not only by what they are able to do but also by what they are able to refuse to do. As a result, it supports reasoning about the potential for deadlock. A process $Q$ refines $P$ in the failures model (written $P \leq_{SF} Q$) if $P \leq_T Q$ and every failure of $Q$ is also a failure of $P$.

We also introduced the model checker FDR2 [For97], which provides automated support for applying these notions in practice. The advantage of using a model checker is that one can analyze much larger systems than is possible by hand. In addition, model checkers can be useful in debugging designs: for example, when a desired refinement $P \leq_T Q$ fails, FDR2 produces a witness (i.e., a trace of $Q$ that is not allowed by the specification $P$).

The final third of the course is spent on using CSP and FDR2 to analyze several different problems and protocols, such as the alternating-bit protocol and a distributed-database cache-coherency protocol. For three class periods, students worked in small groups of 4-5 students to specify and implement a one-lane bridge that safely supported bi-directional traffic. We also spent two lectures on the Needham-Schroeder key-exchange protocol and Gavin Lowe's use of CSP and FDR2 to uncover a previously unknown flaw in it [Low96]. This analysis uses CSP to model the system as the parallel composition of an initiator, responder, and intruder; CSP is also used to describe the desired authentication properties. FDR2 can then be used to try to validate refinement relationships between the system and the two desired properties. The result of FDR2's analysis is a witness trace that highlights a possible man-in-the-middle attack.

## 3.2   Assessment Methods

Grades for CIS 632 were based on an equally weighted combination of homework assignments, quizzes, a final exam, and a final project. The purpose of homeworks was to keep students up-to-date with the material discussed in class and to familiarize them with the tools. The homeworks also served as simple formative-assessment tools: if several students had questions while working on the assignments or did poorly on particular questions, there was indication that certain topics needed to be reviewed again.

In total, there were six homeworks. The first two homeworks concentrated on sequential processes. The first homework required students to write CSP processes for a variety of scenarios, including one of their own choosing. For the second homework, students wrote machine-readable CSP and used the process animator ProBE [For98] to interact with their processes and to test their understanding of the CSP transition rules. The third and fourth homeworks focused on the various parallel operators of CSP: the third homework assessed basic understanding of the operators, while the fourth homework challenged the students to use the operators to introduce constraints on a system. The final two homeworks assessed students' understanding of the primary abstraction operators (i.e., hiding and renaming), as well as their mastery of the traces and failures models.

The quizzes and the final exam—all closed book and closed notes—served as summative-assessment tools, letting students demonstrate their understanding of the fundamental concepts. The quizzes were relatively lightweight and intended primarily as sanity checks. Typically, 60-75% of a quiz's points were for basic understanding of fundamentals (e.g., drawing transition graphs of processes, identifying a process's set of traces or failures, determining simple refinement relationships between processes). The remaining points tested students' deeper understanding of the concepts, such as writing a CSP process to model a scenario, validating or refuting claims about refinement relationships, and generating CSP processes that have (or fail to have) certain properties. The final exam placed more weight on these latter sort of questions: 34 points (out of 100) were for fundamentals, 30 were for writing CSP to model a scenario, and 36 were for validating/refuting a variety of claims about refinement relationships. Two examples of these claims follow:

- If $f(P) \leq_{SF} f(Q)$ and $f$ is a renaming function, then $P \leq_{SF} Q$.
- For all processes $P$, $Q$, and $R$, and for all sets $X$ and $Y$, the following are trace equivalent:

$$P \underset{X}{\|} \left( Q \underset{Y}{\|} R \right) \text{ and } \left( P \underset{X}{\|} Q \right) \underset{Y}{\|} R.$$

The first claim states that every failures-refinement relationship that holds between renamed processes (the process $f(P)$ behaves like $P$, except for a renaming of events via the function $f$) must also hold between the original processes. The second claim states that distinct parallel-composition operators are necessarily associative with one another. Both claims happen to be false.

The final project required students to use machine-readable CSP and FDR to model and reason about a nontrivial system or protocol. Students were required to submit annotated machine-readable CSP scripts containing descriptions of their system and of the desired behavioral properties, as well as the assertions (e.g., refinement or deadlock checks) necessary for validating those properties. Students were also required to submit 8–10 page project reports containing the following features: a high-level description of both the problem they were solving/analyzing and their CSP solution; a description of their use of refinements (e.g., explaining why trace refinements were used instead of failures refinements, or vice versa); and some analysis of their experience (e.g., unexpected results or design choices that were particularly good or bad). This paper was graded for grammar, spelling, and style, as well as for content. Students analyzed a variety of protocols and algorithms, including the Bully election algorithm, the Needham-Schroeder and TMN security protocols, the two-phase commit protocol for distributed transactions, and a distributed-sum algorithm.

## 3.3     Observations

We have found it useful to introduce the automated tools early in the semester: it helps students view CSP more like a programming language (and therefore "real") than just a mathematical notation. While grading homeworks early in the semester, we noticed that the undergraduates seemed to write higher quality CSP code: the graduate students wrote code that was technically correct, but it had a very strong imperative flavor (e.g., large numbers of nested conditionals). We postulate that, because the undergraduates all had functional-programming experience, they were better prepared to think about computational solutions in a non-imperative way.[3]

We have also found that students at both the graduate and undergraduate levels have difficulty grasping the distinction between the *properties* one wishes to prove about a system and the *constraints* imposed upon a system through parallel composition. The properties are described as CSP processes,

---

[3]   A student from the Fall 2001 class made a similar observation a few weeks later in an unsolicited comment to the CIS 632 instructor. The student was using Scheme in another class, and he suggested that functional programming should be a prerequisite for CIS 632.

and one can check whether the system satisfies those properties by checking whether a refinement relationship exists. Constraints are also represented by CSP processes, placed in parallel with the system to *enforce* certain properties. The confusion seems to arise because the same language is used both to express properties and to describe the system design: students have difficulty maintaining that distinction.

On the CIS 632 final exam, students had very little difficulty with drawing transition graphs or identifying a process's traces and failures. The average grade (out of 10 students) for the combination of these questions was 85%, with a high mark of 100% (two students), a low of 62%, three students between 74% and 77%, and the rest between 85% and 97%. Students were also asked to write a CSP process to describe a banking account that allowed deposits, withdrawals (with limited overdraft protection), and queries, as well as requests to change the overdraft limit. Students then had to add a parallel constraint to the system to limit the number of rejected overdraft-change requests. On this question, the average grade was 74%, with a high of 93% and a low of 53%; five students received between 60% and 73%, and three received between 87% and 90%. The final question required students to judge the validity of various claims and to provide convincing explanations for their answers. Students had much more difficulty with this question: most students correctly identified the truth or falsity of the claims (worth a third of the points) but provided insufficiently convincing explanations. Here, the average was 63%, with a high of 89% (two students) and a low of 36%; the remaining students received grades between 39% and 86%, in a fairly even distribution.

## 3.4    Adjustments

The results from the final exam suggest that students have good intuition about the concepts but need more practice in justifying answers rigorously: for example, many students would give a specific example to justify that a general claim was true. We plan to structure homeworks and lectures to give students more practice in providing rigorous and logical justifications for answers, as well as to review common logical fallacies.

The confusion between constraints and properties has triggered changes in two successive years. Having identified the problem in Fall 2001, we made a concerted effort in Fall 2002 to mediate it. In the bridge project, two groups were charged with identifying the desirable properties and describing them in CSP; the remaining groups were to model the bridge and a traffic-light system in accordance with a proposed solution. We would then, as a class, combine both parts in a single file and check the necessary refinement relationships. The expectation was that, by separating the tasks, students would concentrate on either properties or the system and be able to see how they relate to each other. However, both groups charged with writing properties repeatedly asked for clarification of their task: they had trouble comprehending how their properties were related to the overall system.

We plan to use the process algebra CCS in the next offering of this course. The CCS notion of synchronization differs from the CSP notion in a way that avoids the constraints idiom. Furthermore, the available automated tools for CCS (e.g., the Concurrency Workbench [CPS93]) support the use of temporal logic for describing desirable properties. We believe that the use of different notations will help students distinguish between system-level descriptions and their behavioral properties.

## 4.    CSE 774: PRINCIPLES OF NETWORK SECURITY

*Principles of Network Security* is an analytical course that uses predicate calculus, higher-order logic, and specialized logical systems to describe, specify, and verify the correctness and security properties of network security protocols, algorithms, and implementations. Students use formal logic to rigorously analyze cryptographic algorithms, key-distribution protocols, delegation, access control, electronic mail, and networks of certification authorities.

This course is open only to graduate students. Because this course is fairly novel even among IA curricula and has no standard textbook, we describe its contents in more detail than the course in the previous section.

### 4.1    Educational Outcomes and Course Outline

Both the educational outcomes and our discussion about this course make use of a modified Bloom's taxonomy [Blo74] to classify and distinguish the many kinds of knowledge and abilities. Some kinds of knowledge are at relatively low levels (e.g., *recalling* that $15_{16} = 21_{10}$), while others are at very high levels (e.g., *evaluating* whether an implementation meets a specification and requirement). The outcomes, which appear in the course's online syllabus, are listed in Table 2.

The first part of the course (outlined in Table 3) deals with network security fundamentals and covers the standard topics: basic security properties, cryptographic algorithms (e.g., DES and RSA), authentication and hash functions, digital signatures, protocols and certificates. The primary reference is William Stallings' classic text [Sta99].

*Table 2.* CSE 774 Educational Outcomes

---

**Comprehension**
Define the meaning of security services such as confidentiality, integrity, non-repudiation, and authentication
Describe the characteristics of private key and secret key cryptographic systems
Describe cryptographic algorithms for encryption, hashing, and signing
Describe cryptographic protocols for session-based security such as Kerberos, and store-and-forward security such as Privacy Enhanced Mail
Describe basic principles of trust topologies and networks of certification authorities

---

**Application**
When given a block diagram or functional description of an implementation, you should be able to represent the implementation using predicate calculus
When given protocol descriptions and trust hierarchies, you should be able to use specialized security calculi such as the logic of authentication for distributed systems to describe the protocol and trust relationships
When given a trust topology, determine the necessary certificates for establishing trust in a key

---

**Analysis**
When given a set of assumptions and a goal to prove, you should be able to prove, using formal inference rules, if the security goal is true or not
When given a set of certificates, you should be able to formally derive whether a key is associated with a particular principal

---

**Synthesis**
When given a description of a system or component and its specification and security properties, you should be able to construct a theory that describes both, and show if the security properties are supported
When given a description of a trust topology, you should be able to create a formal description of certificates and trust relationships for the certification authorities

---

**Evaluation**
When given a theory, inference rules, and a proof, you should be able to judge if the proof is correct
When given a specification and implementation, you should be able to judge whether the implementation satisfies its specification

---

*Table 3.* CSE 774 Topics in Security Fundamentals

| Topic | Primary References |
|---|---|
| **Basic Security Properties:** confidentiality, authentication, integrity, non-repudiation, access control, availability; mechanisms; attacks | [Sta99] §1 Also: [SS75], [Lam71] |
| **Conventional Encryption:** DES, Electronic Code Book, Cipher Block Chaining | [Sta99] §3.1 – §3.3, §3.7 |
| **Confidentiality:** placement of encryption, traffic confidentiality, hey distribution | [Sta99] §5.1 – §5.3 |

| Topic | Primary References |
|---|---|
| **Public-key Cryptography:** principles of public-key cryptosystems, RSA, key management | [Sta99] §6.1 – §6.3 |
| **Message Authentication and Hash Functions:** authentication requirements, authentication functions, message authentication codes, hash functions | [Sta99] §8.1 – §8.4 |
| **Hash Functions:** Secure Hash Algorithm (SHA-1) | [Sta99] §9.2 |
| **Digital Signatures and Authentication Protocols:** digital signatures, authentication protocols, digital signature standard | [Sta99] §10.1 – §10.3 |
| **Authentication Applications:** Kerberos, X.509 authentication service | [Sta99] §11.1 – §11.2 |

The second part of the course (see Table 4) deals with reasoning about freshness of protocols, replay attacks, and role-based access control. We use the BAN logic [BAN90] to reason about freshness and potential replay attacks. We also introduce the formal definitions and properties of role-based access control (RBAC), as described by Ferraiolo, Sandhu, and Kuhn in [FBK99, FSG+00] and [FK92]. The knowledge expected of students is at the levels of *comprehension, application, analysis* and *synthesis*. Specifically, when given informal descriptions of key-exchange protocols, students are expected to be able to describe the protocol abstractly in the BAN logic; postulate initial beliefs about key associations, scope of authority, freshness of nonces, and so on; and show that, at the end of the protocol, belief in the distributed keys has been established. A similar set of skills is expected related to RBAC: when given an organizational structure of roles, students are expected to write down role-containment relations and derive the membership relations that are implied by a specific organizational structure.

*Table 4.* CSE 774 Topics in Belief Logics and Role-Based Access Control

| Topic | Primary Reference |
|---|---|
| **BAN Logic** | [BAN90] |
| **RBAC Definitions and Properties** | [FBK99] Also: [FSG+00], [FK92] |

The third part of the course (outlined in Table 5) focuses on authentication, delegation, and access control in distributed systems. Nine weeks is spent on this topic, the major focus of the course. The technical content of this part centers on the Abadi calculus [ABLP93, LABW92] for reasoning about principals, their statements, and their beliefs.

*Table 5.* CSE 774 Topics in Authentication, Delegation, and Access Control

| Topic | Primary References |
|---|---|
| Underlying Semantics and Model | [HK00] §1 – §3 |
| | Also: [ABLP93] §3.3 – §3.4 |
| Axioms for Principals and Statements | [LABW92] §3, [HK00] §4.1 – §4.3 |
| | Also: [ABLP93] §3.1 – §3.2 |
| Channels and Encryption | [LABW92] §4 |
| Group Names | [LABW92] §5.3 |
| Roles and Programs | [LABW92] §6 |
| | Also: [HK00] §4.4 – §4.5 |
| Delegation | [ABLP93] §5 – §6.1 |
| | Also: [LABW92] §7, [HK00] §4.6 |
| Interprocess Communication | [LABW92] §8 |
| Access-Control Decisions | [ABLP93] §6.2 |
| | Also: [LABW92] §9 |
| Reasoning about Credentials and Certificates | [WABL94] §1 – §4.3 |
| Extensions to the Logic | [HK00] §6 |

## 4.2 Assessment Methods

We used Socratic-style question-driven lectures as one means for formative assessment. For example, when introductory concepts on RBAC were presented, students were called upon to answer questions related to the definitions, properties, or applications of RBAC. To ensure the participation of all students and to randomize the order in which they are called, names are drawn from a deck of cards. Students are allowed to say "I don't know." There is no attempt to intimidate; rather, the intent is to provoke a thoughtful response. Generally speaking, if three successive students are unable to answer a question, the instructor can reasonably conclude that the class is unclear about the current topic. At that point, the instructor can decide whether more time or a different approach is needed. Similarly, if students are able to answer the questions, they have feedback that they answered the questions correctly. Students who couldn't answer the questions know that they need to study those particular topics more.

Summative assessment is accomplished through four open-book, open-notes exams. Students receive written solutions as they turn in their exams. The questions are formulated with the educational outcomes at the various levels of knowledge previously described (*comprehension, application, analysis, synthesis*, and *evaluation*). While the course emphasizes the use of formal analysis, more weight is typically given to questions that ask students to set up the formal assumptions, definitions, and goals when given an informal problem description.

## 4.3     Observations

**Fundamentals** The first exam occurred four weeks into the course. Two questions dealt specifically with comprehending cryptographic algorithms (DES and RSA): given particular inputs, students had to compute the outputs. Little class time was devoted to these topics, and the average grades on these questions (out of eighteen students) were 71% and 82%. At the levels of application, analysis, and synthesis, students were asked to model cryptographic algorithms in schemes such as electronic code book and cipher block chaining. Here, the results were less satisfying. For example, students were asked to model ECB encryption as a recursive function (where the particular encryption function and key are parameters) and prove that ECB inverts itself. In this case, the average score was 50%. However, the distribution of grades was bimodal: 25% of the students received full or close to full credit, 25% received no credit, and the remaining students received between 20% and 70%, with most of these students getting more than 50%. All of the students who received no credit had failed to take the prerequisite course in predicate calculus.

**BAN Logic and Role-Based Access Control** The BAN material was also assessed in the first exam, at the application, analysis, and synthesis levels. Specifically, one question at the analytical level asked for a proof that, in the context of the X.509 protocol, one principal believed that another principal believed in a particular statement. The initial assumptions about keys and nonces were given. The average for this question was 76%, with seven students getting 100% and one student getting 0%. Another question asked students to consider how beliefs would change if X.509 timestamps could not be checked accurately, and to justify their answers using the BAN logic. The average for this question was 70%: ten students got 100%, and three students got 0%.

RBAC was assessed in the second exam, which was given after seven weeks. By this time student enrollment had dropped from eighteen to fifteen. RBAC was assessed at the levels of application, analysis, and synthesis. Students were shown an organizational chart of company roles and asked to formally prove or disprove mutual exclusivity of various roles. The average on this problem was 66%, but the distribution was again bimodal. Five students earned 100%, six students earned between 70% and 95%, one student received 20%, and the remaining three students received 0%.

**Authentication, Delegation, and Access Control** The underlying semantics of the principal calculus of Abadi and colleagues [LABW92, ABLP93, HK00] is based on Kripke structures. A Kripke structure comprises a set $W$ of *possible worlds*; an interpretation function $I$, which maps each propositional variable to a subset of $W$; and an interpretation function $J$, which maps each principal name to a binary relation over $W$. Intuitively, $I(p)$ is the set of worlds in which the propositional variable $p$ is true, and $J(A)$ is the accessibility relation for principal $A$: if $(w,w')$ is in $J(A)$, then principal $A$ cannot distinguish between worlds $w$ and $w'$.

Questions on the second and third exam focused on assessing the students' understanding at the comprehension and analysis levels. Specifically, they were given a particular Kripke structure and asked to evaluate the beliefs of principals in various worlds. The average grade on Kripke structures in the second exam was 58%, with three students receiving 100% and four students receiving 25% or less. These grades improved on the third exam to an average of 65% with five students receiving 100%, one student receiving 93%, and the remaining students receiving between 27% and 53%.

Students were also asked on both the second and third exams to prove an axiom of the calculus (e.g., "if $(A \land B)$ *says* s, then $A$ *says* s and $B$ *says* s"). The average grade for this question on the second exam was 48%, with two students receiving 100% and three students receiving 0%. On the third exam, grades improved to an average of 60%, with five students receiving 100%, one student receiving 80%, one student receiving 0%, and the rest receiving between 20% and 60%.

The fourth and final exam (given to fourteen students after fourteen weeks of class) focused on reasoning about certificates, delegations, and authority and on proving properties of credentials used in the Taos operating system [WABL94]. This time, students were presented with a client/server system where the server receives a message " $C_{Alice}$ *says* $RQ$" within the context of boot, delegation, and channel certificates. The students first had to set up a theory whereby the server could conclude that *((Machine as OS) for Alice) says RQ*, and then they had to carry out a formal proof to justify their conclusions. This problem was very similar to the extended example of [LABW92]. The average score on these questions was 67%, with seven students scoring 80% and above (two at 100%, one at 97%, and four at 80%), and the remaining seven students with scores from 33% to 60%.

## 4.4 Adjustments

This course has evolved much over the last six years. In this latest offering, we were interested in seeing how far and how deeply our students could learn to use the principal calculus of Abadi and colleagues. We were pleasantly surprised. The mid-course corrections we made were based on our observation that many students were not facile with the use of discrete mathematics (sets, relations, algebraic properties). This observation caused us to devote more time to reinforcing discrete mathematical notions at the expense of reasoning about additional protocols, such as electronic banking protocols. In the future, we plan on rectifying the lack of facility with discrete math by incorporating more applications such as RBAC and modal logic into the predicate-calculus course that is a prerequisite for this course.

Overall, the students were satisfied with the course, although some would have preferred less theory and more applications. In our view, limiting the time spent on cryptographic algorithms to devote time to the authentication logic was well worth it: students gained knowledge that enables them to think rigorously about authentication, certificates, delegation, and access control.


## 5.     CONCLUSIONS

We have described two courses that illustrate out efforts to introduce rigorous foundations for assurance into an IA curriculum. Specifically, we have presented not only the material that we cover, but also how we assess students' mastery of that material and how they are doing. The statistics that we have provided are not by themselves statistically significant. However, we believe they shed light both on how we are doing so far and on what is possible in a Master's-level IA curriculum. Furthermore, students have responded positively to these courses: in fact, in each of the past two years, undergraduates have expressed interest in our Master's CASSA program as a result of analyzing security protocols in the concurrency course.

Based on our experiences, we advocate using an outcomes-based approach to develop courses and curricula. We are not assessment experts, but rather users who have found value in adopting practices put forward by experts in the field of Higher Education. We have tried to demonstrate that the process does not have to be painful or cumbersome. Even a lightweight approach as in CIS 632 offers a lot of benefits. A course's educational outcomes are suggestive of the appropriate assessment techniques, and both outcomes and assessment are in the instructor's control. Another advantage of writing outcomes is that information is communicated more precisely, both to students and to other faculty. Because we have thought about educational outcomes, several faculty across several courses have developed consensus regarding our Computing Engineering and Computer Science Master's programs. We are moving towards a common core for these two programs that includes logic, functional programming, and concurrency. This common core would help prepare students for the two courses discussed here, as well as for the rest of our Master's programs.

# ACKNOWLEDGMENTS

This work is partially supported by the National Science Foundation under Grant Number DUE-0241856, as well as by the Information Assurance program of the New York State Center for Advanced Technology in Computer Applications and Software Engineering (CASE).

# REFERENCES

[ABLP93]   Martin Abadi, Michael Burrows, Butler Lampson, and Gordon Plotkin. A calculus for access control in distributed systems. ACM Transactions on Programming Languages and Systems, 15(4):706–734, September 1993.

[BAN90]   Michael Burrows, Martin Abadi, and Roger Needham. A logic of authentication. Technical report, SRC Research Report 39, Systems Research Center, Digital Equipment Corporation, Palo Alto, CA, 1990.

[Blo74]   Benjamin S. Bloom. The Taxonomy of Educational Objectives: Affective and Cognitive Domains. David McKay, New York, 1974.

[CPS93]   Rance Cleaveland, Joachim Parrow, and Bernhard Steffen. The Concurrency Workbench: a semantic-based tool for the verification of concurrent systems. ACM Transactions on Programming Languages and Systems, 15:36–72, 1993.

[Dia98]   Robert M. Diamond. Designing & Assessing Courses & Curricula: A Practical Guide. Jossey-Boss, revised edition, 1998.

[FBK99]   David F. Ferraiolo, John F. Barkley, and D. Richard Kuhn. A role-based access control model and reference implementation within a corporate intranet. ACM Transactions on Information and Systems Security, 2(1):34–64, February 1999.

[FK92]   David Ferraiolo and D. Richard Kuhn. Role based access control. In Proceedings of 15th Annual Conference on National Computer Security, pages 554–563, Gaithersburg, MD, 1992. National Institute of Standards and Technology.

[For97]   Formal Systems (Europe) Ltd, Oxford. Failures-Divergence Refinement: FDR2 User Manual, October 1997.

[For98]   Formal Systems (Europe) Ltd, Oxford. Process Behaviour Explorer: ProBE User Manual, March 1998.

[FSG+00]   David F. Ferraiolo, Ravi Sandhu, Serban Gavrila, D. Richard Kuhn, and Ramaswamy Chandramouli. A proposed standard for role-based access control. Technical report, National Institute of Standards and Technology, December 2000.

[HK00]   Jon Howell and David Kotz. A formal semantics for spki. Technical Report TR 2000-363, Dept. of Computer Science, Dartmouth College, Hanover, NH, March 2000.

[Hoa85]   C.A.R. Hoare. Communicating Sequential Processes. Series in Computer Science. Prentice Hall, London, 1985.

[LABW92] Butler Lampson, Martin Abadi, Michael Burrows, and Edward Wobber. Authentication in distributed systems: Theory and practice. ACM Transactions on Computer Systems, 10(4):265–310, November 1992.

[Lam71]   Butler Lampson. Protection. In Proceedings of the 5th Princeton Conference on Information Sciences and Systems, Princeton, NJ, 1971.

[Low96]   Gavin Lowe. Breaking and fixing the Needham-Schroeder public-key protocol using FDR. Software Concepts and Tools, 17:93–102, 1996.

[Mil80]    Robin Milner. A Calculus of Communicating Systems, volume 92 of Lecture Notes in Computer Science. Springer-Verlag, 1980.

[OC02]    Susan Older and Shiu-Kai Chin. Building a rigorous foundation for assurance into information assurance education. In Proceedings of 6th National Colloquium for Information Systems Security Education, volume 1. George Washington University Journal of Information Security, 2002.

[Ros98]    A.W. Roscoe. The Theory and Practice of Concurrency. Series in Computer Science. Prentice Hall, London, 1998.

[Sch00]    Steve Schneider. Concurrent and Real-Time Systems: The CSP Approach. John Wiley & Sons, 2000.

[SS75]    Jerome Saltzer and Michael Schroeder. The protection of information in computer systems. Proceedings IEEE, 63(9):1278–1308, September 1975.

[Sta99]    William Stallings. Cryptography and Network Security, Second Edition. Prentice-Hall, 1999.

[Syr98]    Syracuse University Department of Electrical Engineering and Computer Science. Developing curricula to meet the needs of the next millenium: Preliminary report of the EECS Curriculum & Course Development Committee, 1998.

[WABL94] Edward Wobber, Martin Abadi, Michael Burrows, and Butler Lampson. Authentication in the Taos operating system. ACM Transactions on Computer Systems, 12(1):3–32, February 1994.

# EVALUATION THEORY AND PRACTICE AS APPLIED TO SECURITY EDUCATION
*An Overview*

Melissa J. Dark
*Purdue University*

**Abstract**: This paper will overview general evaluation purposes, elements, and steps for designing an evaluation in order to provide foundational information that can be used to conduct an evaluation of any security awareness, training, or education programs. An example of evaluation principles discussed in this paper as applied to an information security education program has been provided in the appendix. This paper is a tool for individuals who have little to no formal training in educational evaluation.

**Key words**: evaluation, evaluation design, formative evaluation, summative evaluation, measurement, metrics, program logic, validity, reliability.

## 1. INTRODUCTION

The information assurance environment is shaped by new technologies, unknown threats, increasing vulnerabilities, a national security workforce crisis, and a lack of sufficient security education. The lack of human resource is the most critical because it underlies each of the other issues. In response, new security education initiatives and programs are rapidly being established to expand our human resources capacity. While several initiatives intend to address this need, there will be many unasked and unanswered questions about the impact of such programs and the extent to which these initiatives succeed. A common misconception in education is that evaluation does not need to be seriously considered until the end of the awareness, training, and/or education program. However, this fallacy contributes to educational programs that are less effective than needed and less efficient than they had to be. This paper will overview general evaluation purposes, elements, and steps for designing an evaluation in order to provide foundational information that can be used to conduct an evaluation of any security awareness, training, or education programs. An extensive example is provided in the appendix wherein the principles presented in this paper are applied to a security education program.

## 2.        DEFINING EVALUATION

What is evaluation? Evaluation is concerned with the investigation of the worth or merit of an object and conducted for purposes of improving, informing, and/or proving (1). In the broadest sense, evaluation "includes all efforts to place value on events, things, processes, or people" (3). Evaluation is both the process of conducting an evaluation or a program as well as the resulting product, e.g., an evaluation report. Evaluation of educational programs utilizes social research procedures to systematically investigate the effectiveness of the programs. Evaluation spans the life cycle of any program including the diagnosis of the social problems being addressed, conceptualization and design, implementation and administration, outcomes, and efficiency (3).

Evaluation is generally conducted for the purposes of informing, improving, and/or proving. Evaluation that is conducted to identify needs and to understand the nature of the need(s) is known as needs evaluation/analysis. Needs analysis is usually done prior to program development and includes investigation that both quantifies and qualifies the nature of the need. Evaluation that is undertaken to furnish information that will guide improvement to the educational program or activity is known as formative evaluation. For example, a formative evaluation might be intended to a) help management improve community acceptance of a security awareness program, b) improve a security training program through the use of a new laboratory activities, or c) help an organization improve the cost effectiveness of a security education program by converting it to self-paced, computer-based instruction. Formative evaluation is conducted in the early stages of developing an educational product or program or in the early stages of implementation when there is still sufficient time to make use of the evaluation results. In contrast to formative evaluation, evaluation undertaken to render a final judgment is known as summative evaluation. Examples of summative evaluation might include a) judging the effectiveness of a faculty development program that intends to develop faculty knowledge and skills; or b) show the extent to which security vulnerabilities were reduced as a result of a new training program. Summative evaluation is conducted at the end of the educational program, activity, module, etc.

## 3. THE EVALUATION SYSTEM

The evaluation of a program will only produce relevant, useful, and accurate information if the evaluation 'system' is designed to ensure that this happens. We'll start by looking at elements common to all evaluation systems and proceed to an overview of steps that can be followed to design any evaluation.

Evaluation systems are comprised of metrics and measurement systems. These terms are often used interchangeably or misused in education, so it is worth clarifying the differences and relationships. The purpose of the measurement process is to establish the degree or amount to which a characteristic, trait, or feature exists. The measurement process almost always includes a measurement instrument of some sort that produces a measure (e.g., a score, rating, ranking, etc.). The result of the measurement process is a measure that serves as an indicator of the desired trait, skill, ability, etc. Most measures are meaningless until they are contextualized by a measurement system (e.g., a scale of some sort). A measure that is contextualized by a measurement system is a metric. The measurement system is critical in evaluation because it allows program mangers, policy makers, evaluators, and other stakeholders to ascertain the degree or extent to which the desired property, trait, process, etc., exists across programs, across time, relative to expectations, etc. Measurement always involves three common steps: 1) identifying and defining the quality or attribute that is to be measured, 2) determining a set of operations by which the attribute may be made manifest and perceivable, and 3) establishing a set of procedures or definitions for translating observations into quantitative statements of degree or amount (4). Error can be introduced into the measurement process at each of these steps; erroneous measures and measurement lead to inappropriate evaluations.

While measurement and metrics are an essential part of evaluation, evaluation goes beyond measurement. Evaluation is the systematic process of collecting, analyzing, and interpreting information (2) in order to render judgments. As previously mentioned, these judgments might be in regard to improvement (formative evaluation) or to render final judgment (summative evaluation). In addition to measurement error, error can also be introduced through a poorly designed evaluation. The remainder of this paper outlines recommended steps and associated considerations for designing an effective evaluation. An example of each of the following steps as applied to an information security education program has been provided in the appendix.

## 4.     STEPS FOR DESIGNING AN EVALUATION

Following is a discussion of five steps to consider when designing an evaluation. I will discuss each step in detail and have provided a detailed example of each step as applied to security education in the appendix.

The first step is to determine whether the purpose of the evaluation is needs analysis, formative, or summative. Needs analysis, formative, and summative evaluation questions are distinctly different in nature as exemplified by the evaluation questions shown in table 1.

*Table 1:* Needs Analysis/Formative/Summative Evaluation

| Needs Analysis | Formative | Summative |
|---|---|---|
| What learning goals are not being met? | What problems are students having learning the content and why? | How well were goals/objectives met? |
| How/why are current programs insufficient? | Are the awareness campaigns having the desired impact and why/why not? | Did any changes made have the desired impact? |
| Are current programs adaptable for a new/different learner population? | | Is it worth teaching again? |
| | | Was it cost effective? |
| What changes are needed to programs to meet the needs of a new learner population? | How should the curriculum be updated to meet industry needs? | To what degree did the training program alter employee behavior and mitigate our security risk? |
| | Where is this program least cost effective and what can be done to improve cost effectiveness? | How many students passed the exam? |

Lack of proper focus will inevitably lead to an inappropriate evaluation; when this happens decisions based on the evaluation are bound to be error-ridden. In addition to poor focus, another grievous mistake is to attempt to take one type of data (e.g., data that were collected for a formative evaluation) and use these data for another purpose (e.g., to answer a summative evaluation question). Data for the most part are meaningless. Data only become meaningful when used in a context and for a purpose; the appropriate reuse of data is dependent upon the degree of alignment between the original and the new context and purpose. The evaluator needs to clearly determine the purpose of the evaluation and adhere to it throughout the evaluation process.

The second step is to frame the evaluation. This step is critical to beginning the evaluation properly. In a way, conducting an evaluation is like building a house; one should not build a house without a design that specifies what goes where and why. Likewise, when conducting an evaluation, a design is needed that serves as a blueprint for what the evaluation will accomplish. The design of the evaluation should reflect the purpose (needs analysis/formative/summative) of the evaluation. When the evaluation is a needs analysis, the object of the evaluation is to ascertain the nature and scope of the need so that programs can be developed that will address the need, i.e., fill the gap. By nature, a needs analysis is an evaluation of a state or condition. The purpose of a formative or summative evaluation is to evaluate a program that has been established in response to a known need. By nature, formative and summative analyses are evaluations of a program, initiative, etc., developed in response to the needs. Therefore, formative and summative evaluation should also reflect the framework of the security awareness, training, or education program being evaluated.

The framework of any program can be determined by identifying the program logic, which consists of antecedents, transactions, and outcomes, as well as the underlying beliefs, assumptions, and theories (figure 1).

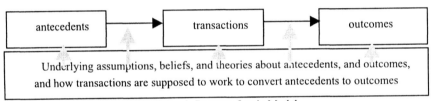

*Figure 1:* Program Logic Model

Antecedents are the inputs into the program. Outcomes are the goals and objectives that the program is trying to achieve. Transactions are the activities within the program that convert antecedents into outcomes. Educational antecedents, transactions, and outcomes can include policies, programs, curricula, courses, instructional software, instructional materials, delivery systems, learners, and so on. By identifying underlying assumptions, beliefs, and theories about how transactions are supposed to work to convert antecedents into outcomes, the evaluator can fully define the conceptual framework of the program. There is not a standard process for identifying and documenting program logic, however, there are several models that can be utilized to guide this process; some of which are the Provus Discrepancy Model, the CIPP (context, input, process, product) model, Stake's countenance approach, Eisner's connoisseurship and criticism approach, Stake's illuminative evaluation, and so on. Which model is most appropriate depends upon several factors including, but not limited to the purpose of the evaluation, the evlauand (the program, persons, etc., being evaluated), the audience for the evaluation, the required degree of rigor, and the existence of predetermined and widely accepted standards. Once program logic is manifest, the evaluator is in a position to 1) use this information as a blueprint for determining the extent of program implementation, 2) identify gaps and contradictions in the conceptual framework and causal links, 3) identify unrealistic expectations for the program, and 4) reveal possible side effects of the program.

After critical aspects of the program have been defined and documented, the next step is to determine evaluation questions, i.e., what questions is the evaluation seeking to answer. When drafting evaluation questions, you will want to attend to the tone and style of the questions, as well as the content focus of the questions. The tone and style of the evaluation questions reflects whether you are conducting a needs analysis, formative, or summative evaluation. The content focus of the questions reflects program logic (antecedents, transactions, and outcomes, and underlying assumptions, beliefs, and theories).

I like to use two levels of evaluation questions. The first level question is a comprehensive evaluation question that cannot be answered in and of itself, such as the example provided in figure 2. Level one questions guide the evaluation, are generally timeless, and aligned to level two questions.

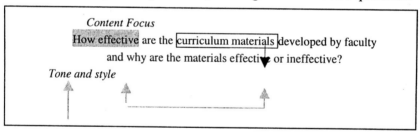

*Figure 2:* Level One Evaluation Question

Second level (level two) evaluation questions are more specific. The collective answers to the second level questions paint a picture that answers the first level question. Level two questions are based on underlying assumptions, beliefs, and theories. Level two questions often change as the program is modified and improved, but remain aligned to level one. Good level two questions: 1) indicate specific criteria of merit, 2) orient you toward a measure(s) of performance outcomes, 3) focus on only one aspect of a goal, 4) are designed with thought toward the information that could be collected to inform them, 5) consider any subpopulations that need to be examined separately, 6) are actionable so that they guide improvement or decision-making, 7) are reliable (i.e., can be measured by a variety of people and across time, and 8) are comparable (i.e., measures developed from level two questions should be able to be compared to measures developed from similar questions in the past).

Following are sample statements about effective curriculum materials that demonstrate guiding assumptions, beliefs, and theories: 1) curriculum materials should be current in order to provide students recency of content, 2) curriculum materials should have content validity. 3) curriculum materials should have construct validity, 4) curriculum materials should include opportunities for active learning, 5) curriculum materials should specify intended learning outcomes. These statements can easily be transformed into level two evaluation questions as shown in figure 3.

---

To what extent are the curriculum materials current?
To what extent do the materials have content validity?
To what extent do the materials have construct validity?
To what extent do the materials provide opportunities for active learning?
To what extent do the materials specify intended learning outcomes?

---

*Figure 3:* Level Two Evaluation Questions

With evaluation goals identified and questions formulated, the fourth step is to figure out what information is needed to answer evaluation questions. More specifically, measures and a measurement system need to be defined. The evaluator should identify and define the qualities or attributes that are to be measured, determine indicators of the attributes that are manifest and perceivable, and 3) create, adopt, and/or revise instruments to collect data. While a comprehensive discussion of measurement is not possible in this paper, there are a few key points I want to reiterate. The qualities or attributes that are to be measured should be derived from the program logic model. By now, these qualities and attributes should be evident in your level two evaluation questions. If these qualities and attributes are not evident, then you should go back to step three. If you do not know what you qualities you are assessing, then it will be impossible to know what measure will serve as indicators of these qualities. Good indicators are 1) oriented toward a measure of performance, 2) specific, 3) operational definitions of the attribute you are trying to assess, 4) theory-driven, 5) valid, and 6) reflective of the program goals, questions, elements, assumptions, beliefs, etc. Indicators can be viewed incrementally or as a fixed target. For example, in some cases it makes sense to report an increase in pass rate on the national examination (pass rates increased by 1% every year for 4 years), but in other situation it makes more sense to report a fixed target (all students passed at or above proficiency levels).

When measuring improvement incrementally, it is necessary to establish a baseline as a starting point. In this instance, you will need some type of comparative design in order to detect change, such as a cyclic or pre/post design. While the observed change is often sufficient evidence of program effects, it is possible that observed effects are due to other factors, such as maturation, other conditions, another program happening at the same time, and so on. If evidence based on a pretest/posttest design is not conclusive enough, then it might be necessary to use a pretest/posttest comparison group design. The pretest/posttest comparison group design collects information for both groups (treatment and control) both before and after the program. With this design, both the treatment and the control group will experience change due to maturation, testing, history, etc., making it possible to attribute differences between the two groups to the security education program. The addition of a control group will require that the available participant group be larger. As the need for rigor increases, the evaluation design becomes more sophisticated and the resources required to conduct the evaluation also increase. Occasionally, the measurement step is complete once sufficient indicators have been identified. For example, if student test scores on a national certification examination are an indicator of well-prepared graduates and if one indicator is sufficient, then it might not be necessary to create, adopt, or revise an instrument to collect indicator data. However, in many evaluation situations, the required indicators are a combination of existing measures as well as new measures making it necessary to create, adopt, and/or revise an instrument(s).

The fifth step in the evaluation design process is to establish a systematic method(s) for collecting the information. There are many different methods for collecting information. Again, a comprehensive discussion is not possible; instead I will provide tips and techniques for improving data collection and overview various data collection methods.

Pilot testing is a trial run of the instruments that you plan to use and can be invaluable in collecting 'good' data. Pilot testing gives the investigator an opportunity to identify and address instrument error, can save you time and money, and give you an idea how long data collection might take. Pilot testing can range from sending the instrument to a few of the intended users and then calling them to discuss the questions to actually conducting a pilot study. The effort put into pilot testing usually is dependent upon availability of resources and required degree of rigor in the evaluation. When pilot testing, your goal is to discern sources of measurement error in the instrument. Measurement error is an attribute of the instrument that keeps the user from correctly and completely responding, which in turn biases your data.

Triangulation is the utilization of many indicators and sources of data. Many sources are often better than one when looking for evidence. For example, if you are looking for evidence of well-prepared students and your students obtain above average national certification examination scores, reports from alumni that they were well-prepared for their first job in the occupation, and data from employers that graduates are well-prepared, you have in essence controlled for measurement error and increased the degree of confidence with which you can ascertain that your students are in fact well-prepared. The more sources of evidence you have, the more faith you can have in a result or finding.

Sampling is sometimes required in an evaluation study. This is usually a result of a large population and/or limited resources. Depending upon the nature and purpose of the evaluation, the evaluator will need to make decisions about sampling. When attempting to make generalizations about the entire population based on the sample, principles of sampling, including representativeness and sample size, will need to be considered. When investigating unique cases or seeking detailed information about transactions or outcomes, purposive sampling techniques will be more appropriate.

There are a variety of different methods for collecting data, e.g., surveys, tests, etc. Regardless of the method used to collect data, evaluators need to attend to the validity and the reliability of their instruments. Validity refers to the degree to which an instrument measures what it is supposed to measure. Due to the fact that instruments are usually designed with a specific purpose, the validity of the instrument is a function of that purpose. Validity is an important issue both when you create your own instrument, when you adopt another instrument for use, and when you make interpretations based on results. Validity is not a number, it is a matter of degree. A test is not valid or invalid; it is more a matter of having high validity, moderate validity, or low validity. Reliability refers to the consistency of the evaluation results. If we give a test to a group on two different occasions and receive the identical or very similar results, then the instrument is fairly reliable. If two evaluators conduct a focus group and report very similar findings, then the there is said to be rater or interviewer reliability. While reliability is conceptually distinct from validity, there is a relationship between the two. Reliability is a necessary, but not sufficient condition, for validity. You can have an instrument that measures the wrong thing (invalid), but does so with great consistency (reliable). It is possible to have reliability without validity, but it is not possible to have validity without reliability. Both validity and reliability are needed to base interpretations on the data that is collected.

When designing instruments to collect information that will be used in an evaluation, you will also want to consider the characteristics, advantages, and disadvantages of various methods for collecting data. Surveys can vary along a number of dimensions such as how questions are asked and how the instrument is delivered. Questions can be asked in a closed-ended versus open-ended manner. Surveys can be mailed, distributed in person, conducted over the telephone, or in a group setting. Determining what to ask on a survey and how to ask it is not an easy task. There are entire books devoted to this topic. For the sake of this paper, here are a few basic tenets. First, identify exactly want type of information you want responders to provide. Generally, questions can be classified into two types: 1) behavior or attribute questions, and 2) beliefs or attitudes questions. For example, in a study designed to assess instructor effectiveness, you need to decide in advance what type of information you want/need to collect. If you want to know about behavior, then the following questions would be appropriate: 1) My instructor utilizes a variety of strategies to teach this class, or 2) My instructor allows me to ask questions and gives me timely feedback. However, if you want to know beliefs, such as how students feel about the course, then the following questions might be appropriate: 1) In your opinion, how effective were the instructional strategies at helping you learn, or 2) I believe that this instructor is among the best I have ever known. Second, think about exactly what you want to know and ask it as directly as you can. Be specific, use simple words, avoid jargon, and keep it as short as possible. Third, eliminate bias from your questions. Bias in questions leads your respondent to answer in the positive light, regardless of whether it is accurate or not. Take for example the following questions: 1) Do you agree that instructor's who offer test review sessions are more effective than instructors who do not, and 2) Graduates of the National University program are generally more prepared today than they were 3 years ago. Have the graduates that you have hired been more prepared?

As opposed to surveys, tests are instruments designed to assess learning. Instruments can vary from written tests, oral examinations, to performance evaluations. Within those categories, tests often include a variety of formats for items, including multiple choice, true-false, short answer, and essay. Determining what to include on a test is not a simple procedure. There are some basic tenets that can be used to construct tests that are more valid and reliable. First, identify the purpose of testing. Tests can be used for a variety of reasons including placement, formative evaluation, diagnostic testing, summative testing, or prediction. Placement testing will focus on a minimum amount of knowledge, whereas formative evaluation will focus on a predetermined segment of instruction, and summative testing will focus on an entire course or program. Second, develop a set of test specifications. A set of specifications will ensure that the test has content validity. To build a set of specifications, you will need to delineate intended learning outcomes, corresponding course content, and prepare a specification chart that details and weights outcomes by content area. Third, select appropriate items. Types of items can be classified as two general types: objective items and essay items. Objective test items include any type of question where response options are supplied, and essay items include any type of question where the learner must generate and present the answer in some format. Objective items are efficient for measuring facts, understanding, and on a limited based more complex outcomes, whereas essay items are appropriate for more complex outcomes. Scoring is relatively easy on objective test items and high reliability is more likely. Scoring on essay items tends to be slow and subject to more inconsistencies, thereby becoming a potential threat to reliability.

Interviews are well suited to collecting detailed information from a smaller group of participants. Interviews are generally more time-consuming and costly than a survey, but well written interviews can produce a wealth of information. Interviews can range from very structured, where the questions are written out and are to be covered verbatim, to extremely unstructured (where a list of general topics to be covered is followed). The decision on which type of approach to use depends upon the nature of the evaluation and the type of information that you are trying to collect.

Focus groups are an effective way to collect large amounts of detailed information on a restricted budget. A focus group is like a group interview and can also be conducted using a structured or unstructured approach. However, in focus groups it is difficult to ensure that you get the input of all participants. When conducting a focus group, you should: 1) identify what information you are trying to collect, 2) create a focus group guide to follow, 3) be prepared to take copious notes....you might even want an audio tape so you can capture it all, and 4) seek out the opinion of quiet participants.

Sometimes the best way to collect information about people's behavior is to watch them. Observation allows you to collect information without burdening the person providing the information. However, observation is limited in its use to what you see. Observation is not an effective method for collecting information about attitudes, feelings, etc. When conducting an observation, you should: 1) identify what information you are trying to collect, 2) determine specifically what behaviors will serve as indicators, 3) create a checklist for use during observation, and 4) train observers on what to look for and how to accurately record observations on the checklist.

Evaluating any educational program can be a challenging endeavor and the same will be true in security education. As more and more institutions, organizations, schools, and programs launch security education programs in an attempt to meet needs that are emerging in a rapidly changing environment, evaluation will be more difficult, yet even more important in order to ensure that programs are having the desired impact. The need to embrace this challenge will be even greater. The questions facing us are many and varied. How do we assess educational programs that vary in: 1) types of students served, 2) curriculum areas, 3) facilities, 4) policies, 5) stakeholders served, and so on? My hope is that this paper can guide users from a variety of institutions and programs through the process of educational program evaluation with the goal of raising the quality of security education evaluations with the subsequent goal of bettering security education programs.

# 5.      APPENDIX

## 5.1      Step 1: Determine the Purpose of the Evaluation

### 5.1.1      A Capacity Building Program in Information Security Education

Micheal Hanes is the Director of the Information Security Consortium. The goal of the Information Security Education Consortium was to develop, delivery, disseminate and evaluate a multidisciplinary program to develop faculty expertise and capacity in teaching Information Assurance and Security at the undergraduate and graduate levels. By doing so, they hoped to improve the capacity and capability of higher education to address the critical shortage of Information Assurance and Security specialists.

In order to develop faculty expertise and capacity in teaching Information Assurance and Security, they had the following objectives:

- Develop a Core of Multi-Disciplinary Faculty Mentors

- Experts will be recruited to serve as mentors from academia, industry, and

- Mentors will attend a mentor workshop to structure guidelines for the design and development of curriculum materials and the faculty development institute.

- Faculty mentors will work with recruited faculty for two years to facilitate integration of information assurance and security into their academic programs.

- Develop Curricular Materials to be used in Faculty Development Institute

    - Materials will be current in information assurance and security subject matter.

    - Materials will be current in educational methodology for effective undergraduate and graduate education.

    - Educational methodology for using the materials in undergraduate and graduate programs will be explicitly addressed so that participating faculty understand and know how to use the materials most effectively.

- Develop Subject-Matter Expertise of Participating Faculty through a Faculty Development Institute led by Faculty Mentors

  - Institute will utilize current educational methodology for effective faculty development.

- Dissemination of Curriculum Materials

- Curriculum materials will be made available through publishers, presentations at professional conferences such as NCISSE, and NISSC, and through related journals.

In addition to leading the project, Michael was responsible for assessing the effectiveness of the program. One of the first things that Michael asked himself was why was assessment necessary in the first place? Michael realized that different people had different reasons for wanting an assessment. The consortium had certain reasons, the mentors had other reasons, and the sponsor had yet other unique interests and reasons.

Upon talking with these groups, Michael learned that the consortium wanted to find out to what extent their program was building capacity, how many educators were participating, which activities were most and least effective, and how these activities were contributing to capacity building. The mentors specifically wanted to find out to what degree their materials were utilized in other classrooms and how, their effectiveness, and suggestions for improvement. The sponsor was interested in knowing the cost benefit of the program as well as ways to improve the cost benefit ratio.

So why was Michael assessing this program? The answer to this question had two major parts:

- To find out the extent to which the program is producing the intended results, and

- To find out where is in performing as planned, where it is not, and methods for improvement so that it does perform as planned in the future.

## 5.2    Step 2: Frame the Evaluation

### 5.2.1    The Conceptual Framework for Information Security Education Program

### 5.2.2    Antecedents

- Expertise of those chosen to be mentors in information and security assurance content areas

- Faculty attendees will want and need to integrate topics into their curriculum

- Curriculum development model

### 5.2.3     Transactions

- Mentor workshop to teach mentors curriculum development format
- Development of curriculum materials to integrate information assurance and security into other curriculum areas
- Faculty members attend institute and work within their own fields as well as with experts in the field of information assurance and security
- Mentors assist faculty in integration.
- Materials are integrated into existing curricula
- Materials are disseminated to a wider audience

### 5.2.4     Outcomes

- Mentors enhance their curricula with materials developed during institutes
- Effective curriculum materials
- Curriculum materials disseminated through various channels to a wide audience
- Faculty members integrate information assurance and security information into their curricula
- Students in core courses gain experience and knowledge in the field of information assurance and security
- Students are able to use skills in the field of information assurance and security in order to enhance their work and increase their potential value in the job market

### 5.2.5     Underlying Assumptions, Beliefs, and Theories

Current instruction in information assurance and security is insufficient to support the workplace need for skilled workers in this field. Institutions and faculty see a similar critical need for this type of instruction as the proposal's authors. There is an established link between instruction in information assurance and security and increased use. Participating institutions will pay for half of the costs incurred by faculty attending the development institute. A faculty institute is the best method for serving the proposed clientele. Instructors will be able to or willing to modify their curricula to reflect information security instruction. Institutions see a need for a change in cross-curricular preparation in this area of technology. Development of curricular materials will have an impact at the classroom level. The field of information security has far-reaching implications in all fields. Faculty mentoring is an effective way to facilitate curriculum changes. Faculty and curriculum development will increase capacity.

## 5.3 Step 3: Determine Evaluation Questions

### 5.3.1 Assessment Questions for the Information Security Program

Michael had already asked himself why different stakeholders wanted an assessment and what they wanted from the assessment. He had come with two major reasons for the assessment. He had also reviewed the conceptual framework of the program and identified the intended antecedents, transactions, and outcomes. With the broad purpose in mind and the key components of the program laid out, Michael was able to frame key assessment questions that were well grounded. The following is a result of his work:

| Program Goal | Level 1 Questions | Level Two Questions |
|---|---|---|
| Curriculum development | How effective is the curriculum development process and the resulting materials? | To what extent are mentors experts in the field? To what extent did the mentor workshop specify curriculum development criteria. To what extent were the criteria based on instructional theory? To what extent do the curriculum materials specify learning outcomes? To what extent are the curriculum materials valid and usable? |
| Faculty development | How effective is the institute at helping educators integrate IAS into their curriculum? | To what extent do faculty attendees gain knowledge and skills in IAS topics. To what extent do faculty attendees gain knowledge and skills in using curricular materials? To what extent do faculty mentors facilitate successful integration with faculty attendees? |
| Curriculum dissemination | How effective are dissemination efforts? Why or why not? | To what extent do faculty attendees integrate materials into their curriculum? To what extent are materials made available and used outside the institute? |
| Cost benefit | How effective is the program at maximizing benefit of cost investment? | What are the most/least beneficial aspects of the program and why? What is the cost investment? How can the program cost/benefit be improved? |

Michael reviewed the questions to determine if there was anything he was leaving out based on his priorities and those of other stakeholders. He determined that the goals and questions he had were valid questions and went on to determine the design of the assessment.

## 5.4 Step 4: Determine What Information is Needed to Answer Evaluation Questions

What Information Did the Information Security Education Consortium Need to Collect?

| Level Two Questions | Indicators | Existing | TBD |
|---|---|---|---|
| To what extent are mentors experts in the field? | Number and type of publications of mentors | X | |
| To what extent did the mentor workshop specify curriculum development criteria? | Number and quality of curriculum guidelines | | X |
| | Usability of guidelines | | X |
| | Adherence to guidelines | | X |
| To what extent were the criteria based on instructional theory? | Congruence between learning outcomes and appropriate instructional strategies | | X |
| To what extent do the curriculum materials specify learning outcomes? | % of materials that bear evidence of learning outcomes | | X |
| To what extent are the curriculum materials valid and usable? | Faculty ratings of validity and usability | | X |
| | Faculty use | | X |
| To what extent do faculty attendees gain knowledge and skills in IAS topics? | Test scores | | X |
| | Integration rates | | X |
| To what extent do faculty attendees gain knowledge/skills in using curricular materials? | Test scores | | X |
| | Integration rates | | X |
| To what extent do faculty mentors facilitate successful integration with faculty attendees? | Amount of time mentors work with faculty | | X |
| | % of integration | | X |
| To what extent do faculty attendees integrate materials into their curriculum? | % of integration | | X |
| | Length of integration | | X |
| | # of students exposed | | X |
| To what extent are materials made available and used outside the institute? | # and methods of dissemination | | X |
| | # of requests for materials | | X |
| | reported use of materials | | X |
| What are the most/least beneficial aspects of the program and why? | Outcomes of materials | | X |
| | Outcomes of faculty development institute and Outcomes of curriculum dissemination | | X |
| What is the cost investment? | Cost per activity | | X |
| How can cost/benefit be improved? | Cost/benefit ratio | | X |

## 5.5      Step 5: Method(s) for Collecting Information

**How Did the Information Security Education Program Collect Information?**

Michael listed possible ways to collect information pertinent to his measures and came up with the following:

| | | |
|---|---|---|
| To what extent are mentors experts in the field? | Number and type of publications of mentors | Records |
| To what extent did the mentor workshop specify curriculum development criteria? | Number and quality of curriculum guidelines Usability of guidelines Adherence to guidelines | Records and Materials Survey Records and Materials |
| To what extent were the criteria based on instructional theory? | Congruence between learning outcomes and appropriate instructional strategies | Records and Materials |
| To what extent do the curriculum materials specify learning outcomes? | % of materials that bear evidence of learning outcomes | Records and Materials |
| To what extent are the curriculum materials valid and usable? | Faculty ratings of validity and usability Faculty use | Survey Survey/observation |
| To what extent do faculty attendees gain knowledge and skills in IAS topics? | Test scores Integration rates | Test Survey/observation |
| To what extent do faculty attendees gain knowledge/skills in using curricular materials? | Test scores Integration rates | Test Survey/observation |
| To what extent do faculty mentors facilitate successful integration with faculty attendees? | Amount of time mentors work with faculty % of integration | Records Survey/observation |
| To what extent do faculty attendees integrate materials into their curriculum? | % of integration Length of integration # of students exposed | Survey/observation Survey Survey |
| To what extent are materials made available and used outside the institute? | # and methods of dissemination # of requests for materials reported use of materials | Records Records |
| What are the most/least beneficial aspects of the program and why? | Outcomes of materials Outcomes of faculty development institute and Outcomes of curriculum dissemination | Observation/Survey/ Records Observation/Survey/Records Observation/Survey/Records |
| What is the cost investment? | Cost per activity | Records |
| How can the program cost/benefit be improved? | Cost/benefit ratio | Records |

## REFERENCES

1.  Evaluation Center. (May 10, 2000). <u>About evaluation</u>. (On-line). Available: http://www.wmich.edu

2.  Gronlund, N. (1985). <u>Measurement and evaluation in teaching</u> (5<sup>th</sup> ed.). New York: Macmillan.

3. Rossi, P., Freeman, H., Lipsay, M. (1999). *Evaluation: A Systematic Approach.* 6th edition. London: Sage Publications.

4. Thorndike, R., & Hagan. E. (1977). <u>Measurement and evaluation in psychology and education</u> (4<sup>th</sup> ed.). New York: Wiley.

# TEN YEARS OF INFORMATION SECURITY MASTERS PROGRAMMES
## Reflections and New Challenges

Chez Ciechanowicz, Keith M. Martin, Fred C. Piper and Matthew J. B. Robshaw
*Information Security Group, Royal Holloway, University of London, Egham, Surrey, TW20 0EX, United Kingdom*

Abstract:     Royal Holloway launched its MSc programme in Information Security in 1992. In the subsequent ten years this programme has grown steadily in popularity, with just over 250 students registered in the current 2002-2003 session. In this paper we reflect on the apparent success of the first ten years of the programme and comment on a number of issues that we feel have wider relevance to information security education programmes in general. We also discuss some challenges facing such programmes in the future and how we propose to address them.

Key words:   postgraduate training, masters programmes, programme design, industrial relationships, distance learning

## 1. INTRODUCTION

The developments in electronic information handling over the last ten years have resulted in an unprecedented demand for information security skills and awareness. This demand is no longer only from specialised sectors such as defence and finance, but it is now coming from all business environments, public sector organisations, government departments, and to a certain extent from private citizens themselves.

Royal Holloway, University of London, launched a postgraduate Master of Science programme in Information Security in 1992, and has witnessed the results of this change in the profile of the subject over the subsequent decade. This paper is not concerned with the drivers for such change, which should be self-evident, but with the ways in which higher education programmes can best try to embrace and satisfy the demand for information security skills.

We will first present some background to the development of our own programmes in information security. We will then look at a number of programme design decisions that we have faced and that we feel have relevance beyond our own borders. We end by taking the opportunity to discuss several breaking issues and challenges that we feel need to be addressed to meet future needs for postgraduate information security education.

## 2. INFORMATION SECURITY PROGRAMMES

In this section we will examine the current situation on our own information security programmes. We will go on to discuss a little bit about the background of students on these courses and then look at relevant growth patterns.

The interest in information security at Royal Holloway grew out of a strong research base in cryptography, stemming from the academic interests of individual academics within the Mathematics Department. In 1992 the formation of the Information Security Group (ISG) formalised a broadening of the research focus across both Mathematics and Computer Science. The ISG launched the MSc Information Security in 1992, the first postgraduate qualification of its kind in Europe, and it is now in its eleventh year. In 1999 the ISG, now an autonomous group, launched a second related MSc in Secure Electronic Commerce.

## 2.1 Current Range of Programmes

### 2.1.1 MSc Information Security

This is an advanced MSc degree that is designed to introduce the technical, legal and commercial aspects of Information Security. The degree is intended as a foundation for a professional career, as well as for postgraduate research. Graduates of the degree are expected to find employment in both industry and commerce as security experts.

The MSc degree is taught in course modules. Each module usually consists of thirty-three hours of lectures (three hours per week for eleven weeks), sometimes with tutorials and practical work. The curriculum for the MSc degree consists of six taught modules and a project. Of the six taught modules, four are mandatory core modules and the other two are optional modules chosen by the student from a list of options. Alternatives to the standard mode of delivery are currently being developed (see Section 4.1).

A list of the modules for this programme are shown in Tables 1 and 3. Full details can be found at [3].

### 2.1.2 MSc Secure Electronic Commerce

This advanced MSc degree has very similar aims and intentions as the MSc Information Security, but has a slightly different focus. The main differences are that whole core modules are devoted to business issues and the law, with a reduction in the amount of technical content. The structure of both MSc programmes is identical, with most of the optional modules shared between the two degrees (see Tables 2 and 3).

*Table 1.* MSc Information Security Core + Specific Option

| IC1 | IC2 | IC3 | IC4 | OPT5 |
|---|---|---|---|---|
| Security Management | Introduction to Cryptography and Security Mechanisms | Network Security | Computer Security | Secure Electronic Commerce and other Applications |

*Table 2.* MSc Secure Electronic Commerce Core + Specific Option

| SC1 | SC2 | SC3 | SC4 | OPT6 |
|---|---|---|---|---|
| Business and Security Issues | Introduction to Cryptography and Security Mechanisms | Secure E-commerce: Infrastructure and Standards | Legal and Regulatory Aspects of Electronic Commerce | Current Developments in Secure Electronic Commerce |

*Table 3.* Options common to both MSc courses + Compulsory Project

| OPT7 | OPT8 | OPT9 | OPT10 | |
|---|---|---|---|---|
| Standards and Evaluation Criteria | Advanced Cryptography | Database Security | Computer Crime | M.Sc. Project |

### 2.1.3 Postgraduate Diploma

The ISG, in co-operation with QCC InfoSec Training Ltd, also runs a postgraduate diploma that is intended for students who do not have the time to attend a whole MSc programme. This consists of a number of short courses, supplemented by the writing of three essays and a project. The focus of the diploma is more on training than on comprehensive education.

Currently there are over 60 registrations. The diploma is particularly popular with students who wish to study over an extended time period.

### 2.1.4    Other Programmes

The ISG has a large PhD programme, with almost 40 students currently registered. We also run specific information security training courses on demand.

## 2.2    Student Background

Students on the two MSc programmes at Royal Holloway come from a variety of backgrounds, including both management (business and economics) and technical (information sciences, computer science and mathematics). Part-time students, who take the degrees over two years, have been particularly encouraged to apply. We are willing to consider relevant industrial experience as a replacement for conventional academic qualifications on our MSc programmes, and regularly accept high quality students with industrial backgrounds onto the programmes. Although management students tend to find the technical aspects of the programmes initially challenging, the provision of background classes and tutorial support tends to bring them up to speed.

Most students on the MSc programmes fall into one of the following three categories:

1. Recent graduates: students fresh from an undergraduate degree who wish to spend a year engaging in further specialisation.
2. Sponsored students: part-time students currently in employment within the I.T. sector (but occasionally full-time students on year-release) whose employers are at least partially supporting them in their studies.
3. Career changers: mature students, often with extensive I.T. or business experience, who are seeking to update knowledge or seek fresh career opportunities.

Sponsored students and career changers have joined the programmes from many different industrial sectors, including hi-tech companies, military, government, public services, financial organisations, specialist security companies and telecommunications.

Both MSc programmes have proved very attractive to overseas students. To date students from almost 40 different countries have completed one of the two programmes, with around 20-30% of students in a typical year coming to Royal Holloway from outside the European Union. Within the E.U. the programmes seem to be particularly popular with students from Greece, Germany and Ireland. Beyond the E.U. we have had significant numbers of students from China (mainland and Hong Kong), Japan, Korea, Malaysia, Singapore and Taiwan. Most years we have several students from the United States. Currently we are seeing a big increase in interest from Central and South America, India, and the Middle East.

## 2.3    Growth Patterns

The number of students attending the two M.Sc. courses at Royal Holloway is shown in Figure 1.

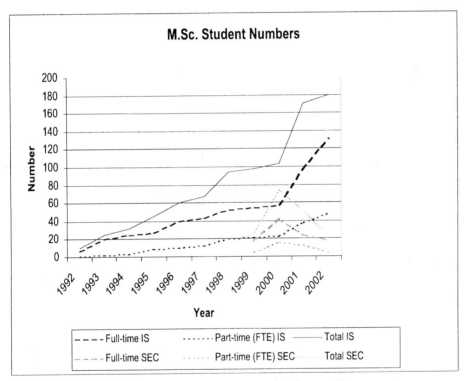

*Figure 1.* Numbers of students attending Royal Holloway MSc programmes

Although the upwards trend in the total numbers of students attending Royal Holloway MSc programmes is to be expected given the technological developments during the period over which the programmes have been running, the continual steady increase in interest in such programmes has surprised us. Numbers may currently be "artificially high" on the MSc Information Security due to the present downturn in the I.T. sector resulting in an extra demand for retraining. The reverse in fortune of the MSc Secure Electronic Commerce is almost certainly due to a "branding problem" following the failure of "e-commerce" to live up to much of its anticipated hype (we discuss this issue in Section 4.3). Nonetheless the growth in total numbers provides strong evidence that interest in postgraduate qualifications in information security is still high, and likely to remain so for the foreseeable future.

# 3.     PROGRAMME DESIGN ISSUES

We now review a number of programme design issues that we feel have been influential in the planning of our MSc programmes. We do not claim to have got any of these exactly right, but the current success of the programmes suggests that at least some of the decisions that we have made must have been fairly sound. We will also reflect on some decisions that we perhaps did not get quite right.

## 3.1     Involving the Information Security Industry

The MSc programmes at Royal Holloway are heavily influenced by the requirements of the information security industry and the ISG works closely with industrial partners to maintain the standards required in the workplace. This is done in a number of different ways.

### 3.1.1     Programme Planning

From the very first stages of planning of the MSc programmes, the ISG has worked very closely with the information security industry to make sure that the learning outcomes of the degree programmes closely match the professional security skills that are required by employers. From the outset, the basic structure of the MSc programmes was widely discussed with more than thirty institutions; these included government departments, large IT companies, and many financial organisations. This exercise has ensured that the overall structure of the MSc remains stable.

### 3.1.2     Curriculum Development

To ensure that the course is completely up to date, many of the modules involve significant input from recognised security experts from industry. Furthermore, all of the academic staff have links with external organisations that are involved with information security and secure electronic commerce, including many of the largest such organisations in the country.

The courses are also overseen by a Steering Committee that consists of the members of the ISG as well as a number of visiting professors that include some very influential experts from industry. Although this latter group has no formal powers their opinions are highly regarded and all their suggestions are therefore taken very seriously and acted upon.

### 3.1.3    Teaching

The ISG makes quite considerable use of presentations by security industry experts on a number of modules. The use of external speakers is normally made when
- The topic does not lend itself to an academic treatise and is most suited to presentation by a practitioner (this applies to areas such as e-business security and security management).
- The topic contains significant amounts of specialised state-of-the-art material that is either not accessible to academics, or is more readily available from practitioners active in industry research forums or development projects.

The involvement of security professionals in the delivery of course material has a number of significant benefits for all involved parties, some of which are not immediately obvious:
- Involving security professionals in the course helps to cement the relationships between Royal Holloway and external organisations.
- Students benefit by having direct access to practitioners.
- External organisations gain exposure to a specialist recruitment base.
- Students and security professionals both have the opportunity to establish industrial project placements
- Most security professionals thoroughly enjoy coming to Royal Holloway and often comment on the thrill they get from exposure to a security aware audience who often ask thought-provoking questions.
- In our experience (and often in contrast to University management expectations), most of our selected security professionals are outstanding speakers who deliver careful and relevant presentations.

There are of course a number of drawbacks to using external presenters, which need to be carefully managed:
- It is not always easy to control the content of a presentation by an external speaker (we overcome this by careful selection of presenters).
- It can be difficult to provide context and structure to a module that heavily uses external speakers (we address this by careful design of each lecture programme and, if necessary, outside the lecture environment by the provision of supplementary material).

There are in fact two entire modules whose subject areas are so specialised and beyond our academic skills base that we contract them out to ISG consultants. These concern Computer Crime and Legal Aspects of Secure Electronic Commerce. It is questionable whether we would offer these topics within the MSc programme if we were restricted to use of our own internal knowledge base, and there is no doubt that the programmes would be weakened by their exclusion.

### 3.1.4    Establishing and Maintaining Industrial Relations

In our opinion, the success of our programmes has largely been based on our strong relationships with the local information security industry. Establishing and nurturing such relationships is not an easy task, and this has been an ongoing and intensive priority of the ISG since its inception.

While individual personalities and involvement in projects have played a considerable part in this success, we cannot ignore the role of geography in establishing the ISG as an information security hub within the U.K. Proximity to London itself, and to London Heathrow Airport, has made getting to Royal Holloway a relatively straightforward exercise for anyone based in, or visiting, London or the South-east of England, which is home to a considerable percentage of both the U.K. population and business headquarters of U.K. organisations. (The same argument also applies to the ability of the programmes to recruit part-time students on day-release from places of employment.) This has even facilitated some part-time students to "commute" from Belgium, Denmark and Italy to attend our MSc programmes!

The MSc programmes are now also a major source of further industrial links as our growing alumni find employment in the information security industry throughout the world. The ISG continues to nurture its industrial relations through its web page, alumni mailing lists and further networking activities such as informal dinners.

## 3.2    Getting the Syllabus Balance Right

Deciding exactly what to include in a Masters programme in Information Security is not easy, as the subject spans a vast number of wide ranging and disparate disciplines. In particular, getting a suitable balance between technical issues and business/management issues is a major challenge.

The approach taken by the ISG at Royal Holloway is largely an accident of circumstance. Due to its origins as a centre for cryptographic research, it would seem inevitable that an ISG hosted programme would have a technical bias. However, from the outset the ISG recognised that such an approach would neither be likely to attract a large number of students nor supply the needs of the information security industry at large.

As a result we have tended to adopt an approach of teaching technical material in house, and inviting external input in order to cover business and management issues (see Section 3.1.3). This seems to work quite well because technical topics lend themselves well to a single integrated approach, whereas the ambiguity of many management issues are more suited to a diverse coverage from different voices and business environment perspectives.

One interesting development that reflects the fragility of this balance concerns the core module on Cryptography and Security Mechanisms. Many students from non-technical backgrounds commence their MSc programme by regarding this module with considerable trepidation. However, the result of teaching cryptography to students from diverse backgrounds for ten years has been that the focus of this module has drifted considerably from technical details to management issues. In fact this module is now a non-technical cryptography module - a concept that some students, and academics, sometimes have trouble comprehending! An optional module on the technical aspects of cryptographic algorithm design now balances this shift in emphasis.

## 3.3 Encouraging Student Diversity

Another area where we feel that our current programmes have gained strength over the years has been in the participation of students from wide ranging backgrounds. This has acted as a strong area of compensation at a time when increasing numbers of students have inevitably resulted in a less personalised learning experience for students following the programmes.

We have encouraged diversity of experience within the student community by:
- Developing a programme structure that is particularly suited to part-time students, by concentrating lectures on certain days of the week to facilitate study by means of day release.
- Supporting applications from high quality (mature) students with relevant industrial experience, irrespective of whether they have previous academic qualifications.

In Section 2.2 we noted that students on the programmes typically fall into one of three categories. While "recent graduates" are often academically strong, they typically lack the practical or industrial experience of "sponsored students" and "career changers". This results in a student community with mutually compatible skill sets, and by encouraging the students to form informal study groups as well as to participate in organised course activities, we try to foster an environment in which these different student communities can interact and share their skills and experience. This seems to us particularly important in a discipline such as information security, where there are rarely any "correct answers" and where opinions and debates can be just as insightful as the relevant facts.

## 3.4    Hands On or Hands Off?

There is no doubt that it is desirable to provide a practical component to any information security qualification. While theory is arguably longer lasting and of greater significance, it is most certainly enhanced by practical "hands on" sessions, regardless of how ephemeral the technology on which it is demonstrated may prove to be. There is also no doubt that providing such a component is incompatible with supporting large numbers of students on a taught programme. This is one demand that our current approach cannot satisfy.

However it is interesting to report a fairly commonly observed pattern in student response to our openly "classroom-based" approach to information security training (it should be noted that this pattern relates only to the minority of students who comment on the theoretical bias to the course). Students typically start with an open mind, but then as they learn about various technologies it is common for a minority of students to express a desire for more "hands on" access to technologies. While we do our best to facilitate such a demand (such as running hacking courses and firewall configuration sessions) we notice that this demand often falls away as students realise the sheer mass of material that they need to cover to satisfy the programme. By the end of the course they tend to be satisfied with the overall balance and have recognised the difficulties that greater access to practical work might have involved.

It is also worth emphasising that as with most academic courses, as well as knowledge transfer, successful students should complete the course with a number of transferable skills in the area of learning, information processing and report writing. Many employers regard these as more important than extensive practical experience.

We are continuously seeking new opportunities to provide managed practical sessions. Currently we are developing a penetration-testing laboratory where students can experiment with various tools within a localised and controlled environment. We are also developing a smart card centre where students can get more closely involved with projects relating to security hardware tokens. Students with a keen desire for "hands on" are also often encouraged to pursue a practical MSc project. However we do recognise that on this issue we are responding to our constraints rather than to some notion of an ideal course. We believe that our current approach is the most suitable one to follow with the large student numbers that are attracted to the programmes.

## 3.5     The Shifting Syllabus

Probably the major challenge faced by any courses attempting to provide a comprehensive overview of information security issue is the problem of the shifting syllabus. The developments over the last ten years in this area have been dramatic, and during the typical running schedule of a course module (in our case eleven weeks) there is very likely to be at least one or two developments that have the potential to impact module content.

The challenge is of course to harness these developments and use them to enhance the learning experience, rather than to view them as potential obstructions. Including real time incidents and contemporary events as illustrative examples is greatly appreciated by students. The only difficulty is keeping abreast of developments in order to accommodate the latest information.

There are a number of ways in which we try to do this at Royal Holloway:

- External speakers: the use of external speakers on some modules does bring in the latest information from people who are often at the "coalface" of developments in their particular field.
- Optional seminars: each semester we run a series of optional seminars, which can be used to plug syllabus gaps should issues arise during the year that are not adequately covered by the main syllabus.
- Mailing lists: we provide open access to several student mailing lists, which allow staff, current students and alumni to post relevant links and articles concerning breaking issues.
- Using news stories: several of the modules on the MSc programmes incorporate current events directly into their syllabus by requesting comment on newspaper/magazine articles (for example).

In addition to a "running review" of the programme syllabus, most modules need to undergo an annual retrospective review process, where content is updated and amended for the following session. As a rough estimate, we plan for a syllabus change each year of approximately 10% per module. Obviously this varies depending on the module content. The Cryptography and Security Mechanisms module, for example, is reasonably stable. The Computer Security module has a stable theoretical core that has been designed explicitly to be as timeless and technology independent as possible, however application security topics change on an annual basis. Current Developments in Secure Electronic Commerce, in contrast, undergoes annual reviews that can lead to changes in up to 50% of the module content, depending on what issues have emerged and which have faded over the previous twelve months.

## 3.6    Scalability

The issue of scalability of a postgraduate course is one that we feel, retrospectively, we perhaps did not get quite right. While in 1992 the ISG recognised the potential demand for information security postgraduate education, the expectation (and initial reality) was of student numbers of around 10-20, not 100-200. A number of problems have arisen from the rapid increase in student numbers:

– Timetabling issues: One feature that was built into the programme that made sense initially, but now pose restrictions on current operation is our "bundling" of modules together to allow part-time students to only attend on certain days of the week. Since there are now significant numbers of students, many of whom are attending over two years, we have found it very difficult to make any timetabling adjustments and find ourselves restricted to the initial course timetable that we offered in 1992. This restriction makes it particularly difficult to make changes to the ways in which the core modules are offered on campus.

– Impacts on staffing: The format of the MSc programme, particularly the existence of a significant project component, has resulted in considerable pressures on staffing resources throughout the twelve months of the year. With a couple of dozen students it is possible to arrange emergency supervisory cover over the summer months, but with approaching 200 students this becomes much harder. Although the ISG has been permitted to recruit extra staff in the last three years, there are still very high demands placed on the current staff. This puts inevitable pressures on research time, and has also made it very hard for research staff to take sabbaticals. Had it been possible to predict the demand, we might have been able to plan staffing resources more effectively.

– Impacts on the student experience: The classroom-based approach to teaching the main syllabus material (formal lectures and supporting tutorials) has also probably suffered by the increase in numbers. Quite simply, lectures become more formal and it becomes less possible to offer quality staff-student time with larger student numbers. Of course this problem is offset slightly by the greater capability for active study groups and peer learning to take place amongst the students themselves.

## 4. FUTURE DEVELOPMENTS

Given the speed at which developments in information security take place, it does seem at times that operating information security educational programmes is an exercise in "running to stand still". However, as well as keeping track of future syllabus content, there are a number of other issues that we feel are important to address in order to maintain our claims to meet the training needs of the information security industry.

## 4.1 Flexible Learning

A major area of development at Royal Holloway is to try to meet the needs of future learners, especially those whose geographical and financial constraints limit their ability to attend a campus in the U.K. for several days a week over the period of one (or two) years. There are two major initiatives underway, both driven by direct demand, which we hope will result in a more flexible programme that will open up our programmes to new student markets.

### 4.1.1 Distance Learning

We are in the process of "converting" our MSc Information Security into distance learning format for remote delivery. The initiative is backed by the External Programme of the University of London [1], who have extensive experience of delivering paper-based distance learning degree courses. This programme is going to be launched in September 2003 and includes the following features:
- Course content is presented using a mixture of interactive web pages, audio recordings and reading resources.
- Courseware will be delivered in electronic form, either through CDRoms or web downloads.
- Students interact with courseware through a custom built virtual learning environment.
- Students are supported online via electronic offline seminars (bulletin boards) and email support from course tutors.
- The course is structured identically to the campus based MSc and students assemble their degree on a modular basis.
- Students will be examined using the External Programme's worldwide network of examination centres and will sit examinations of identical standard to the campus based MSc programme.

The distance learning programme comes with its own set of challenges. These include:

- Finding qualified support. Providing qualified support for distance learners in a specialist area such as information security is not particularly easy. Such support is needed to manage the running of a distance learning module, to moderate online discussions and to support the extra work generated by assessment and project supervision. Academics within the ISG could provide this support, but are already stretched in workload and so such an expansion of our programme involves finding extra assistance. We are currently looking into the involvement of alumni and security professionals in these activities.

- Updating material. Given the annual turnover in syllabus material described in Section 3.5, keeping distance learning material up to date is likely to be very challenging. It is inevitable that distance learning courseware may lag behind some of the content delivered on campus, but on the other hand the resource base of learning materials developed over time may well compensate for this.

- External presentations. For topics such as security management, where we make heavy use of external speakers on the campus course, creating suitable distance learning material is challenging. Our current approach has been to take the best of the campus presentations and present them as "supported audio lectures", where PowerPoint slides, audio clips and supporting text / exercises are blended into a multimedia package. For some learners this may even be a preferable experience to sitting in a live presentation, however student feedback on using these materials is not yet available.

### 4.1.2    Intensive Modules

Another direction we are starting to move in is to provide certain modules in more intensive formats. Rather than attending an entire module on campus on day release, students would attend several intensive sessions (possibly lasting several days). Where numbers of students from an external organisation or from a specific geographical location are sufficiently high, we also intend to offer these intensive modules on site.

This is essentially an alternative format for part-time students, and recognises that fact that different organisations prefer different types of schedule concerning the release of employees for educational courses. Such intensive modules of course still need to be supported over a longer period.

The main drawback with this format is that it is only appropriate for modules that are entirely taught "in house". For this reason we anticipate that students preferring intensive modules will be required to assemble their final degree by also "attending" modules delivered either on campus or at a distance. The details of how this might be done in practice have not yet been fully worked out, but we are convinced that flexibility of delivery is going to be a high priority for future information security students, and that programmes will need to match this demand if they are to be successful in tomorrow's higher education market.

## 4.2 Professional Qualifications

The increasing interest in information security has led to a proliferation of professional qualifications in this area, which clearly is something that academic institutions need to monitor. We have been particularly interested in the increased profile of the CISSP qualification from (ISC)$^2$ [2]. CISSP is an interesting example because there is some considerable overlap between what is offered by this qualification and what is offered within the ISG. The CISSP qualification requires that the individual have four years of relevant industry experience and that they have performed well in an examination. They also need to maintain their qualification by completing accredited course work. The scope of examinable material is probably about the same as that offered at Royal Holloway, although the depth of coverage by the ISG is much greater and the CISSP does not have a project requirement.

Rather than being regarded as "competitors", a CISSP qualification and an MSc from Royal Holloway appear to complement each other very well. It is the practical experience that some view as being lacking from the MSc's, yet it is this practical experience that the CISSP qualification claims to recognise (exactly how such industrial experience can be quantified is a difficult issue that we have also encountered during our admissions selection process). We have been investigating the possibility of exploiting this synergy between the MSc and the CISSP qualification and hope that it may be possible to offer some arrangements in the future that will facilitate some students obtaining both qualifications. We will also be watching carefully the development of other related professional qualifications.

## 4.3 Tomorrow's Programmes

The demand for higher education information security training that we have experienced suggests a preference for general programmes that equip students with a solid grounding in issues across different business sectors, but we believe that there is also a demand for more specialist training targeted at precise industries.

In 1999 we launched our MSc Secure Electronic Commerce, in response to the rising demand for direct training relevant to this area. As can be seen in Figure 1, this course was extremely successful from launch, but suffered a significant downturn in student numbers in direct response to changes in the fortunes of fledgling "dot.com" businesses. It would seem likely that other information security topics may lend themselves to short term increases in demand, however it does not seem justifiable to launch programmes to meet needs that may turn out also to be rather ephemeral in their high levels of demand.

We are currently reviewing the status of the MSc Secure Electronic Commerce programme, which in our opinion remains a viable and attractive degree, but may have to be restructured and perhaps re-branded. (It is worth noting that a taught Masters programme with over 20 full-time students is not normally regarded in U.K. universities as a "failure"!) Part of the current curriculum review process is also looking at information security specialisations that may have a more stable future, such as secure telecommunications.

## 5.      CONCLUDING REMARKS

We have reviewed some of the issues that we feel have arisen from our ten years of experience of delivering postgraduate MSc courses in information security. We have had a very positive experience of involvement in this area over the last decade, but recognise that success can only be maintained by hard work and constant retrospective review. If we had to identify one area on which to concentrate when designing information security programmes it would certainly be involving the security industry throughout the process of creating and delivering courses. While information security is an academic discipline in its own right, it is more importantly a practical topic, whose skills are in high demand. Meeting those skills in the future may need a re-assessment of the ways in which course content is delivered to students, and we believe that they key to continued future success will be the ability to deliver programmes in as flexible and adaptable a manner as possible.

## REFERENCES

1. University of London External Programme, (accessed 12th December 02), http://www.londonexternal.ac.uk
2. International Information Systems Security Certification Consortium, Inc., (accessed 17th December 02), http://www.isc2.org
3. Information Security Group MSc Programmes, (accessed 12th December 02), http://www.isg.rhul.ac.uk/msc/msc_home.shtml

# NETWORK SECURITY SCIENTIFIC AND RESEARCH LABORATORY

Natalia Miloslavskaia, Alexander Tolstoi
*Moscow Engineering Physics Institute (State University), milmur@mephi.edu, ait@mephi.edu*

Abstract:     Importance of Network Security Scientific and Research Laboratory in an educational process of a modern university is examined. A two-part laboratory structure and topology with respect to the initial requirements are described. Laboratory activities are discussed in detail. Designing and using of the laboratory in the Moscow Engineering Physics Institute (State University) is summarised.

Key words:   security education, network security, scientific and research laboratory, distance learning

## 1.     INTRODUCTION

The Information Security Faculty of the Moscow Engineering Physics Institute (State University) (MEPhI) has felt the necessity of designing new educational environment for teaching information and network technologies. A testing area for student practices today is more urgent than ever. This is not surprising as he/she has pretty high theoretical foundation and at the same time has lacked any practical training. Of course, students were taught lectures and recommended literature. Various ways of implementing the obtained knowledge in everyday practice are described. Nevertheless one has to admit that all those activities are not sufficient nowadays. When applying for a job, a person who worked with the real equipment, who designed and implemented even a small project, and more or less familiar with software in use, will undoubtedly have advantages as compared with other applicants. In fact, till now the students could gain practical experience only by themselves, mainly because it had been obtained with their own hands at the expense of other activities during their free time.

## 2.    PREHISTORY

MEPhI together with the Moscow Microsoft representatives and some Russian commercial companies (such as STC Electron-service and CROC) has already designed and implemented the Network Security Scientific and Research Laboratory. Its main goal is to implement the "education-science-business" approach in practice.

The aims of the Laboratory usage are the following:

- examination of system vulnerabilities and analysis of unauthorized access to computers and networks;
- security testing and computer-aided testing facilities;
- extending students' knowledge of security concepts and principles;
- familiarization with instruments used for ensuring system security;
- design of secure systems and subsystems;
- which, in turn, means
- a new level of scientific and research activities of the MEPhI faculty;
- an increase of efficiency of specialist training in the group of "Information security" specialties and refreshing stuff training in the field of security of information technologies, and
- adjustment of new educational technologies.

With such a Laboratory MEPhI is fully prepared to participate in the Russian federal programs on "Electronic Russia 2002-2010" and "Uniform Educational Environment". Besides it is possible not only to continue training specialists in Complex Protection of Informatization Objects, Complex Information Security of Computer-Based Systems and Computer Security, but to increase its qualitative level as well. In monthly personnel retraining courses for the Bank of Russia, Sberbank, Vnesheconombank, etc. on the basis of the faculty, results of the training with the help of expansion of practical training or carrying out extra laboratory works become more substantial.

Owing to a considerable support we are ready to put new educational technologies, for example, distance learning and progress testing and informational support of an educational process into operation.

There is an evident increase of efficiency of specialist training and progress in adjustment of new educational technologies. Students and even instructors get assistance in improving their theoretical and practical professional skills.

## 3.    LABORATORY DESIGN

Every project is fulfilled in definite stages. With limited financial resources thorough planning and design are a must for the most effective utilization of the resources and high-quality implementation of the project. All the stages were developed and realized by the students.

At the *preproject stage* the Laboratory design premises were explored and its necessity was motivated. The *project stage* followed the first one, when goals & tasks of laboratory, objects & methods of studies, educational courses to use it, preliminaries & knowledge and skills, configurations of the workplaces of the administrator, instructor and a typical intruder, the laboratory structure, hardware & software, firmware requirements and specifications, educational, methodical & technical maintenance and topics for scientific and research work were defined.

The project stage related to compiling the logical structure of the Laboratory and firmware requirements. At the same time the following main tasks of the Laboratory were worked out:
- research of the hardware, operating systems, data warehouses, software and firmware and technical means of network protection;
- design of operational models of protected networks on the basis of new information and network technologies on different platforms;
- adjustment of main methods and scenarios of distance learning and progress testing;
- information database of security technologies;
- education of users and students;
- detection of local and remote network attacks;
- analysis of mechanisms and means of attacks;
- discovery of channels of unauthorized information leaks from the system;
- definition of security policies and measures;
- elimination of consequences of unauthorized intrusion into computer systems;
- evaluation of the system protectability;
- installation, configuration and administration of security equipment;
- development of new methods and systems for information protection;
- "sandboxes" for temporary software and new technologies testing.

To carry out all those tasks successfully the Laboratory should meet some requirements. For example, when modeling secure networks it is essential to have sufficient flexibility of configuration and scalability, whereas when evaluating the system protectability and designing new methods of information protection demands a capability to react to new operational environment. The complete list of project requirements should include maximum flexibility, simulation of various attacks, heterogeneity, low cost and availability.

The resulting logical structure of the Laboratory satisfying all the given requirements and able to carry all the tasks is depicted in figure 1.

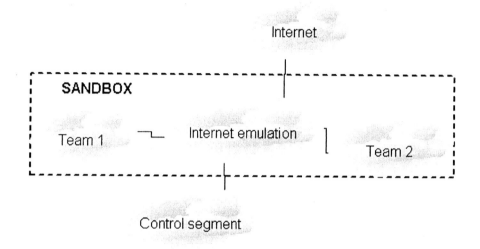

*Figure 1.* Logical structure of the Laboratory.

The Laboratory consists of several logical segments performing different functions which increase flexibility of the Laboratory as a whole and allows to modify it easily and/or expand it to fit new needs:

1. The Internet emulation segment, a model of public data network.
2. "Team 1" and "Team 2" segments for mutual attacks and defense.
3. Control segment, a workplace of the administrator/instructor and entrance to the Internet.
4. Transport medium, connecting all segments.

All the segments include security equipment, the specific setup being defined by the problems being solved.

The Internet emulation segment plays the role of public data network and is a transit area, passing all the traffic of participating parties, that is why it becomes a proper location for various informational warehouses, "public" servers (DNS, proxy, Web, etc.) and a management system. The management system controls operations of the segment and executes the established security policy.

The team segments simulate different corporate subnets and play the roles of networks under attack, attacking networks etc (e.g. serve as mini-

sandboxes for temporary software testing). Accordingly the team segments should contain such firmware as:
- workstation software (OS on popular and usable platforms –Microsoft, Unix, Novell; as well as Web-browsers and other software necessary the problem solutions);
- communication facilities (they may be absent if the segment is used as an "isolated" area);
- databases (Oracle, Informix, MS SQL, MySQL, etc., the ultimate choice is defined by the problem being solved);
- e-mail facilities (servers and client software);
- different servers (application, Web-, file- and others, not yet defined);
- security subsystems and firmware security facilities;
- programming tools (for analysis of the available and design of security facilities of their own, for analysis of vulnerabilities and various technologies);
- adaptive network security and management tools, including systems for evaluation of protectability, monitoring user activity, traffic analysis and intrusion detection.

The control segment is the workplace of the administrator (an instructor participates in the laboratory works) and controls access of participants to external (relative to the Laboratory) services (for example, the Internet). This area should include adaptive network security and management tools, security subsystems and firmware security facilities, e-mail facilities and other servers.

All segments are linked into a single complex with the transport medium built on popular technologies used in networks at present. In our case the transport medium is Ethernet because it is flexible, cheap and scalable technology to satisfy nearly all the speed and quality-of-service requirements.

The team segments (and the control segment) use various software from freeware, downloaded from the Internet for analysis, to licensed operating systems and security facilities (for example, network audit tools, software firewalls, antiviral software, etc.). Besides, design and permanent update of the unified database of investigated vulnerabilities, methods of defense and used firmware, as well as maintenance of centralized support server in the control segment are of special interest.

The *implementation stage* follows the project stage. The faculty could not to afford a self-dependent Laboratory because of limited financial resources. That is why the next stage was the *search for partners*. The partners were to be interested in the Laboratory maintenance because they could shift their research and testing activities onto students and post-graduates. The partners, the Moscow Microsoft representatives, the STC Electron-Service and the

CROC Company introduced some modifications into the initial Laboratory topology so that it would be more flexible and effective to solve various problems. The project of the Laboratory compiled by the joint efforts is depicted in figure 2.

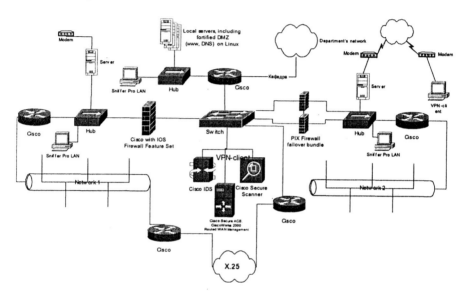

*Figure 2.* Laboratory topology.

After search for partners and adjustment of the project, the participants started the *start-and-adjustment stage* to equip the rooms, lay the communications, install and configure the equipment. Again it should be stressed that all the works were carried out only by the students.

Then the Laboratory was ready for *presentation and operations test*.

Figure 3 shows the Laboratory that is divided in two main parts.

The first part of the Laboratory is designed to carry out all the works listed above.

The second part is intended for improvement of the basic techniques and scripts of distance learning and progress testing. The basis of this part of the Laboratory was earlier developed at the MEPhI Distance Learning and Testing Systems (DLTS). The MEPhI DLTS is a complex of hardware, software and methodology tools for distance learning and certification based on the advanced Internet technologies and modern educational and testing techniques and specially trained personnel. Interactive DLTS Web site is constructed upon the Microsoft ASP technology. The Internet Information Server 5.0 provides the ASP support. VBScript language is used for writing ASP scripts. The DLTS information environment consists of the educational material in the HTML format and the centralized database under the

Microsoft SQL Server 2000 control. The tools for the development of new educational course, the test tools and DLTS operation support tools are implemented as the Internet and Delphi applications. All DLTS resources must be protected and located in the Laboratory.

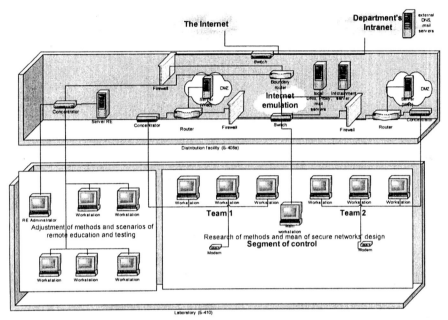

*Figure 3.* Equipment and configuration of the Laboratory.

## 4.    LABORATORY ACTIVITIES

There is a list of requirements for trainees who work in the Laboratory: network protocols & services, operating systems (Unix, Windows, Netware...), database management systems, computer viruses (malware), programming languages (Java, ActiveX...) and basic security principles.

The objects of the Laboratory are network hardware & software, protocols & services, standards, legal and norm documents, standalone computers or groups of computers in the internal and external networks with specific hardware platform and installed software — primary (for example, OS) and applied (network), with the Internet access. As for the protection hardware & software, the students should study means of intrusion detection, security monitoring and audit, protection means (such as firewalls, encryption tools), access control implementation, security policy development and, of course, regulation of information security. To this end the following methods of research are used:

- emulation of intruder's activities and examination of standard attacks described in different publications;
- discovery of system vulnerabilities by scanning and probing;
- intrusion detection and elimination of consequences;
- experiments with security facilities and means of unauthorized access detection to determine the functional capabilities and to work out recommendations for installation and improvement;
- control of network information flows through traffic analysis;
- evaluation of functioning systems' protectability and recommendations for its enhancement;
- assessment of protection of computers, networks, services, protocols, hardware and software in accordance with fixed procedures and Russian standards and guidelines;
- testing system security policies and new procedures of protection to determine their comprehensiveness and validity;
- analysis of documents regulating information security;
- design, installation, configuration and administration of security facilities and patches for software and hardware.

The Laboratory participates in students training in the specialized educational courses on Information security basics, Theoretical foundations of information security, Operating system security, Network security, Database security, Complex information security of computer-based systems, Cryptographic tools of information protection, Technical methods and tools of information security, Firmware methods and tools of information security, Legal aspects of information security, Organization of information security and Building secure computer-based systems.

The subjects of the laboratory works are different. For example, the work on buffer overflow attacks is designed for the Programming technologies course, functioning of packet filters, channel encryption devices and other hardware for the Computer hardware course. Spotting leakage paths is a good illustration for the Communication networks and systems course. Analysis of OS's protectability and setup of configuration files corresponds to the Operating systems. Specific DBMS threats and built-in protection capabilities are the main topics for Database management systems. Network attacks and methods of their detection best fit Computational networks. The Management basics imply designing security policies and study of the main administrator's responsibilities, etc.

On the basis of the Laboratory there are plans to introduce the new courses on Secure network technologies, Monitoring of network security,

VPN management, Informational and mail systems, Information security administrators, Building data networks and Network management tools.

The knowledge that trainees can gain through the Laboratory is of prior importance. For example, it allows to study the areas of:

- unauthorized computer access;
- network attacks;
- procedures and means for performing attacks;
- threats for information computer systems;
- vulnerabilities and bugs in systems, services and network protocols through which the adversary's intrusion can be expected;
- channels of unauthorized information leaks from the system;
- network security monitoring;
- access isolation systems providing a controlled access to informational and network resources;
- secure informational systems;
- system's security policy;
- measures and procedures of accident prevention;
- eliminating the consequences of unauthorized intrusion into a system;
- system protectability;
- defining the purpose, basic functions and place of information security standards in the system; usage peculiarities of the specific standard;
- evaluating the functional capabilities of the existing security equipment and determine the applicability of firmware in network architectures;
- configuring the security facilities built into many systems;
- ensuring the secure operation of system applications;
- administering security equipment;
- methods of defense;
- implementing new systems and means of information protection;
- basic regulations and standards in information security;
- preparing documentation for a new security equipment for further state level certification.

This is not a comprehensive list. Every student chooses his/her own specialization and questions that he/she will thoroughly study. It is impossible to be a specialist in every possible field. Nevertheless all students can obtain a necessary minimum of knowledge in their own problems mentioned to continue independent studies and research.

On the basis of the typical basic tasks as well as our personal experience the following scientific and research topics were suggested as subjects of student's research.

1. *Design of a Network Security Scientific and Research Laboratory (complex project):* Goals, tasks, and requirements. Hardware and software. Laboratory structure. Objects and methods of research.

2. *Laboratory equipment:* Marketing research. Start-and-adjustment works.

3. *Laboratory maintenance:* Educational and methodical maintenance. Information support, resources & interfaces. Glossary. Intruder's models and workplace of an attacker. Workplace of network security administrator. Instructor's interface for dynamic reconfiguration of Laboratory depending on the attack under study. Instructor's interface for monitoring Laboratory operations.

4. *Laboratory practice:* Emulation of specific attacks. Emulation of secure network protocols. Interfaces emulating operation of security facilities. Network topology _ attacks & Transport medium in use _ attacks dependencies. Peculiarities of telephone channel & fiber-optic attacks. Peculiarities of attacks from the Internet. Attacks on network hardware & software. Vulnerabilities and protection of workstations. Attacks on firewalls & proxies. Vulnerabilities of client/server architecture. Vulnerabilities of databases and database management systems. Attacks on electronic document interchange. Vulnerabilities and protection of Web-servers and applications. Application-level attacks and protection. Vulnerabilities of network services and commands. Crypto protection. Digital signature. PKI. Firewalls. Adaptive network security. Antiviral software. Virtual private networks. Protection against an unauthorized access. Security policy development and management. File and session encryption. Network-based & host-based intrusion detection systems. Attacks on IDS. System & network security scanners. Security services: intrusion tests. Trusted operating systems. Design of own means and methods of defense.

## 5.      CONCLUSION

Development of Network Security Scientific and Research Laboratory allows not only to improve student's training in the set of information security specialties, but it also raises educational and research activities of the faculty to a new standard which results in increased efficiency of training and retraining courses on old and new educational programs and participation in the Russian federal programs. It permits online exchanges of experience with foreign partners and to joint investigation and research (the so-called exterior projects). With a mutual agreement it is possible to participate even in the joint laboratory works when, for example, Russian, American [1], Australian [2] or Greek [3] students can compete in network protocols, technologies and network protection tools.

# REFERENCES

[1] White G.B., Sward R.E. Developing an Undergraduate Lab for Information Warfare and Computer Security. Proceeding of the IFIP TC11 WG11.8 First World Conference on Information Security Education. 17-19 June 1999, Kista, Sweden. Pp. 163-170.

[2] Armstrong C.J., Armstrong H.L. The Virtual Campus. Proceeding of the IFIP TC11 WG11.8 Second World Conference on Information Security Education. 12-14 July 2001, Perth, Australia. Pp. 161-168.

[3] Gritzalis D., Tryfonas T. Action Learning in Practice: Pilot delivery of an INFOSEC University laboratory course. Proceeding of the IFIP TC11 WG11.8 Second World Conference on Information Security Education. 12-14 July 2001, Perth, Australia. Pp. 169-182.

# A COMPREHENSIVE UNDERGRADUATE INFORMATION ASSURANCE PROGRAM

Gregory Conti, John Hill, Scott Lathrop, Kenneth Alford, and Daniel Ragsdale
*Information Technology and Operations Center (ITOC), Department of Electrical Engineering and Computer Science, United States Military Academy, West Point, NY*

Abstract: This paper describes the experience of our institution in creating a comprehensive undergraduate information assurance (IA) program. An interdisciplinary approach was undertaken in order to include a larger portion of the student body and faculty and thus influence a broader audience. The program includes a wide variety of mutually supporting information assurance activities including a research center, coursework, an information warfare laboratory, a cyber defense exercise, an outreach program, conferences, trips, summer internships, a guest speaker program, a National Security Agency Liaison program, summer student internships, faculty sabbaticals and a student information warfare club. This paper organizes discussion of these activities into the student experience, building faculty expertise, and organizational support. The catalyst for these activities has been the formation of the Military Academy's dedicated information assurance research center, the Information Technology and Operations Center (ITOC), and the continuing support from and interaction with the National Security Agency. The primary goal of this paper is to provide a descriptive resource to educators who wish to implement an undergraduate or graduate level information assurance program. It is our sincere hope to inspire and aid others in starting similar programs.

Keywords: Information Assurance, Education, Information Warfare, Computer Security Education, Computer Security

# 1.　INTRODUCTION

## 1.1　Motivation

Business, government, military, public utilities, and academia all take advantage of the efficiency, speed, computational abilities, storage, and transport capabilities provided by information systems. These systems are so ingrained into everyday operations that the functions and services they provide would be difficult, if not impossible, to perform without them.

Gene Spafford, the director the Center for Education and Research in Information Assurance and Security (CERIAS), is well known in the information security community. He was called upon in 1997 to testify before congress on the subject of information security education. In no uncertain terms he told the committee that security must be built into information systems, and that in order to make that happen we must properly educate our students: "To ensure safe computing, the security (and other desirable properties) must be designed in from the start. To do that, we need to be sure all of our students understand the many concerns of security, privacy, integrity, and reliability." [1]

It is easy to describe why there is such a need for information security education. As Spafford testified, "Our students and soon-to-be students will be designing our information technologies of the future. We are endangering them and ourselves because the majority of them will receive no training in information security." The way to achieve secure information systems is to provide the appropriate information security education to the people who have to build them.

By November of 1996 (according to Spafford) there were only four "declared, dedicated computer security research centers in degree-granting departments at universities in the United States." Other institutions were performing valuable work in this area, but perhaps didn't have the same institutional or financial support. Fortunately, since that time, information security has been added to numerous programs, new research centers have been established, and additional research funding has been made available. Unfortunately, there is still much to be done. In 2000, Matt Bishop identified the following weaknesses (among others) in our overall efforts: we continue to repeat well-known errors (e.g., buffer overflows), we have not improved how we design systems and programs to account for security constraints, and we don't fully understand how security problems arise from human interaction with systems. [2] Clearly, each of these weaknesses can be addressed by information security education.

Bishop makes clear distinctions in information security education between public awareness and academic education. He further divides academic education into four broadly stated types: training, undergraduate education, terminal master's education, and doctoral education. [2] Our institution provides education primarily at the undergraduate level (we have no post-graduate program). However, our Information Assurance program and research efforts serve as an effective training ground for our faculty with masters and doctoral degrees.

Recent events in American and world history clearly demonstrate that the demand for information assurance is waxing, not waning. It is our contention that all undergraduate students, regardless of their major or areas of specialization, should receive appropriate levels of information assurance education. At the United States Military Academy, our long-term goal is to introduce *all* of our students to the principles of information assurance and provide in-depth information assurance education to as many students as possible. This paper discusses the actions we are taking to realize that goal.

## 1.2    Background

The United States Military Academy (USMA) is a medium-sized undergraduate academic institution located at West Point, New York.. There are approximately 4,100 students, all of whom will serve in the military upon graduation. Approximately 200 students are Computer Science, Electrical Engineering, or Information Systems Engineering majors. There are approximately 400 other students taking a three-course engineering sequence (similar to a minor) in either Computer Science or Electrical Engineering. All students take a core information technology (IT) course as a freshman. Beginning in the Fall of 2003, all juniors will be required to take a second IT course.

Information assurance, information security and computer security are of vital importance to the nation, the military, and to us as individuals. It is due to the awareness of this importance and extensive interest by both our faculty members and our students that this program was implemented. Until 1999, our academic program lacked any cohesive information assurance activities. Information assurance education was presented minimally and in an ad-hoc manner. The coalescence of new faculty members with IA experience, increased resources, senior decision-maker support, world events, and heightened public awareness provided the momentum required to establish and build up the current IA program.

## 1.3    Program Components

In a 2000 report, Corey Schou, the director of the National Information Assurance Training and Education Center (NIATEC) at Idaho State

University and chair of the National Colloquium for Information Systems Security Education (NCISSE), noted that the need for information security professionals still couldn't be met by the output of existing academic programs. [3] Clearly, our academic programs must reach out to more students. He also identified several initiatives for improvement of information security education. Among these were more internships to provide students and faculty with practical information assurance experience, exchanges of government and academic professionals, and improved training resources for students and faculty.

At our institution, we are trying to reach out to as many students as possible. Also, the three initiatives mentioned above represent just a few of the many components that make up our information assurance program. Many of these components started as small faculty member initiatives. Over time, the components have helped us to define what makes a successful overall program. This paper describes the components from the student, faculty, and organizational perspective, and seeks to aid other academic programs avoid the hurdles we experienced as the components matured into a cohesive program

## 2.     RELATED WORK

There is much ongoing work in the area of information assurance education. This activity has dramatically increased due to heightened national awareness and by programs such as the National Security Agency's Information Assurance Center of Excellence program, the Federal Cyber Service Initiative, the Information Assurance Scholarship program and greater overall resourcing of information assurance research. Prior to the recent emphasis, several institutions established computer security and information assurance programs. Recently, many other programs have been formalizing and stepping up their activities in information assurance education. The majority of these activities are at the graduate level. We believe that the interdisciplinary nature and undergraduate focus of the work presented in this paper will help other undergraduate institutions rapidly prototype and implement similar IA programs.

## 3.     THE STUDENT EXPERIENCE

The heart of every academic information assurance program is the student experience. This experience is built upon an overarching framework for information technology and information security education. Hung upon this framework is an interlocking series of activities that provide mutually supporting information assurance education. The student-focused portion of our IA program includes a student information warfare club, coursework, lecturers, guest speakers, an information warfare lab, an interschool information assurance competition, summer internships and educational trips.

## 3.1     Framework for Information Technology and Information Security Education

**Information Technology Goal:** Information technology is a key component of the military's strategy. USMA intends to provide graduates for the military who can operate in an information-rich environment, take advantage of existing information technology, and are prepared to explore and exploit future technology — "The overarching goal of the Academic Program is to enable its graduates to anticipate and to respond effectively to the uncertainties of a changing technological, social, political, and economic world." Additionally, an IT goal was recently added to the overarching goal — "graduates will demonstrate proficiency in information technology." Within the context of our Academic Program, information technology (IT) is defined as encompassing "the knowledge, skills, processes, and tools by which the state of the physical world is sensed and, along with other knowledge, is disseminated, stored, transformed, processed, analyzed, presented, used to make decisions about actions, and used to initiate and control actions." [4] Information technology is embedded in the academic program, and so is information security education. This integration can be seen in most of the course descriptions.

**Daily experience:** One of the earliest experiences in each student's first academic year is the setup and configuration of their mandatory-purchase student computer. [5] From that moment forward students are immersed in an ubiquitous computing environment — all 4,100 student computers are networked together. Wireless networking is expanding rapidly, energized by the introduction of laptop computers to the Class of 2006. Every academic department and agency on the institution is "wired in" as well. Students are exposed to and intimately engaged with Information Technology as an integral part of their daily routine. The vast majority of courses the students are required to take (*core* courses) take advantage of information technology, ranging from the use of web sites and e-mail for communication through the use of sophisticated automated tools within the classroom. In addition, certain core courses are designated to provide the primary instruction leading to proficiency in specific applications. Other courses are then able to rely on that proficiency. "Throughout their core courses, students learn to use, evaluate, and select appropriate computing system tools to solve real-world problems. They develop personal skills in the effective use of fundamental computing applications such as word processing, spreadsheet analysis, desktop publishing, database management, presentation graphics, computer security, and telecommunications software." [4]

**Dedicated IT instruction:** This institution has long required that every student take an "Introduction to Computer Science" course, which has recently been reconfigured to focus less on the specifics of computer science and programming and more on information technology. The first year course (IT105) lays a good foundation for students in understanding and using Information Technology. [4] To support the emphasis of the IT goal mentioned above, a new course (IT305), mandatory for juniors, was created to "develop further understanding of the physical and mathematical principles governing sensors and communications as they apply to IT systems" and to "develop their abilities to describe, analyze, and evaluate information systems and their components to build comprehension of selected current and emerging information technologies." A significant component of this course is that "students acquire skills and knowledge relevant to effective information assurance and develop the ability to make informed and rational decisions involving the legal and ethical dimensions of IT." [4]

**Majors and Minors:** Every USMA graduate receives a thorough grounding in information technology (IT) and an exposure to information assurance (IA). In addition, there are several majors in the academic program that provide special emphasis on IT and on IA. The Computer Science (CS) major develops capabilities in designing, testing, and building computer and information systems, integrating and applying those systems, and being effective users of those systems. CS majors get a thorough grounding in information assurance. [6]. The Electrical Engineering (EE) major focuses on digitization – the exchange of information using computers networked together by digital communications systems, and see information assurance from that perspective. [7] The Information Systems Engineering (ISE) major focuses on providing students with a solid foundation in the development, integration and use of information systems, and focuses attention on the defense of information systems. [8] The equivalent of a minor at the institution is a "core engineering sequence" that focuses on the design-build-test methodology and allows students in any field to expand their knowledge of IT and IA.

## 3.2    Student Information Assurance Organization

A student information warfare club was formed in February 2001 under the auspices of the Association for Computing Machinery (ACM) Special Interest Group for Security Audit and Control (SIGSAC) and quickly grew to 80 members. It has continued to grow at a rapid pace and now numbers 450+ students (more than 10% of the student population) and six faculty advisors. This is particularly significant when one considers that there are approximately 80 computer science majors at this institution. It was formed due to a realization of the potential of such a club by faculty and extensive interest by students. It was the first student chapter of its kind out of the more than 600 ACM student chapters worldwide. The chapter includes a wide range of interdisciplinary activities and has members from every academic department. It is this wide range of activities and interdisciplinary focus that allow the club to reach a wide audience. It has proven to be an effective vehicle in increasing information assurance awareness, facilitating ethical education and debate, providing leader development opportunities and generating excitement in students for information assurance.

SIGSAC members participate in virtually every aspect of the institution-wide IA program. Members receive invitations to hear guest speakers discuss information assurance topics. This has proven to be very popular, frequently drawing large numbers of students. Members also receive early information about IA-related course offerings and summer internships. During a recent offering of MA489 Mathematical Cryptology over half of the students in the course were chapter members who learned of the course from the SIGSAC mailing list. SIGSAC members are almost exclusively those who compete for and win the IA-related summer internships. Resources can be scarce and SIGSAC is an ideal venue to identify candidates and select those who are most interested and prepared.

The institution participates in an annual collegiate information assurance competition called the Cyber Defense Exercise. While the Cyber Defense Exercise is not a SIGSAC activity, chapter members have been among the most prepared and stood out as leaders. A few members of the faculty draw the analogy that SIGSAC is the junior varsity team, while students in the senior-level CS482 Information Assurance course are the varsity. Trips are another popular activity - chapter leaders coordinate with existing trip organizers and are frequently able to secure seats for SIGSAC members. Using this strategy, students have visited the National Security Agency, the Blackhat Briefings, InfoWarCon, the United States Army's 1st Information Operations Command, the Pentagon and the White House. Recently students have begun a program of Internet safety awareness training for local schools.

This strategy has resulted in a great deal of enthusiasm and participation. As a result of these activities, the chapter won a 2001-2002 ACM Outstanding Activities Award. More details can be found at http://www.itoc.usma.edu/sigsac/.

## 3.3     Courses Providing Breadth and Depth in Information Assurance

Information Assurance coursework is at the heart of the program. Some courses are primarily information assurance related, others have a large information assurance component or otherwise play a supporting role.

**CS482** *Information Assurance*: CS482 is the flagship information assurance course in the curriculum. It provides depth and is taught in the Information Warfare (IWAR) laboratory. This lab contains an isolated network designed to allow a much greater range of action beyond what would be allowed in a traditional lab on the official academic network. The course teaches students how to employ strong network defenses by exposing them to core information assurance principles as well as the tools and techniques of attackers. This course is highly technical and is limited to students with a substantial background in Computer Science or Electrical Engineering. It is offered each spring and culminates with a demanding three-day Cyber Defense Exercise (CDX), which is described in more detail later in this paper.

**SS490 Policy and Strategy of Cyberwar** This course is offered by the Department of Social Sciences and provides additional depth and complements CS482. While CS482 focuses on the technical aspects of information assurance, SS490 focuses on the political, economic and social issues. The course is open to a much wider population of students and is offered each fall. The prerequisites are the mandatory IT105 course and SS307 *International Relations*.

**MA489 Mathematical Cryptology:** This course is offered by the Department of Mathematical Sciences and exposes students to manual and machine cryptosystems, the history of the art, and cryptanalytic techniques.

**LW489 CyberLaw:** This course is offered by the Department of Law and exposes students to the legal issues associated with information technology and cyber war.

**Information Security Integration Throughout the Curriculum:** While CS482, SS490, MA489 and LW489 provide specific and in-depth exposure to information assurance, a variety of other courses (primarily in the CS and IT programs) provide support. A deliberate decision was made in these courses to weave security throughout applicable lessons rather than relegate the subject to only a lesson or two at the end. The core information technology courses, IT105 and IT305, expose freshmen to information assurance and include an information warfare lesson and exercises in the IWAR lab, and addresses security throughout the spectrum of military information systems. CS385 *Analysis and Design of Algorithms* covers the mathematical foundation for encryption algorithms. The CS481 *Operating Systems* course delves into threats against computer system assets and operating system design issues associated with countering those threats. CS484 *Computer Networks* teaches information assurance and network security by complementing traditional theory based instruction with hands-on exercises utilizing white hat and hacker tools and techniques. Every layer of the OSI model can be exploited and these exercises illustrate to the students the respective strengths and weaknesses.

## 3.4 Lectures and Guest Speakers

Formal classroom instruction is augmented with a wide range of lectures and guest speakers. Student attendance is typically optional for the majority of the student body and for SIGSAC members. In some instances, CS482 *Information Assurance* in particular, students taking the course were required to participate. In 2001 and 2002 speakers came from several activities, including the Defense Advanced Research Projects Agency (DARPA), the National Security Agency (NSA), White Wolf Security Consulting, the Secret Service Electronic Crimes Task Force, a Department of Defense Computer Crime Investigative Unit, the Department of Defense Joint Task Force for Computer Network Operations, and the Honeynet Project. Bringing in outside speakers helped to build bridges with other organizations as well as foster enthusiasm among the students and faculty. For the general student population, this series of speakers proved to be the most successful portion of the IA program.

## 3.5 Information Warfare (IWAR) Laboratory

We decided early in the process of building our Information Assurance program that simply discussing Information Assurance topics was not enough. In order to meet the institution's goal of providing an "active learning" approach to education, only a facility where students could obtain hands-on experience with cyber attacks and technical countermeasures would suffice. The Information Warfare Analysis and Research (IWAR) laboratory has evolved over the last two years to provide such an environment and is the centerpiece of our IA education.

Consisting of over 200 computers and networking nodes, the IWAR lab is an isolated network of heterogeneous operating systems, applications, and networking equipment where students enrolled in our courses and members of our ACM SIGSAC student chapter can learn about the capabilities of known computer attacks and discover the technical countermeasures to defend an information system against such exploits. Except for a few administrative machines, the students are given full administrative privileges on systems within the lab. This enables them to experiment with offensive and defensive tools such as port scanners, vulnerability scanners, Trojan horses, worms, viruses, firewalls, intrusion detection systems, password crackers, and any published exploits without running the risk of releasing malicious code onto our production network or into the "wild." Just as a soldier would only fire a weapon on the range or in combat, our policy only permits users to experiment with the malicious tools in the controlled confines of the lab.

Currently the IWAR lab supports CS482 *Information Assurance,* CS484 *Computer Networks*, SS490 *Policy and Strategy of Cyber War*, several lessons in IT305 *Military Information Systems* and one lesson in LW489 *CyberLaw*. Faculty members reserve the lab and use it to teach components of their courses that would best not be done on the official academic network. A good example is running the Ethereal software package (http://www.ethereal.com). Ethereal is packet sniffing software that is very useful for demonstrating encapsulation techniques within the OSI network stack and for demonstrating network protocols in action. The risk is that it also can capture personal information and capture passwords. The IWAR lab provides on ideal venue for such a tool.

The lab is also used as a focal point for congressional, academic, military, and other visitors interested in observing or replicating our work; and is used for information warfare demonstrations during a once-per-semester "technology tour" for the freshmen students. The purpose of this demonstration is to motivate the freshmen to take advantage of the lab and Information Assurance courses during their time as students. Finally, the lab provides a facility for faculty members to conduct research and work on projects in Information Assurance topics. The website at http://www.itoc.usma.edu provides more information and includes labs used in the IA course as well as the standard operating procedures.

## 3.6    Cyber-Defense Exercise (CDX)

The Cyber Defense Exercise (CDX) is the most demanding activity in our IA program. As the capstone project in the CS482 *Information Assurance* course, the exercise is an intensive three-week competition allowing students to apply their IA skills in a team setting. Given a set of constraints and required network services, students from each of the military academies (Military, Air Force, Naval, Coast Guard, and Merchant Marine) and the Naval Postgraduate School design, build, harden and defend their network against attacks by professional red teams from the NSA and the 1$^{st}$ Information Operations Command. The primary sponsor of the event is the National Security Agency who awards the Information Assurance Director's Trophy to the undergraduate team whose network provides the required functionality while proving to be most resilient to attacks. This annual event has been held twice, with USMA winning the trophy both times. The Naval Postgraduate School participates in the exercise and does very well, but is not involved in the competitive scoring of the undergraduate institutions.

During the first two weeks, or preparation phase of the exercise, students build their network and secure their systems. Certain constraints in the exercise directive require the students to use several different operating systems on one or more of their end systems. For example, in last year's competition student's employed Solaris 8.0, Linux kernel 2.4.8, Windows 2000 Advanced Server, and Windows NT 4.0. Certain services such as web, email, and file servers must be provided by the students' system. In order to establish a defense-in-depth and defense-in-breadth posture, security measures are limited to open source tools to include, but not limited to, open-source port scanners, vulnerability scanners, network monitoring tools, intrusion detection, and host-based and network-based firewalls. For example, in the recently completed exercise, the students established an intrusion detection system using Snort running on a Linux machine. In order to prevent traffic from leaving their network interface card, they built a one-way Ethernet cable that allowed only one-way traffic into their intrusion detection machine, aptly named *Narc*. More information on the exercise can be found at http://www.itoc.usma.edu.

## 3.7    Summer Internships

Many students are given the opportunity to participate in three to four week summer internships. This is a longstanding program at this institution, but until recently, there were no internships within the information assurance community. The institution's information assurance research center actively develops relationships with external organizations and coordinates a wide variety of information assurance related opportunities for students. Recent internships included assignments at the newly established Homeland Security Office in order to assist the creation of national policy for the nation's critical infrastructures; the evaluation of network security with the National Security Agency; research of wireless tracking devices with the Secret Service; and investigation of hackers breaking into military networks at a Department of Defense Computer Crime Investigative Unit (CCIU).

Students are encouraged to bring back the work they begin on these summer internships and to continue the work as either part of an individual study class or as part of their senior project. These internships reinforce in the students' minds the emphasis and priority Information Assurance initiatives receive in real world settings and motivate the students to continue to delve deeper into their studies.

## 3.8　　Student Trips

Trips to Information Assurance conferences and to governmental agencies working in Information Assurance also contributes significantly to motivating students and faculty to start or continue their educational experience in IA topics. Conference participation provides a source of new ideas. Each trip brings both direct and subtle thoughts as well professional contacts and exposure that benefit the program. Although some of the material being presented may be somewhat over their heads, students begin to appreciate the complexity and issues associated with securing information systems.

Within the past two years there have been four major trips scheduled each year. Participation in conferences is carefully synchronized with other program activities and the academic year to provide maximum impact. Table 1 displays this careful timing. Approximately 30 students and four to five faculty members accompany the students on each trip. The priority for the trips is to those students who are either enrolled in one of the IA course or actively involved in the SIGSAC program.

*Table 1:* Conference/Trip Timeline

| When | What | Why |
|------|------|-----|
| September | InfoWarCon/Visit D.C. Area Agencies | Motivate Students to pick IA topics for their senior projects. Build underclass (SIGSAC) understanding of the issues. |
| February/ March | Blackhat/SANS type conference | Provide instruction and motivate students enrolled in Information Assurance Course for upcoming Cyber Defense Exercise. |
| March/ April | NSA Trip | Provide overview of NSA's priority on IA to students involved with SIGSAC. |
| June | IEEE Information Assurance Workshop | Contribute to the education of the IA community. Promote our own program and faculty. |
| July | Blackhat/Defcon | Stimulate faculty interest and keep them up to date on the latest exploits coming from the BlackHat community. |

A trip in the fall centers on the InfoWarCon, www.infowarcon.com, conference in Washington D.C. In conjunction with the conference, the students visit with a senior Department of Defense Chief Information Officer (CIO) at the Pentagon, discuss network security issues with the Pentagon's Computer Network Security Defense team, receive a presentation and tour of the Homeland Defense Office's Critical Infrastructure Protection, and view the 1$^{st}$ Information Operations Command and control center for military computer network defense. There are two trips scheduled in the spring: one is to tour the National Security Agency's Information Assurance operations, and the other trip is to a conference. Last year the students attended the Blackhat conference in New Orleans (http://www.blackhat.com/). The topic of discussion was focused on Windows Security, which proved beneficial to the students in the Cyber Defense exercise. This year the students will attend the SANS conference (http://www.sans.org/).

## 4. BUILDING FACULTY EXPERTISE

The success of the student experience depends in large measure upon faculty expertise in Information Assurance. Information Assurance, like many areas of computer science, is fast moving and faculty members require constant maintenance to remain current. To facilitate continued development, our program includes an aggressive program of outreach, publication, trips and professional exchanges.

## 4.1 Faculty Outreach

An important aspect of building faculty expertise in information assurance is the integral outreach activities to government, academia, industry and the local community. The relationships built provide a give-and-take of ideas, professional contacts and possibly even identification of resources or funding. Some of the government agencies involved in the faculty outreach effort are the National Security Agency (NSA), the Defense Advanced Research Projects Agency (DARPA), the Defense Information Systems Agency (DISA), the Army's First Information Operations Command (formerly the Land Information Warfare Activity (LIWA)) and the Department of Defense's Joint Task Force for Computer Network Operations (JTF-CNO). These agencies (and others) have active information assurance programs, and have provided valuable support ranging from simple collaboration through provision of expertise and funding.

Faculty members participate in professional organizations such as the Association for Computing Machinery (ACM), the ACM Special Interest

Group for Security Audit and Control (SIGSAC), the NSA Information Assurance Center of Excellence program, the IEEE Computer Society, the IEEE Task Force on Information Assurance, the Federal Information Systems Security Educators Association (FISSEA), and the National Colloquium on Information Systems Security Education (CISSE). Faculty members also participate in information assurance conferences and work with some of the leading information assurance research centers, in particular Texas A&M University and the Center for Education and Research in Information Assurance and Security (CERIAS) at Purdue.

There is a growing awareness of the need to pass information assurance principles beyond the professional community to the population at large. Students and faculty members are building information security and Internet safety training packages and plan to teach students at local schools.

## 4.2     Faculty Publications, Conferences and Trips

Faculty members submit their work to professional journals and to conferences to share their ideas, successes, and lessons learned. Conference participation is the source of new ideas for the information assurance program. Each trip brings both direct and subtle ideas as well professional contacts and exposure that benefit the program. Our institution directs resources to support the widest possible participation by both students and faculty. To the maximum extent possible, funding is provided to send at least one author of an accepted paper to present it and to encourage faculty members to attend IA-related conferences. Participation in such conferences is carefully synchronized with other program activities and the academic year to provide maximum impact.

Several members of the faculty attend the Blackhat conference in Las Vegas with some staying on for the hacker convention, DEFCON (http://www.defcon.org/). The Blackhat Briefings are an excellent source for an update on the current state of the Information Assurance community. Faculty members have participated during the past several years and brought back a wide variety of tools and techniques. The Blackhat Briefings occur several times per year and our faculty members have participated in both the summer and spring offerings. DEFCON provides invaluable cultural exposure to some of the more visible members of the underground hacker community.

It is the program's goal for each computer science faculty member to attend at least one Blackhat and DEFCON conference. Again, this not only stimulates the faculty intellect but also keeps them current with the latest exploits and serves as a motivational tool to emphasize the necessity to continue improving our program. The Blackhat Briefings organization and

DEFCON freely distribute the briefings and tools via their websites. Faculty members frequently use these tools to create in class exercises for the information assurance aspects of their courses.

In addition to trips to other conferences, the ITOC organizes and executes the annual IEEE Information Assurance Workshop. This event has been held for three years and includes presenters who are subject matter experts in a wide variety of IA topics such as wireless networking, honeynets, agent architectures in coalition environments, intrusion detection and response. The conference targets academia, business, and government employees and thus provides a balance between theoretical and practical application of the Information Assurance topics. It has proven to be a very effective means of outreach and interaction with the larger Information Assurance community. This institution is unique in that it selects military officers for advanced schooling with follow-on military teaching assignments. It has proved to be successful to invite the soon to be faculty members and their advisors to participate. More information can be found at www.itoc.usma.edu/workshop.

## 4.3    Professional Exchange

**Sabbaticals:** Tenured faculty members are offered the opportunity to participate in a sabbatical once every seven years. Typically of one-year duration, they allow faculty members to step away from traditional responsibilities and gain a fresh perspective by working at another academic institution (even outside the U.S.) or at agencies within the United States government. The most recent participant in the program worked with members of the ITOC to arrange their sabbatical at the National Security Agency working in their research and engineering program. While this is a first attempt at tying in the sabbatical program with information assurance there is much future potential. The insights gathered from working at the front line of information assurance and personal contacts made are expected to prove very valuable.

**NSA Fellow:** The Department of Electrical Engineering and Computer Science hosts a Visiting Fellow from the National Security Agency. This NSA Fellow brings a wealth of experience and expertise in information security and is actively involved in both the academic and research programs in the department. The current NSA fellow contributed in the following ways:

- taught CS407/CS408 Information Systems Design and CS482 Information Assurance

- directed research in support of the ITOC.

- developed and shared IA curricula with academic programs at other military academies

- participated in the successful effort to obtain NSA certification as a Center of Academic Excellence for Information Assurance Education

- helped establish the annual Cyber Defense Exercise.

**Endowed Chair:** The Department of Electrical Engineering and Computer Science has an endowed chair (The Adam Chair) that allows the department to bring in a faculty member with significant qualifications in an area of interest. The current occupant of the Adam Chair is actively involved in supporting the research efforts of the ITOC.


# 5.     ORGANIZATIONAL SUPPORT

For an academic information assurance program to be successful it must be supported with adequate personnel, financial, and physical resources. Successful programs also require two additional components—a champion and additional outside help. The IA program at this institution is fortunate to receive adequate resources in each of these areas.

The Information Technology and Operations Center (ITOC) has served as our "IA champion." This center is the driving force behind the success we have experienced. Formally, the center's mission is to "support the educational mission through curriculum development, research, and outreach to the Army that addresses the acquisition, use, management, and protection of information."

With only four full-time and several part-time positions (which include a National Security Agency fellow and chaired professor), the center is a lean organization, but it has been able to accomplish a great deal in tying independent IA initiatives into an integrated whole. The computer and research scientists in the center are responsible for:

- conducting information assurance research

- maintaining outreach programs

- coordinating guest speakers

- maintaining the IWAR lab

- organizing participation in the annual Cyber Defense Exercise

- teaching CS482 Information Assurance

- developing IA course materials for other courses

- having primary responsibility for the IEEE Information Assurance Workshop held each summer

- coordinating faculty and student attendance at IA conferences
- arranging IA educational trips for faculty, staff and students
- assisting in teaching other IA courses or lessons
- providing essential support to the student Information Warfare club (ACM SIGSAC)
- coordinating IA related student internships and faculty sabbaticals

The center's staff is augmented by support from faculty and staff of the Department of Electrical Engineering and Computer Science and others from across the institution and country in support of their IA program. These "augmentees" support the Information Warfare club, organize IA trips, assist in coordinating summer internships, assist in the planning and execution of the IEEE Information Warfare Conference, conduct IA research and arrange for guest speakers.

We are deeply indebted to the support and resources provided by the National Security Agency (NSA) which include a full-time fellow, co-sponsorship of an annual IEEE Information Warfare Conference, an annual student and faculty "field trip" to visit NSA headquarters, NSA summer student internships, sponsorship of the annual Cyber Defend Exercise, program certification through their Information Assurance Centers of Excellence program, and research assistance.

In addition to resources provided by the institution and NSA, several other organizations have been extremely supportive in establishing a viable IA program. These include the Defense Information Systems Agency, the Department of Defense Joint Staff, and several Department of Defense program and project managers.

## 6. FUTURE WORK

The IA program continues to evolve and improve as lessons from past experiences are learned. There is a large amount of future work that needs to be done across all aspects of the program, to include:

- Establish a fellowship program for recent top information assurance graduates in order to allow these graduates to continue their education
- Develop "IWAR in a box" — create a virtual IWAR laboratory inside a single computer.
- Implement Honeypot within the IWAR lab in order to capture live attacks.
- Expand the Cyber Defense Exercise to include coalition forces and insider attacks.
- Increase the number of summer internships and include stints at Computer Emergency Response Teams (CERTS) located around the world.
- Continue education of faculty members from all academic departments

## 7.     `CONCLUSIONS

This paper described the methodology, implementation and results from the creation of a comprehensive undergraduate information assurance program. The interdisciplinary approach is very successful in reaching a large portion of the student body and faculty. The overall program of mutually supporting information assurance activities is successful in fostering a high degree of learning by both students and faculty. Hopefully this will prove useful to other undergraduate institutions considering the development of their own information assurance program.

## DISCLAIMER

The views expressed in this article are those of the authors and do not reflect the official policy or position of the United States Military Academy, the Department of the Army, or the Department of Defense or the U.S. Government.

## REFERENCES

Spafford, Eugene H. (1997). "One View of A Critical National Need: Support for Information Security Education and Research." Testimony Before the US House of Representatives Committee on Science. Washington, DC, February 11.

Bishop, M. 2000. "Academia and Education in Information Security: Four Years Later." Fourth National Colloquium on Information System Security Education, Washington, DC.

Schou, C., D. Frincke, et al. 2000. "Meeting the Information Assurance Crisis - Now." EDPACS: The EDP Audit, Control, and Security Newsletter.

Office of the Dean. "Educating Future Army Officers for a Changing World." United States Military Academy. Available online [accessed December 24, 2002] at http://www.dean.usma.edu/AAD/EFAOCW.pdf

Office of the Dean. "Computing@West Point." United States Military Academy. Available online [accessed December 29, 2002] at www.dean.usma.edu/dean/computingatwestpoint

Ray, C. "Computer Science Program." United States Military Academy. Available online [accessed December 29, 2002] at www.eecs.usma.edu/programs/cs/default.htm

Dudevoir, G. "Electrical Engineering Program." United States Military Academy. Available online [accessed December 29, 2002] at www.eecs.usma.edu/programs/ee/default.htm

Blair, J. R. S. "Information Systems Engineering Program." United States Military Academy. Available online [accessed December 29, 2002] at www.eecs.usma.edu/programs/ise/default.htm

# TRAINING THE CYBER WARRIOR

J.D. Fulp
*Naval Postgraduate School*

Abstract:     This paper suggests the major educational components of a curriculum that is
designed to educate individuals for job assignments as Information Assurance
professionals – also known as: cyber warriors. It suggests a minimum common
body of knowledge for all cyber warriors along with two major specialization
categories: cyber tacticians and cyber strategists. The paper describes the
distinction between tactician and strategist and offers a rough outline of the
education each should receive.

Key words:   Education, Cyber Defense Exercise, Information Assurance Curriculum,
Cyber Tactician, Cyber Strategist, Cyber Warrior

## 1.     INTRODUCTION

Though the wide scale interconnection of automated information
systems (e.g., the Internet) has been a boon to U.S. military and economic
power, it also presents a soft underbelly to present and future adversaries.
U.S. reliance upon the ever-expanding National Information Infrastructure,
in conjunction with an increasingly wired world, exacerbates the U.S.'s
vulnerability to cyber threats. Sensitive information could once be protected
using relatively easily understood physical, personnel, and communications
security mechanisms. The advent of interconnected automated systems now
requires that such information receive the additional protections afforded by
computer and network security mechanisms. The education of individuals to
understand the complexities inherent in such mechanisms, so that they can
effectively implement them is the central theme of this paper.

It is natural to invoke military principles and terminology to discuss
elements of this new era of increased cyber vulnerability. Though those
involved may not wear uniforms, or fight along linear geographic

boundaries; there is clearly a high stakes adversarial environment that is conducive to well understood military conceptualization. Therefore we have such analogies as: de-militarized zones (moderately protected public service networks), security perimeters (boundaries between different data risk levels), and cyber warriors (IA professionals). This paper suggests an education regimen for cyber warriors, and suggests that these warriors be divided into two categories: cyber tacticians and cyber strategists. Cyber tacticians would focus on reducing the risk of existing fielded systems primarily through the application of appropriate safeguards (e.g., firewalls, intrusion detection, redundant configurations, data backups, etc.). Cyber strategists would focus on reducing the risk of future systems primarily through the application of structured and formal system design techniques that reduce system vulnerabilities.

## 2.    BOOT CAMP: TEACHING THE FUNDAMENTALS

Cyber tacticians and cyber strategists should both receive the same basic core education. We can refer to this as cyber boot camp in keeping with the military analogy. Cyber boot camp should address all of the core subject matter encountered in modern information systems, and do so in a bottom-up order. Cyber boot camp should also introduce the core principles of information assurance.

## 2.1    Subject Matter Ordering

The minimum set of core subject matter courses I suggest are: 1) Discrete Mathematics, 2) Computer Hardware/Architecture, 3) Programming, 4) Operating Systems, and 5) Algorithms. These choices will be elaborated upon below. By bottom-up order, I suggest introducing the courses in the order presented above while allowing that Programming and Operating Systems may be presented in any order due to their logical interdependency. Teaching these courses in the order suggested should reduce much of the confusion often experienced by novice students who find themselves working with an abstract logical concept (e.g., pointers) before they have seen the underlying physical level implementation (e.g., a 32 bit address indicating a physical memory location). Upon completion of this course of study, students should have a clear understanding of the problem-to-solution process in its entirety. That is; real-world problem statement → algorithm to solve it → program to implement the algorithm → operating

system that will load, schedule, and allocate resources for the program →
hardware that electrically executes the instruction-cycle and runs the loaded
program that solves the problem. And this entire process can be conceptually
described or modeled with the most basic layer, i.e., Discrete Mathematics.
Throughout the presentation of these five core courses, we also introduce the
students to the core principles of information assurance that are described in
section 2.3.

## 2.2    Subject Matter: Courses

Cyber warriors should begin with the solid conceptual understanding that
computers are ultimately nothing but physical structures that provide a
means for mathematics to be brought to corporeal life. For example,
numbers translate into; pixilated screen images, hard drive armature
displacements, pointer offsets, IP address masks, etc. Discrete Mathematics
provides the descriptive tools necessary to discuss, define, design, and
analyze the behavior of computer hardware and software. It is the logical
starting place for the study of information processing systems, and provides
the necessary tools for describing system design and functionality.

Next in the sequence is computer hardware and architectural design. At
this layer students learn about the binary switch (transistor) that is at the
"atomic level" of computer processors. They learn about logic gates that
realize Boolean relationships that make the controlled movement and
manipulation of digital data possible. They are introduced to combinational
circuits, storage devices, encoders, decoders, multiplexers and the other
basic digital building block components. The capstone instruction in this
course should consist of a demonstration of how a high level language code
fragment must be converted to machine code that is supported by the
underlying target hardware's instruction set; followed by a clock-cycle-by-
clock-cycle analysis of what happens as the hardware processes each fetched
instruction from memory.

We follow the hardware layer with a course in either Operating Systems
(OS) or a contemporary programming language. On the one hand, OSs are
programs, thus we would expect programming to precede the OS course. On
the other hand, application programs rely upon an appropriate OS
environment upon which to run. This classic "chicken or egg" relationship
should not be a major point of contention as it pertains to the quality of our
cyber warrior curriculum. As indicated above, I suggest that instruction in
programming follow directly behind the hardware course. This allows
students to immediately "use" their newly understood knowledge of
hardware by writing instructions that will ultimately run on it.

With the rudiments of hardware, and software design understood, we should next instruct our students in the features and functionalities of operating systems (OS). Students come to understand the central role that the OS plays in choreographing the interaction between special purpose application programs and the host platform (hardware) it is being run on. It is also at this point that our students should begin to see how a well designed OS can play a crucial role in a cyber defense strategy via such mechanisms as: file system support for access control, subject/object labeling, locking mechanisms, security domains, and segmentation.

We finish the coursework with our students being indoctrinated into the world of complex problem solving with a course in advanced algorithms. Students learn that size and speed matter in computer systems just as they do on the battlefield. They also obtain enhanced understanding of the complexity of the myriad protocols employed to bind systems in an inter-operative networked environment. Our cyber warriors are now mentally armed to scrutinize the complexities of such topics as: key space search efficiency, path finding, tree pruning, shortest path determination, signature matching, etc.

## 2.3      Core Principles of Information Assurance

Throughout boot camp we inculcate the students with the seminal concepts in information assurance methodology. Though many concepts, principles, models or theoretical postulations may legitimately vie for inclusion in this category, I suggest the following four as an absolute must: the Reference Monitor Concept, the Risk Management Equation, the Defense-in-Depth paradigm, and the Principle of Least Privilege. The Reference Monitor Concept is at the heart of virtually every technical mechanism (hardware or software) that has ever been devised for the purpose of enhancing the security of information. The Risk Management Equation provides a high level management framework by which cyber warriors can organize and allocate their defensive efforts. Defense-in-Depth dictates not putting all of one's security eggs in one basket, but instead employing multiple, sometimes overlapping, layers of complementary security solutions. The Principle of Least Privilege enjoins all who develop or configure security-relevant attributes of systems to allow no more access to information or computing resources than is absolutely necessary to accomplish each legitimate (i.e., non policy violating) task.

## 2.3.1　The Reference Monitor Concept

The Reference Monitor (RM) Concept, first introduced in the "Anderson Report" [1], provides the most basic and essential technical framework for any information assurance solution. I will make no attempt at a complete description here, but I will offer a synopsis that highlights the importance of this concept to the proper education of the cyber warrior.

The concept maintains that access control is at the heart of data protection. An access request is defined as a subject (person or process) attempting to read or modify an object (logical unit of data). The RM is the mechanism that arbitrates such requests, and does so based upon one or more identifiable or otherwise measurable attributes associated with each subject and object. The actual access control policy that a given RM implements is determined by the relationship of the subject and object attributes and the rules that the RM enforces over these relationships. A more thorough examination of this concept can be found in "The Reference Monitor Concept as a Unifying Principle in Computer Security Education" [2].

## 2.3.2　The Risk Management Equation

The Risk Management Equation gives the cyber warrior a big picture management perspective over the extensive problem domain of IA. The equation is derived from the generally accepted notion that safeguards applied to mitigate initial risk will reduce that risk to some degree, resulting in residual risk. This can be expressed relationally as: zero risk <= residual risk < initial risk, and from that the more general relationship is shown:

**Residual Risk = Risk - Safeguards**

Then, applying the notion put forth by Brinkley and Schell [3], we can substitute the product of threats and vulnerabilities (abbreviated "Vulns" below) for risk, to achieve the final risk management equation.

**Residual Risk = (Threats x Vulns) – Safeguards**

When explaining this equation, students must be informed that merely defining information as the subject of this equation yields insufficient granularity. Instead, students learn that there are ultimately four attributes of information that are potentially of interest to protect: confidentiality, integrity, authenticity, and availability. These attributes are so central to IA that we exhort our warriors to always be mindful of these four attributes when investigating any given IA question. We should refer to these attributes so often that the acronym CIAA becomes part of the cyber warrior's lexicon. Note that while some IA practitioners recommend adding non-repudiation to the list of protected information attributes, I recommend omitting it as it is essentially a byproduct of sufficiently implemented authenticity along with integrity of a one or more attendant timestamps.

Now that our students understand that the Risk Management Equation can be defined collectively over all information attributes, or more precisely, over any of the four specific information attributes, we can proceed to discussion of the equation's individual terms and their relationship.

The threat vulnerability product is somewhat intuitive, but deserves a brief explanation for our novice students. Threats indicate malicious intent to attack one or more of the four information attributes. Brinkley and Schell [3] describe six such threats: human error, abuse of privilege, direct probing, probing with malicious software, direct penetration, and subversion of security mechanism. Vulnerabilities indicate design flaws in the security mechanisms of a system. The product of threats and vulnerabilities is equivalent to risk. Expressing risk as the product of threats and vulnerabilities captures the logical conclusion that risk does not exist for systems that have no vulnerabilities, and conversely, that the lack of any threats poses no risk no matter how many vulnerabilities a system may have. Increasing or decreasing either of the two product terms yields a corresponding increase or decrease in risk. To mitigate risk we apply safeguards, which if effective, should reduce the risk by some amount leaving us with residual risk. Since it is generally considered infeasible to achieve a zero residual risk environment, our cyber warriors are taught that their broad mission is to manage the equations' three dependent variables (threats, vulnerabilities, and safeguards) in such a way as to reduce residual risk to an economically (or militarily) acceptable level. This understanding yields a simple big picture IA management matrix.

| | Threats | Vulnerabilities | Safeguards |
|---|---|---|---|
| Confidentiality | | | |
| Integrity | | | |
| Authenticity | | | |
| Availability | | | |

This matrix identifies twelve areas of concern to the cyber warrior. We can teach this as a mental model that the cyber warriors can use in their daily routine. For example, cyber warriors make the checking of new vulnerability alerts (e.g., CERT advisories) a part of their daily routine. As new vulnerabilities are discovered and announced, they are quick to assess which attribute(s) of information the vulnerability applies to, and what the resulting impact will be on the residual risk of information under their protection. Likewise, these cyber warriors will monitor developments among IA vendors for improved safeguards, ready to investigate and perhaps recommend for purchase any products that promise a reduced residual risk return on investment.

### 2.3.3    Defense-in-depth

This core principle dictates that practitioners of IA should not rely on any single device, technology, or security area (e.g., personnel security, physical security, etc.) when working to minimize system risks. Practitioners should instead seek to bolster system defenses by incorporating multiple devices, technologies, and security areas in a synergistic and mutually supportive manner. The new Department of Defense Directive on Information Assurance [4] emphasizes the importance of this core principle by addressing it in its very first paragraph:

1.1. Establishes policy and assigns responsibilities under reference (a) to achieve Department of Defense (DoD) information assurance (IA) through a defense-in-depth approach that integrates the capabilities of personnel, operations, and technology, and supports the evolution of network centric warfare.

The DoD IA Directive also provides a definition for this core principle:

E2.1.11. Defense-in-Depth. The DoD approach for establishing an adequate IA posture in a shared-risk environment that allows for shared mitigation through: the integration of people, technology, and operations; the layering of IA solutions within and among IT assets; and the selection of IA solutions based on their relative level of robustness.

We should emphasize the importance of defense-in-depth with case studies where a seemingly sufficient single layer defense proved insufficient. We should stress to the fledgling cyber warriors the extreme skill and resolve that some attackers will bring to bear in a concerted assault, and the value that a layered defense-in-depth approach provides in countering such attackers.

**2.3.4    Principle of Least Privilege**

The Principle of Least Privilege is the more all encompassing principle that borrows directly from the intelligence community's institutionalized "need to know" personnel security principle. The idea is that sensitive information should receive no more exposure to potential disclosure or modification risk than which is absolutely necessary for mission accomplishment. Cyber warriors should be taught to employ the least privilege principle to the maximum extent practical; including: user account privileges, listening ports on servers, ICMP response messages (e.g., no response to echo request or requests for subnet mask information), and firewall permit rules, to name a few instances. Least privilege is equally applicable in software design where, for example, we would expect the operating system to restrict a given module's instruction space (i.e., branching) to that module's assigned/allocated memory segment; or via the use of "friend" class relationships in object-oriented programming to restrict illicit or otherwise erroneous inter-object message passing (member function calls).

# 3.    TWO CATEGORIES OF CYBER WARRIORS

Though it is possible to educate all cyber warriors the same, the breadth of the IA problem domain coupled with economic realities suggest specialization should be more granular. I suggest that the two top-level categories be: cyber tactician, and cyber strategist. The military analogy is strong here but not exact. Cyber tacticians focus on reducing residual risk predominantly with the application of safeguards, while cyber strategists focus on reducing residual risk by reducing system vulnerabilities. The skill set for each of these risk mitigation solutions is sufficiently different and complex to warrant specialization.

## 3.1    Cyber Tacticians

Basically, cyber tacticians should be educated to protect the systems that are fielded now. Due to economic forces and improperly educated or motivated programmers, computer systems will be fielded with vulnerabilities that run the gamut of type and severity. Since history gives us no hint that threats are subsiding, the risk management equation tells us that these systems are at risk and that the application of safeguards is the only in-field means of risk mitigation.

We should educate the cyber tacticians to become experts in the utility, application and effectiveness of safeguards. An exhaustive list of safeguards is not attempted here, but the broad categories of safeguard tools and technology are.

First on this list is the important though mundane category of secure standard operating procedures and user training. This category covers such items as: password selection and usage, un-attended log-ons, potentially malicious e-mail attachments, the importance of anti-virus signature updates, social engineering attacks, portable PC security, etc.

Second is data backup technology and policy. The efficacy of this safeguard category is widely known, but the confusion encountered by the multitude of media (e.g., tape, disk, CD-R/RW, DVD+R/RW/RAM) and backup techniques (e.g., full, incremental, differential, RAID levels 1-5, compression, etc.) dissuade many well intentioned users from making it a part of their routine data security habits. Cyber tacticians should maintain mastery of this extremely important recovery safeguard technology, and ensure that a backup policy is created and implemented for all valuable data under their purview.

Cyber tacticians should be well versed in the "principle of least privilege" as it pertains to all aspects of information security. This principle should permeate every configurable software setting and every access control decision. Cyber tacticians should know that vendors often practice the "principle of most privilege" as their out-of-the-box default configurations, including generic root logins and passwords. A regular and concerted effort to ensure that a least privilege policy is enforced system-wide should be heavily stressed.

We should educate the cyber tactician to make regular checks for newly announced vulnerabilities, and be proactive in seeking and installing vendor patches as soon as they become available. The tactician should also be able to assess the added risk that any announced vulnerability presents, and be prepared to take other defensive measures until a patch is available. The measures might include a modified firewall rule-set, proxy isolation of the vulnerable service, or even removing the service from the network in extreme cases.

Cyber tacticians should learn the value of redundancy for systems, services and power. They should be taught to assess an agency's high value data or service assets and be able to propose, design, and implement a redundant/failover configuration that enhances data and service survivability.

We should teach our tacticians to do regular vulnerability assessments of their own systems, thereby taking a proactive role in identifying defensive weaknesses before an attacker does.

Cyber tacticians should be educated as experts in choosing and configuring firewalls and intrusion detection devices and software. They should learn the types of filtering (e.g., stateless, stateful, reflexive, proxy-level, etc.), how to understand and build filter rule-sets, and how to interpret packet level information (e.g., TCP flags, TTL values, sequence numbers, etc.). These skills enable the tactician to read and understand network traffic logs, identify anomalies, and react to such anomalies with updated filter rules.

Encryption technology is next on the agenda. Cyber tacticians should know the fundamentals and ramifications of such cryptological concepts as: block versus stream ciphers, chaining, key symmetry, key space, key management, hashing, and common protocols used to implement secure network transactions (e.g., ISAKMP, IKE, SSL, SSH, IPSec, PPTP, etc.). Cyber tacticians should be capable of configuring appropriately secure communication tunnels between any two protected systems.

We should teach tacticians the art and science of post-incident computer forensics so that they can sift through the digital residue left in the wake of an attack. They should learn how information is stored and how it may be deliberately hidden or subverted. They should learn the tools and techniques of logging, disk examination, evidence recovery, and legal preparation.

Finally, we should complete the cyber tactician's education with several practical cyber defense exercises. These exercises would entail the design, installation and configuration of a highly secured service network. This network would then be the target of attack by a team of cyber warrior graduates who would employ their knowledge and all available exploit tools to try and compromise the protected network. The earlier attacks can be escalatory in nature so that the defending students can more easily observe and learn. For example; the attackers would first engage exclusively in reconnaissance or discovery type activity (e.g., foot printing, port scanning, etc.), followed by surreptitious attacks intended to achieve unnoticed account access or observation of data, then attacks that modify data, and finally the more brutish denial of service category of attacks. Later exercises should be "free play" for the attackers while the cyber defenders must be on guard for anything. Attack/defend exercises such as this provide realistic scenarios that puts to practice the previously mentioned areas of cyber tactician education. The cyber tactician that has her network: 1) patched, 2) configured for least privilege, 3) scanned for vulnerabilities, 4) monitored by network and host-based intrusion detection systems, 5) properly isolated with proxies and/or firewalls, 6) backed up, 7) redundantly configured, and is herself capable of 8) forensic analysis; has vastly minimized her network's residual risk with sound defense-in-depth IA safeguards.

Students of IA at several of the Service Academies and the Naval Postgraduate School (NPS) have participated in two such large scale exercises since 2001 [5]. In these two exercises, the IA students at each school (Blue Teams) configured nearly identical service networks, and applied to these networks the security principles learned in their IA courses. A Red Team comprised of information warfare professionals from the NSA, Air Force, and Army, then attacked each network through a VPN tunnel for four consecutive days. Each Blue Team was graded based upon the resilience of its network to attack, and the accuracy of its daily situation reports which identified each day's attack activities, and the success or failure thereof. NPS was the high scoring Blue Team in both of these exercises. A third exercise is scheduled for April of 2003.

## 3.2    Cyber Strategists

As mentioned above, the focus of the cyber strategist is to reduce risk by reducing system vulnerabilities. By referring back to the risk management equation, we can see that a system with no vulnerabilities results in no risk, thereby negating the need for "after-the-fact" safeguards. The zero vulnerability system is the ideal pursued by cyber strategists, and achievement of this requires a much more theoretical skill set than that of the cyber tactician. So unlike the cyber tactician who builds a virtual protective wall around soft systems, the cyber strategist builds hard systems that need no wall.

Cyber strategists must receive intense education in programming, programming languages, processor functionality, technical policy, and the mathematical skills necessary to understand, code, and formally model the behavior of computer code. This is because the cyber strategist's primary function is to oversee system and network design, development, integration and processor (hardware) functionality to ensure that they correctly implement a given security policy.

Cyber strategists are taught that it is infeasible to attempt to design large general-purpose operating systems to be provably devoid of vulnerabilities due to the arduous and exacting nature of the formal methods methodology required. Instead, they are taught to consolidate all Reference Monitor implementing code into a relatively small software module that is referred to as the security kernel. Strategists must learn the tools and methods by which to ensure the kernel code adheres to three necessary attributes: complete, isolated, and verifiable. A complete kernel is one that is always invoked when any security sensitive access control decision is made. That is, it is proven that no artifice exists that might cause the kernel to miss or otherwise not arbitrate a subject to object access attempt. An isolated kernel is one that cannot be subverted by any means. For example; booting off of a virus-infected disk, downloading a Trojan horse, or even a human attacker with user level system privilege should not be able to modify the operation of the kernel. A verifiable kernel is one that is small enough to have had every line of code formally proven to be correct. Since the security kernel is essentially considered the first and last line of defense, no chances are taken with its design.

Cyber strategists should study existing systems that satisfy the requirements outlined above, and be presented with instructional security kernel fragments that test their ability to find flaws or prove correctness.

Finally, we should teach the cyber strategists the process and methodology of performing Certification and Accreditation (C&A) so that they may utilize their analysis skills to not only oversee the design and development of new systems, but be able to assess the threats and residual risks associated with existing information processing sites, and be able to make an informed yes/no accreditation decision.

# 4.    CONCLUSIONS

The need for purposefully educated IA professionals is real, urgent, and not expected to abate in any foreseeable technological future. All enterprises with a stake in the protection of information and information processing resources require a knowledgeable staff of cyber warriors to provide it. For maximum return on education investment, cyber warriors should receive extensive education in the following five courses: Discrete Mathematics, Computer Hardware/Architecture, Programming, Operating Systems, and Algorithms. They should receive inculcation in the core IA security principles; specifically, the Reference Monitor Concept, the Risk Management Equation, the Defense-in-depth concept, and the Principle of Least Privilege. Cyber warriors should then select to specialize as either cyber tacticians who focus on the application of safeguards to vulnerable systems, or cyber strategists who focus on the reduction of system vulnerabilities. Cyber tactician education will be steeped in: scanning, patching, least-privilege configuration, perimeter security with filtering, intrusion detection, backup/recovery technology, system/service redundancies, and forensics. Cyber tacticians should participate in several cyber defense exercises to put all of their skills to practical test. Cyber strategist education should be steeped in: formal methods analysis, programming, programming languages, and the tools of mathematical proofing. Cyber strategists should study the design and integration of secure systems and use this knowledge to design future secure systems. Cyber strategists should also be educated as Accreditors, with a thorough understanding of the complete Certification and Accreditation process and methodology.

## REFERENCES

1. Anderson, J. P., *Computer Security Technology Planning Study*. Technical Report ESD-TR-73-51, Air Force Electronic Systems Division, Hanscom AFB, Bedford, MA, 1972.
2. Irvine, C. E., The Reference Monitor Concept as a Unifying Principle in Computer Security Education. *In Proceedings of the IFIP TC11 WG 11.8 First World Conference on Information Security Education*, pp. 27-37, Kista, Sweden, June 1999.
3. Donald L. Brinkley and Roger R. Schell, What is There to Worry About? *An Introduction to the Computer Security Problem, In Information Security: An Integrated Collection of Essays*, IEEE Computer Society Press, Los Alamitos, CA USA, 1995
4. Assistant Secretary of Defense for Command, Control, Communications and Intelligence (ASD C3I), *Department of Defense Directive 8500.1, Information Assurance (IA),* October 2002.
5. Donald Welch, Daniel Ragsdale, Wayne Schepens, *Training for Information Assurance*. IEEE Computer, Volume 35, Number 4, pp. 30-37, April 2002

# SECURITY EDUCATION FOR TIMES OF NETWAR AND PEACE

Jaroslav Dockal
*Brno Military Academy, K303, Kounicova 65, 612 00 Brno, Czech Republic,*
*jdockal@vabo.cz*

Abstract: Security education has a lot of things in common all over world but there are some differences that distinguish richer countries from poorer ones and military education from civilian contexts. Although the Internet partially removes some of the handicap of restrictions on international personal contact, it does not fully eliminate it. In spite of this, certain aspects of security education in a small country would be interesting for participants of such an important conference as WISE 3/WECS. That is why this paper describes system of security education in the Czech Republic and discusses specific procedures used at Brno Military Academy for training in operative decision-making. The paper supplement comprises two examples of solutions to critical situations by means of Aprisma's SPECTRUM Security Manager (SSM).

Key words: Security education, military education, subject, lifelong learning, hacker, warrior for netwar, decision-making, scenario, SSM

## 1. SECURITY EDUCATION IN THE CZECH REPUBLIC

This paper will start with a description of the situation of security education in the Czech Republic, particularly at the universities in four major cities: Prague, Brno, Plzen and Ostrava. This analysis should give us an answer for the question: Does the Czech military need a special education origram in the area of security or is it better to recruite graduates of civilian universities?

## 1.1    Prague

The oldest Czech University is Charles University in Prague, founded in 1348. It is paradoxical that often ancient universities have a special liking for a modern education. At Charles University, security education is offered by the College of Mathematics and Physics in the subject *Protection of Information* and in the seminars: *Mathematical Principles of Information Activity*, *Security of Information Systems in Practice* and *Implementations of Cryptography*. The seminar form of classes eliminates the rigorousness of classic teaching. The high quality of teachers creates a solid base for cryptography classes. It is possible to follow a program of study, oriented on cryptography, with a statement this field of study written on graduates' diplomas. There are inexhaustible opportunities to use Microsoft software for security education; Charles University devotes the subject such as *Programming for Windows* to exploring these problems. For teaching of practical problems external experts are used; the University exploits the reality of the fact that the majority of important security companies in the country are located in Prague.

The College of Electrical Engineering of the Czech Technical University provides security education in the subjects *Mathematical Fundamentals of Cryptography* (Department of Mathematics), *Data Protection in Informatics* (Department of Telecommunications Engineering) and *Applied Cryptography* (Department of Computer Science). We can also encounter security problems in lectures of other subjects, especially in *Computer Architecture*, *Computer Networks*, *Distributed Systems* and *Operating systems*. In other words, security problems are integrated into the syllabi of other subjects, so that students understand that not only are functionality and reliability important for modern technical system design, but security is also. An example of this approach is the development of encryption hardware with the involvement of the students of the college. This college does not prepare separate branch of study, because the small number of specialists educated at Charles University is sufficient for the requirements of such a small country as the Czech Republic is.

The third important university in Prague is University of Economics. The students at this university are not oriented to the technical problems of security, so much as they are to the areas of security principles of Internet and laws and ethics, mainly in the area of trade. In 2002 the compulsory subject *Information Technology Security* was started.

## 1.2    Brno

The second most important center of college education in the Czech Republic is Brno, with six universities. Brno is the largest city in Moravia, but more will be said about this university later in the paper. In addition to Brno Military Academy there are only two other universities in Brno that are important in the area of security. These universities are smaller than the ones in Prague and have fewer branches of study, but security education is not at a lower level.

The College of Informatics at Masaryk University Brno offers a whole spectrum of subjects in the area of information security. The subject *Data Protection and Information Privacy* is offered as an introductory course to new students of the Bachelors program. Those students who are interested in a deeper knowledge of cryptography problems have rich choice of lectures and seminars, such as *Security of Information Technologies, Coding Cryptography and Cryptographic Protocols, Applied Cryptography, Authentication and Access Control* and *Essentials of Law for Informatics* and *Information Law.* If students choose to study in the field of Information Technology Security then the majority from these subjects are compulsory and this field of study is stated on the diploma of graduates. Students who study for a master's degree in Computer Systems, Information Systems and Theoretical Informatics attend lecture from *Information Security.* Security applications are integrated into the subjects *System Design and Administration, Computer Networks* and others.

Those students, who are interested in a deeper study of the mathematical basics of cryptography, have an opportunity to do it within the bounds of other subjects offered by the College of Science at Masaryk University Brno. The focus of this study is on the complex conception of security problems in the sphere of Information Technology, mathematics and law, and some subjects are taught wholly or partially in English.

The College of Information Technology at the Brno University of Technology is a new college created with a goal to avoid the rigidity of already existing colleges. It incorporates security problems into classes on two comprehensive subjects: *Information Systems Security* and *Cryptography.* These subjects are electives for those students who are interested in studying these problems.

Both in Prague and Brno, study is based on the credit system. Students can collect credits, which can be used for degrees at both universities. Both in Prague and Brno the schools cooperate in preparing combined programs of study. The two other university centers in Plzen and Ostrava, in which the lectures on security are given on a large scale only at one school in town, do not offer combined programs of study.

## 1.3      Plzen/Ostrava

The town of Plzen is known around the world mainly for its beer (Pilsner). This town also has a modern University of West Bohemia, whose former students have established a group of very enterprising security firms, which also operate in the United States. The aim of the Technical University is to use results of these firms in their research. Security models and fundamentals of cryptography are lectured there in the special subjects *Computer Security*, and security applications in subjects *Operating Systems*, *Distributed Systems* and *Computer Networks*.

The Faculty of Electrical Engineering and Informatics at Ostrava Technical University concentrates security education into one elective subject: *Security in Information Technology*, which is offered to students of the Information Engineering branch.

We can come to the particular conclusion that different goals of these universities results in different structure and contents of the subjects, but there is also another trend: convergence of universities and advanced technical study.

In conclusion the answer to the question: Does the Czech military need a special education origram in the area of security or is it better to recruit graduates of civilian universities? Is as follows. Civilian universities in the Czech Republic have a wide range of graduates with different levels and styles of education. This is very useful in the civilian sector and their future employers will welcome a rich selection of graduates' profiles. Theoretical base is in this system good (in the opinion of author of paper) but practical application of this knowledge is very diverse. The Army educational system on the other hand is unified including security methodology, software and hardware. Enlistment of the civilian graduates means not only having to teach them military duties, but also to integrate their knowledge in security and training to that used in military security equipment. However, instead of trying to integrate civilian graduates after graduation we proceed in another way. This way will be described in the next chapter.

## 2.      APPROACH TO SECURITY EDUCATION AT BRNO MILITARY ACADEMY

This part of this article describes specific approaches to security education at Brno Military Academy and involves two scenarios of a critical situation used in the education process there.

## 2.1 Security Education

After the fall of the Iron Curtain and admission of the Czech Republic to NATO, our military educational system underwent a continuous series of reforms. On the one hand, this volatility is an obstacle to conceptual effort, but on the other hand it is exploited for promotion of new ideas in education.

After the fall of the Iron Curtain and admission to NATO, our military educational system underwent a continuous series of reforms. On the one hand, this volatility is an obstacle to conceptual effort, but on the other hand it is exploited for promotion of new ideas in education.

Security is at present lectured at two colleges, one with a command orientation and another with a technical orientation. At the Command College information security is one of many types of security. At the technical college information security is an important component in the study of Special Communication Systems and Special Information Systems. Classes in Special Communications Systems are concentrated on encryption of data transmissions.

Our students complete a three-year bachelor study program and after some practice as an administrator a two years master's study program. They receive elementary fundamentals of information security in the course *Fundamentals of Informatics*. During the bachelor program, students also have to pass an exam for the special subject *Computer Security*, which involves security models and standards, methodology of designing secure systems, e-commerce and theoretical foundations of cryptography (algorithms and protocols, verification and validation). Other security aspects are taught in other subjects: *Operating Systems* (Unix and Windows security), *Computer Programming* (malicious code, writing secure code, antiviral software), *Computer Networks* (attack and defence, routers ACLs, firewalls, VPNs including BGP/MPLS VPNs, IDS, PKI), *Database Systems* (access control, polyinstantiation), *Computer Hardware* (tamper resistance, emission security, biometric techniques and smart cards), *Web Application Programming* (Java, PHP and ASP security) and *Internet and Intranet Technology* (XML security).

The traditional education system in our country is based on practice "from theoretical fundamentals to applied disciplines". The completion of the bachelor's program is a culmination of this practice. After one or more years of practice in military units as a system, network, web, database or security administrator students have enough basic practical experiences and it is the right moment to give them the opportunity to improve their knowledge through a masters program.

In the masters program we lay great emphasis on merging and integrating partial knowledge and proficiencies; graduates must be capable resolving demanding complex problems. We also put stress on creative solutions to problems. This approach is almost impossible without adequate hardware and software that are capable of reflecting the methods and principles being taught.

Study at our Military Academy does not finish at the graduation ceremony. We are preparing "lifelong learning" in the area of information technology and security will be a part of it. One branch will be for commanders and staff officers and a second for specialists in IT. We prepare security experts at these three levels:

- Strategic level: they should be able to design complex security projects, in particular risk analysis, to create and revise security policy (revise whether it corresponds to the actual requirements), to plan and organize the defense of important military information systems and present qualified requests for the purchase of the new technology and devices.
- Supervisor level: they should be able to revise configuration, organize penetration tests as well as training and practice information units, build surrogate targets and solve new security problems as experts.
- Operation level: they should be able to configure firewalls, routers, intruder detection systems, servers and other devices and in real time analyse logs coming from them.

Operation level is the subject of bachelor's level of study, supervisor level is the subject of master study and strategic level is the subject of the postgraduate study. More theoretical security problems are solved as PhD projects and we plan to increase the number of PhD candidates in the future. "Lifelong learning" is a very demanding matter because it is difficult to establish the start, end or sequence of courses. In addition, IT is continually progressing and courses must be revised.

We cooperate very intensely with companies in the Czech Republic that are active in the area of IT security. For example, we cooperate with the company ICZ (http://www.i.cz/en/) in the area of researching side-channel attacks, with AEC (http://www.aec.cz/us/default.asp) in area of building PKI, we use the source code of the Kernun firewall company Trusted Network Solutions in laboratories and we cooperate with GiTy (http://www.gity.cz/index_e.php) in preparing class scenarios. We use Cisco security bundle, Symantec and NAI software and Hewlett-Packard management software for our laboratories. Once every two years we organize NATO registered PfP/PWP (Partnership for Peace / Partnership Work Programme) International Scientific Conference "Security and Protection of Information", see *http://www.vabo.cz/spi/ defaulten.htm*.

## 2.2    Use of Scenarios in Security Education

The application of information security is the similar to the art of war. Analogously, as in military affairs, in information war success depends on the technique used, systematic training and leadership to fight. Modern war is still based more and more on using highly sophisticated weaponry, often connected into networks. But how can students get experience in this area? We have some experiences of hacker attacks but is this enough to win a network war?

The main motivation of hackers is usually exhibition. For example, Czech hackers placed a figure of a famous Czech shirker soldier Svejk (similar to Beetle Baily) on the web portal of the General Staff of Czech Army. This kind of joking, typical for hacker, will not satisfy a terrorist. The aim of a terrorist attack is total destruction. While a hacker's aim is to stay anonymous, a terrorist is capable of self-sacrifice. A hacker's activity is often a game or question of prestige for him, but it's a matter of life and death for a terrorist.

Several years ago it was common to look on network security in terms of binary logic ("realm of evil" and "realm of good"), in our military sphere if was usual to differentiate only between unsatisfied networks and satisfied networks behind reliable firewall. Possible intrusion was in this interpretation any incident that we had to analyze and take appropriate measures against. In contrast the modern approach to network security is proactive, based on predicting and neutralizastioning attacks. But this approach requires more trained and quick-witted staff at the operation level.

Typical system administration is a question day-to-day maintenance, but defence against terrorist attack requires procedures and techniques used in crisis management. Anti-terrorist defence is based on making an operational choice of variants, which have been prepared for and well rehearsed in advance. For this paper two of our simplest scenarios which are used for training Military Academy bachelor students were chosen. In these scenarios Aprisma's SSM (http://www.aprisma.com/products/security.shtml, ref. 1. and 2.) was used and they were prepared in cooperation with David C. Hajicek from the Company GiTy. The goal of these and other scenarios is to prepare our students for both typical as well as unusual situations and so make them able to solve problems in conditions where they have to deal with a flood of information and lack of time.

## 2.3    Scenario 1:

### 2.3.1    Assignment

On a computer network a user has been discovered who seems dangerous. He executes undesirable operations that might cause a security incident. Your task is to find this user, specify his IP address and the location of his computer, if it allowed by system security policy. Specify which operation this user has executed and assess the degree of danger of the incident and decide what procedure to fellow next.

### 2.3.2    Possible Method of Solution

Start SPECTRUM Security Manager (SSM) see graph of events and identification of security incident. Specify IP address of attacking computer. By the color of the alarm decide if the attacker's activities will be audited or if his activities will be denied. Look at the schema of the computer network and specify the location of his computer.

Try to use some of standard Intruder Detection Systems (IDS). Although all information is full and correct, you will not receive enough information to solve this problem, as shown in Figure 1.

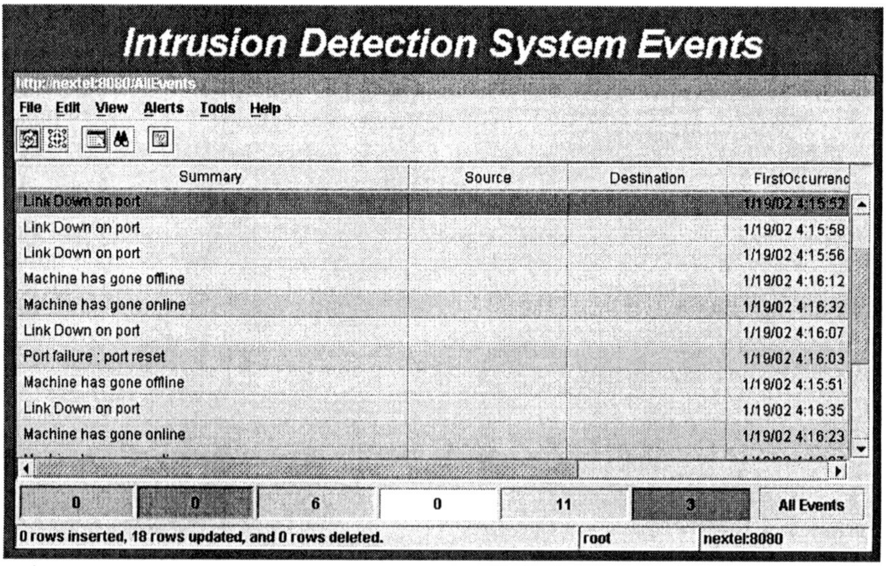

*Figure 1.* Solution of the problem by IDS

Also use the event graph of SSM. In Figure 2 we see a server (red circle on the top of screen), three IDS and security incident: The user with IP address 141.190.129.113 (blue circle in the below left-hand corner of the screen) frequently and within a short period of time tries to access the group of stations. He is maybe looking for some shared files or testing which vulnerable services are running (for example telnet or ftp). In this example we will start with audit because risk value, which was identified by the color of circle, is low.

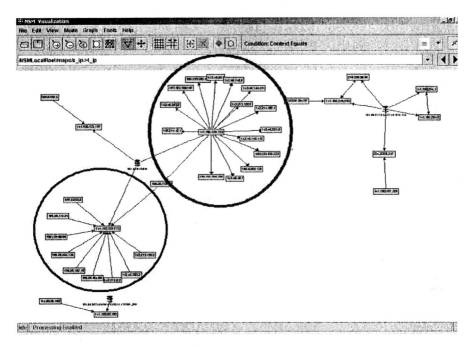

*Figure 2.* Dynamic event graph in SSM

We will make a final decision about what action to take depending on the attacker's previous activity. We use the tool „Reporting Tool" (Figure 3) to identify if our user had other security incidents during his most recent activity.

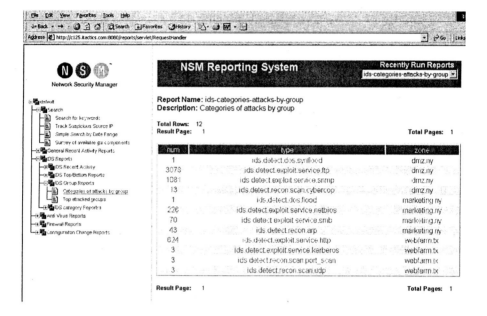

*Figure 3.* Reporting Tool

The Reporting Tool gives us information about security events in the last five minutes. In Figure 3 you can see that in the last 5 minutes no security incident was reported from network 141.190.129.0. This would mean that this attack was accidental and without serious influence on security.

## 2.4    Scenario 2

### 2.4.1    Assignment

Your task is to inspect the functionality of all security devices in a computer network. Specify security incidents in a given time period and suggest what measures should be taken.

### 2.4.2    Possible Method of Solution

Open dialog window of SSM (Figure 4), use "Reporting Tool" (Figure 3), generate a report for the last 5 minutes, specify security problems, and suggest countermeasures depending on security policy of the system.

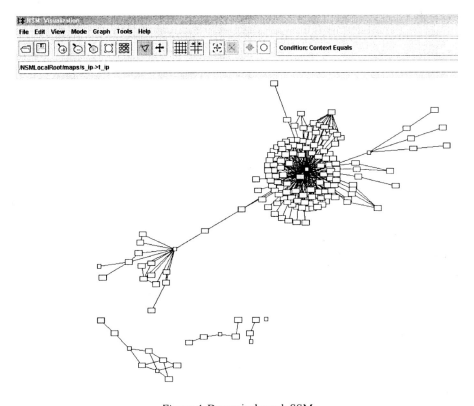

*Figure 4.* Dynamical graph SSM

Use filters and choose output (database, IDS, script execution).

Success of using this type of scenarios is dependent on the student having a good preliminary knowledge of the security tools (such as SSM) and experience with this type of job.

## 3. CONCLUSION

Military security education is in many respects the same as in the civilian sector, but in some respects unique. We cooperate with our civilian universities and learn from their approach to education, but we do not copy them. Apart from other things this paper has described, we use specific procedures for training in operative decision-making based on scenarios to solve exceptional situations.

## REFERENCES

1. User's Manual of iNotary. infocount Brno 2002.
2. Internal Documentation of iNotary. GiTy Brno 2002.

# IMPROVING SECURITY AWARENESS THROUGH COMPUTER-BASED TRAINING

Steven M. Furnell, Alastair G. Warren, and Paul S. Dowland
*info@network-research-group.org, Network Research Group, University of Plymouth, Drake Circus, Plymouth, PL4 8AA, UK, Tel: 44 1752-233521 Fax: 44 1752-233520*

**Abstract**:     Security awareness is a critical issue for all organisations that depend upon information technology. However, significant survey evidence suggests that the issue is often given inadequate attention in modern organisations, leading to problems through security incidents. This paper considers various means that can be used to instil greater awareness, and argues that the most effective method is likely to be via training and awareness programmes. Unfortunately, organisational constraints often preclude the pursuit of such programmes (either in-house or externally) in a traditional manner, and a substitute is needed that can be accessed on-demand, in a self-paced manner. Thus the use of computer-based training is proposed, and the paper discusses the ongoing realisation of an appropriate training tool. The prototype provides an environment that permits the user to explore security problem scenarios, and then select appropriate countermeasures to address the issues identified. It is considered that such an approach would be suitable for promoting day-to-day security awareness for general users, and conducting more specific training for staff with greater security responsibilities.

**Key words**:     Security awareness, Security training, Computer-based training.

## 1.     INTRODUCTION

Although today's society and modern organisations have wholeheartedly adopted the personal computer and the Internet, readily accepting the benefits of such technological advances, the issue of information security has not been so widely adopted, considered, or understood. A major contributing factor here is that many IT users are simply unaware of security in any significant sense. Although they may use baseline technologies such as passwords and anti-virus software, this is often the extent of their awareness of the issue (and it does not even guarantee that these will be used properly). If systems and data are to be appropriately protected, then users at all levels need to be aware of the issues that they are likely to face, as well as what to do about them.

The need for awareness is recognised as one of the main principles of the recently revised Organization for Economic Cooperation and Development (OECD) security guidelines for information systems and networks, which are entitled 'Towards a Culture of Security'. The guidelines state that all participants "should be aware of the need for security of information systems and networks and what they can do to enhance security" (OECD 2002).

This paper examines the problem of security awareness, and presents details of a prototype software tool that is being developed as a means of providing an interactive security training environment for IT users. The next section presents some statistics to illustrate the current lack of security training and awareness in modern businesses. This is followed by a top-level consideration of the means by which security awareness can be promoted in an organisational setting. This leads into the specific issue of security awareness and training programmes, and the discussion of the computer-based tool that the authors' research group is developing.

## 2.     THE PROBLEM OF SECURITY AWARENESS

Although security is often recognised at the business level, it is often found that organisations do not have a full understanding of what they should be doing or how to go about it. The availability and provision of comprehensive security guidelines is not the problem, as appropriate materials can be obtained from a number of sources. The problem is instead one of ensuring that security awareness occurs both in the first instance and as an ongoing factor of an organisation's operation. Indeed, survey results from recent years have consistently conveyed the impression that security awareness and training programmes are distinctly lacking, as illustrated by the following notable examples:

- The KPMG Information Security Survey back in 1998 indicated that only 31% of respondent organisations had security education and training programmes for their staff (KPMG 1998).
- The results from the Department of Trade & Industry survey in 2002 indicated that only 20% of organisations utilised ongoing training (DTI 2002).

- The 2001 IT Abuse survey from the UK Audit Commission found that only about one third (34%) of organisations have any form of computer security awareness training for their staff (Audit Commission 2001).
- Ernst & Young's Global Information Security Survey 2002 found that less than half of the 459 companies questioned had security training and awareness programmes in place (Ernst & Young 2002).

Having said this, organisations have apparently realised that a lack of security training can usher in significant problems:

- Results published by the UK's National Computing Centre back in 2000 cited the problem of inadequate end user awareness as the most significant obstacle to information security, with over 55% of respondents identifying it as a reason (placing it ahead of issues such as budgetary constraints and technical complexity) (NCC 2000).
- The need for training is underlined by a further statistic from the UK Department of Trade & Industry's 2002 security breaches survey, in which 16% of the 1,000 organisations questioned claimed that a lack of training on security issues had been the reason for the most significant incident in the previous 12 months (DTI 2002).
- The aforementioned Ernst & Young survey found that 66% of respondents cited employee awareness as a barrier to achieving effective security (Ernst & Young 2002).

These findings are supported by results from Information Security Magazine's 5th annual industry survey, published in 2002, which suggested that once an installation gets above 100 machines, user awareness becomes the issue with the most impact upon security (Briney and Prince 2002). The findings, which were based upon responses from 215 qualified respondents (filtered from a total of 2,196 responses returned in total), suggested that while the biggest concern in small organisations was preventing intrusions (cited by 44% of associated respondents), all of the other categories cited user awareness of security (scoring 31% in medium organisations, 29% in large, and 42% in very large installations). As such, even though the organisation would seem to have taken a positive step by having specific, named people to look after its security, the practical effect could even be counterproductive because the attention given to it in the environment as a whole is reduced.

With these points in mind, it is relevant to consider how organisations might set about instilling security awareness amongst their employees.

## 3.  METHODS OF INSTILLING SECURITY AWARENESS

Organisations must do something to ensure that their employees are aware of their obligations. Without this, people will in all likelihood assume that they have not got any obligations, and presume that IT security is the exclusive preserve of the IT department. So what are they doing about it? The graph in Figure 1 depicts some further results from the Department of Trade & Industry's 2002 survey, and indicates how the respondent organisations claimed to make their employees aware of their obligations in terms of security.

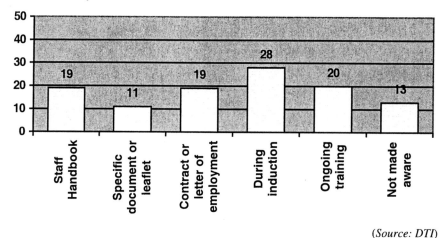

*(Source: DTI)*

Figure 1: How organisations make staff aware of security obligations

If one were to take a hard-line view of the issue, then the result ought to have been 100% positive response in the first five cases, and 0% in the last one. Certainly the methods listed are not mutually exclusive, and it cannot really be argued that doing one of them removes the need to do one of the others. It can consequently be seen that many of the DTI's respondents were doing far less than they could have been. The list below considers some of the things that an organisation could do in order to promote security and boost awareness, including the approaches indicated in Figure 1 and some additional ideas.

– *Corporate endorsement* - All security guidelines and recommendations agree that the lead ought to come from the top, and that an organisation must be seen to consider security as a priority. This is essential in any case, but it will not necessarily get anyone to actually do anything. As such this should almost be regarded as a given, but organisations should not expect it to solve the problem.

- *Clauses in employment contracts* - This again represents a starting point, but the downside is that it will often only raise awareness for a specific instant – after reading (and even signing) their contract, many employees will not remember what it actually said. Evidence for this point is provided by results from Finch et al (2003), who conducted a survey amongst 50 employees from a variety of organisations, and found that 20% of respondents could not remember that they had signed a security policy. Even if they do remember that they are meant to maintain security and have responsibilities in the area, most contracts will not give employees enough detail about *what* they are expected to do.
- *Threatening disciplinary action* - This is basically the use of the stick rather than the carrot, in order to punish users who are found not to be following security appropriately. The approach is not appropriate to all cases (e.g. minor accidental oversights that are exploited), and will only work if the cause of the incident can actually be traced back to an individual. At the end of the day, the ability to invoke disciplinary procedures needs to be there (so that it can at least act as another incentive to staff to take things seriously), but if they need to be used then it still indicates that the employees involved have not taken security on board in the first place.
- *Demonstration* - The idea here is to show employees some practical evidence of what can happen if they neglect security. The most likely way to get them to take notice and buy into the idea is to show them something that is directly to do with them (as it makes it more difficult for them to ignore). However, such overt demonstrations must be handled with care. A typical example of what can go wrong is provided by Cole (2001), who describes an approach that he and colleagues attempted in order to get the users in a large company to choose better passwords (some 95% of them were breakable). In spite of having circulated a password policy in the hope of yielding improvements, and emailing individual users whose passwords were still weak in order to reinforce the point, Cole discovered that more than three quarters of the passwords could still be cracked. He consequently opted for a more public illustration to the problem users – by writing their cracked passwords down on paper and sticking them to their monitors. However, the main effect of this was to make the users irate and abusive, as they felt that approach was too heavy-handed.

Another problem with demonstration is that some things are more difficult to show than others. For example, providing a realistic illustration of what can happen if someone's system gets infected by a virus can carry a significant risk. It could be faked by a system administrator, for example by identifying someone in the organisation who was not using anti-virus software properly, and then temporarily removing all their files and claiming that a virus destroyed them (the files could, of course, be reinstated later). However, although this would be very likely to get people's attention (especially that of the victim), it would be unlikely to endear the administrator to the user community once word got around that it was done deliberately just to prove a point.

- *Written materials, in handbooks and leaflets* - The combination of these approaches in the DTI results (accounting for 30% overall) illustrates that providing staff with material to read is a fairly common way of trying to promote the security message. Unfortunately, creating genuine awareness is not just about putting the information down on paper and assuming that people will read it. It is possible to waste a lot of money on glossy pamphlets that will simply get binned, or put in a drawer and forgotten about. In fact, even if it gets read, there is no guarantee that it will also be understood. Having said this, pamphlets, handbooks, or online reference materials *can* have a valuable part to play in helping users who have experienced a security incident and then require guidance on what to do. The online approach is probably the best, in the sense that the materials will always be there for users to get hold of, plus of course the organisation can save on the associated production costs. All that needs to happen then is for users to actually remember that there are reference materials available when something goes wrong.

- *Awareness programmes* - If people cannot be relied upon to read the things that they are given, then awareness programmes can be one of the best ways to draw their attention to the issues that are relevant to them, and ensure that the information has reached them. As the graph in Figure 1 suggests, this can be undertaken as part of an induction programme and as an ongoing activity. The DTI results show that the former is a somewhat more popular option, but it should not really be a choice – organisations ought to pursue both approaches. A one-off security awareness session is unlikely to be sufficient, because after a while many people will forget what they were told. Another factor, particularly in larger organisations, is that the content presented in a general staff induction programme is likely to have been generalised so that it is applicable to staff at all levels, rather than presenting information specific to individual roles. Employees also need to be aware of security issues that relate to their job, and the applications that they are likely to use. As such, if the business is big enough to warrant it, and budgets can be made to support them, initiatives such as the following ought to be given consideration:

- the inclusion of security-related issues as an integral part of any ongoing organisational training strategy, as well as consideration of mechanisms to promote awareness during day-to-day activities.
- the facility for staff with key responsibilities, such as IT administrators, to attend specialist security training courses. Established training companies, such as Learning Tree International and SANS, typically offer a range of such courses, targeting both general principles (e.g. Learning Tree offers a course entitled "Introduction to System and Network Security", which covers fundamental theory aspects) and more specific technical topics (e.g. "Deploying Intrusion Detection Systems: Hands-On" and "Implementing Web Security: Hands-On", both of which focus practical skills) (Learning Tree 2002).

In many cases, however, it may not be as easy as simply sending staff away on a course if they require training. If nothing else, the cost of doing so could be a significant obstacle – which could again be especially the case for small companies. For example, each of the Learning Tree International courses mentioned above had a standard registration fee of £1,545 per person (for a four day course) – to which participants would typically have to add the costs of travel to the Learning Tree training centre (in London or Edinburgh) and accommodation for the duration of their stay. In my case, for example, living hundreds of miles away from either location, this could easily add another £250 to the overall cost. In the context of the professional training market, these prices are not unusual and the intention here is not to suggest that they are unreasonably high, but such a cost might nonetheless represent a practical barrier to many small businesses (whose staff might of course derive just as much practical benefit as people from larger organisations).

Taking the issue of small businesses further, it is relevant to observe that they will typically face a number of operational constraints that limit their potential to address security. Such constraints will include:
- not having in-house staff with specific security expertise;
- lacking the financial resources to buy in specialist consultancy or provide training for their staff;
- lacking understanding of, or being dismissive of, the risks;
- inability or unwillingness to focus upon security due to other business priorities.

Although there are certainly numerous resources available to provide security advice and guidance without incurring significant expense (e.g. books, web sites, newsgroups and email lists), these offer little facility to test ones understanding in practice. It is desirable to be able to perform such testing before being faced with the task of applying security for real within an organisation. An environment is, therefore, required in which mistakes can be made and learnt from without incurring expense and leaving the system at risk. In response to this requirement, a security training tool is proposed that enables the investigation of available security countermeasures, combined with scenario-based testing and reinforcement. Such a tool represents an example of Computer Based Training (CBT) (Lee and Mamone, 1995).

CBT allows student centred, self-paced learning, enabling users to educate themselves in a time and place that suits them. For employers, CBT can offer benefits with regard to savings in staff being away from the office, reduced traveling costs and times, and saving on expensive accommodation costs that may be incurred for off site courses that require an overnight stay, as well as reduced costs for the training itself.

The use of CBT has certain advantages over conventional methods, especially in company training scenarios. Firstly, CBT is proven to be cost-effective. After the initial set-up costs, what remains is a full-time training facility, available at all times within the organisation. It is also highly appropriate for staff trainees, as they are able to have control of their training and adjust it to their own personal needs. In this way, it is possible for employees to acquire the desired training in specific skills, at their own pace, without having to take time off from work. As such, the training process can be tremendously flexible and personalised. It can also be used to train a large number of employees around the clock. It can run with minimal resource requirements, as there is much less need for a centralised training facility, and different companies or organisations can distribute the same CBT program among their employees.

## 4.　A PROTOTYPE TOOL FOR SECURITY AWARENESS AND TRAINING

The authors have already produced one variant of a prototype training tool, which is described in Furnell et al (2002). The aim of the system is to provide an interactive and user-friendly approach to enhance security awareness and understanding. The training process is based upon a selection of interactive scenario descriptions, in which security countermeasures must be applied in order to solve one or more inherent security issues. The possible solutions must be selected from an accompanying database of security countermeasures, which users can reference in order to obtain explanations of the available security options and approaches. The information held about countermeasures encompasses the type of security issue that they aim to address, along with information about their strength of protection, and the associated impact that their selection might have upon the organisation and its staff (e.g. financial cost, ease of use, disruption to existing practices etc.). Part of the exercise with the tool, when applying the countermeasures to the problem scenarios, is for users to consider these associated impacts (recognising that providing the highest possible level of security is rarely the only consideration).

The original prototype was an exploration-based system, with users selecting particular parts of an onscreen image (i.e. hotspot areas) in order to obtain a textual description that constituted of part of an overall scenario. From this description, the user would need to determine whether any security problem existed, and if so, recommend appropriate countermeasures. The system would then evaluate the overall security strategy that has been suggested, identifying any remaining weak areas or problems that might be introduced as a result. Further work has since been conducted to refine the concept and devise further problem scenarios that can be used as the basis for training activities. The ongoing work has sought to embrace a more multimedia-oriented approach, which will involve the playback of video segments in which problem scenarios will be depicted. This approach will reduce the requirement for users to read and absorb textual information, which many would consider tiresome after a while, increasing the likelihood of them losing interest in the training program. The presentation of information in an audio-visual format is also considered to be a closer approximation of what the task of identifying problems would be like in a real-life scenario (i.e. staff could not expect to be have the relevant information provided to them in a pre-written textual format – they would often be expected to derive it themselves from what they see and hear). Figure 2 shows the resulting remodeled version of the user interface, showing the different characters that participate in the scenario dialogues. In this revised context, selecting the hotspot areas of the image need no longer yield a simple textual description and can instead invoke the playback of a video clip in a Media Player window.

The idea is that users will view the clips and listen to the dialogues in an attempt to identify whether they contain any security-relevant issues. Some clips will contain information about one issue of relevance, whereas others will make reference to multiple security issues. Conversely, some clips may contain nothing of security-relevance at all (on the basis that if the user knows that everything they see will always contain at least one problem, then the exercise becomes somewhat artificial when compared to a real-world scenario in which they would have to use their own judgment in order to extract the relevant details from a lot of other information that is effectively redundant).

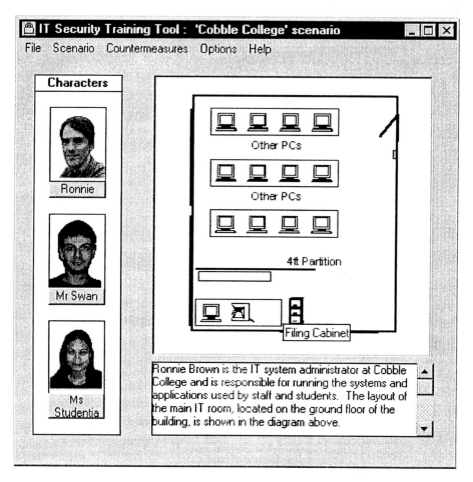

Figure 2: Screenshot from the revised prototype

Selecting the individual characters yields background descriptions about each of them (which can again be in the form of video clips), enabling the user to determine the character's role in the problem scenario that is being explored. Another potential feature (that has not been realised in the problem scenarios currently specified) would be to allow the user to interview the characters, by asking them some preset questions. As with the dialogues from the hotspot areas, some of these questions would yield useful information in the context of the problem scenario, whereas others would simply provide irrelevant details that the user would have to use their judgement in order to filter out and disregard.

The other significant change in the ongoing work relates to the security controls and countermeasures from which the user would select their recommended solutions to any problems identified. The countermeasures in the original project were based upon those from the pan-European ISHTAR (Implementing Secure Healthcare Telematics Applications in Europe) project, which had developed a controls database as one of the deliverables of its research (Davey et al. 2001). Members of the project team had been involved in ISHTAR, and as such the database was a pre-existing resource to underpin an initial prototype of the training tool concept. However, for the ongoing work, it was considered that a more well-known, and widely applicable, foundation could be provided by basing the problem scenarios upon issues addressed by guidelines contained in the BS7799 (ISO/IEC 17799) standard (British Standards Institution 2000).

As a result, twelve sets of problem scenario dialogues have been developed, based around different sections from BS7799 (Warren 2002). Some of these are single problem scenarios, in which the dialogue is focused around a single issue raised in BS7799, and for which the user would consequently be expected to home in on a particular control area in order to recommend the appropriate solution. Other dialogues present multiple problem scenarios, in which the characters mention several security issues, potentially spanning a number of different areas from BS7799. These scenarios would consequently be aimed at more experienced users, wishing to test their wider knowledge of security.

Figure 3 presents an example of some of the dialogue from one of the single problem scenarios, which in this case is set in the context of a doctor's surgery and involves two characters, Dr Grays and her receptionist Judith (remembering, of course, that in the tool itself this would be acted out in a video clip rather than presented textually). In this example, the point that users would be expected to identify is that measures should be taken when disposing of equipment and media to ensure that information is not compromised. Smaller and less technically proficient companies may dispose of their PCs and media without realising the need to ensure that all data has been securely removed. The point relates to section 7.2.6 of BS7799 (Secure disposal or re-use of equipment), which states that machines that contain sensitive information should be physically destroyed or securely overwritten instead of standard delete functions.

| | |
|---|---|
| **DR. GRAYS** | "Morning Judith, how are you finding the new PCs?" |
| **JUDITH** | "Great, I really like these thin screens, rather than the bulky old monitors." |
| **DR. GRAYS** | "Any problems with the software? Are they working OK with the patient records system?" |
| **JUDITH** | "I have not noticed any problems." |
| **DR. GRAYS** | "Where are the old PCs?" |

| JUDITH | "I have stored them in the cupboard until they are collected." |
| DR. GRAYS | "What about any old data that may be on them?" |
| JUDITH | "All gone, I went to the DOS prompt and ran delete star dot star, should be OK." |
| DR. GRAYS | "Good, good. Lets open the doors and see some patients." |

Figure 3: Extract from a single problem scenario dialogue

Multiple problem scenarios may incorporate a number of dialogues, each of which may convey a number of problem issues. An example of a dialogue from one such scenario is presented in Figure 4, and is set within ToolEng Limited, a small (and fictitious) engineering and tool making company. The dialogue takes place during a tea break, and various staff members have congregated in an office that had previously been used by an IT contractor called Brian, who has left the company unexpectedly. A replacement contractor, John, has just started to work for the company. The characters Joe and Jason are fitters who work for ToolEng, while Dennis is the design manager and Janine is an accountant.

| JOE | "John, as Brian's office used to be the rest room, we use it for our breaks, and Brian used to let us surf the web if we wanted during our breaks, is that OK?" |
| JOHN | "I guess so." |
| JOE | "Hey Jason, I know that you are keen to have a look at the web – you know my login and password, don't you. Here is an old floppy you can copy that stuff onto . . . And Jason, do not forget to put your timesheet in the tray outside before lunchtime." |
| JOHN | "So what happens to the timesheets?" |
| JASON | "Oh, Janine collects them, and works them out at home, which is quite good, as once you are logged on you can see every machine on the network, I think" |
| DENNIS | "Joe, have you got a minute? I want to check a design with you." |
| JOE | "Yes, no problem, I'll be there in a minute." |

Figure 4: Extract from a multiple problem scenario dialogue

In contrast to the single problem scenario in Figure 3, there is quite a lot going on here, and it is unlikely that a novice would pick up all of the issues.

For the record, the problems, and the related BS7799 controls, are as follows:

- It seems that there is no control of network access within ToolEng. Control 9.4 (Network access control) states that internal and external networked services should be controlled.
- It would appear, from Jason's use of a floppy disk on Brian's PC, that there are no controls against malicious software. This is contrary to the recommendation of control 8.3.1 (Controls against malicious software).
- Should staff be eating their food in Brian's office near to his PC? Control 7.2.1 (Equipment siting and protection) states that organisations should consider their policy towards eating, drinking and smoking within close proximity to information processing facilities.
- It is not good practice for Joe to allow Jason to login using his name, or divulge his password to Jason. This contravenes control 9.3.1 (Password use).
- It would seem that each user has access to every other machine once logged on. Control 9.4.2 (Enforced Path) suggests that this should not be the case.

Following the selection of the chosen countermeasures, the user is able to have their solution rated by the system against the optimum solution originally conceived by the author of the problem scenario. Through this they will be able to determine the appropriateness of their recommendations. If an incorrect assessment is made (e.g. the user believes there to be no problem when in fact there is one, or vice versa), then their overall score is affected accordingly, before the system automatically guides them in the correct direction. If desired, the system could present additional information, such as a narrative description, to support the countermeasure solutions and ensure that the user understands the rationale behind the scenario author's approach. In some cases, there may be more than one valid solution, via different combinations of countermeasures that achieve the same objectives. The system would be able to assess this by comparing the attributes of the countermeasures chosen (e.g. protection category, disruption level, financial cost, user friendliness) with the attributes of those selected by the scenario author. These attributes are maintained in the countermeasure database along with the basic title and description details.

When it is fully developed, it is considered that the tool will have a number of potential applications. For example, it may be used:

- as an educational awareness mechanism for general staff, which can be accessed on a day-to-day basis. They can attempt to solve the problem scenarios, and then use the database materials to explain points that they did not understand.

- as a training tool for staff with specific security responsibilities within the organisation. They can use the database materials to acquire the background knowledge, and then test their understanding using the problem scenarios.
- as a means for more established security personnel to refresh their knowledge and test alternative solutions to the problems.

Development work is continuing at the time of writing, in the guise of masters and PhD level research projects at the authors' institution.

## 5.     CONCLUSIONS

Security awareness is an essential requirement for any organisation utilising IT systems. However, as the evidence presented in this paper has illustrated, the issue is often given insufficient attention, and is consequently considered to be a significant factor in the ongoing occurrence of security incidents. However, achieving an appropriate level of awareness can be difficult, particularly in smaller organisations with limited funds and in-house expertise that can be drawn upon.

Computer-based training can be used to help inform and educate employees at all levels, exposing them to different security threats, and allowing them to experiment with different countermeasure solutions, within the confines of a simulated environment. It also allows awareness to be cultivated in a more active and engaging manner than simply requiring staff to read pamphlets and other reference material. The principal advantage of the proposed tool will thus be that it enables staff to become familiar with the types of security issue that they may encounter, as well as the countermeasures available, the situations in which they are appropriate, and any constraints that they may impose.

The development of the prototype system, and associated methods, will continue within the authors' research group. Once the software itself has been more fully developed, the intention is to use it as the basis for practical trials, and ultimately determine whether it has a measurable effect upon security awareness within a reference environment.

# REFERENCES

Audit Commission. 2001. yourbusiness@risk - An update on IT Abuse 2001. Audit Commission Publications. September 2001.

British Standards Institution. 2000. Information technology. Code of practice for information security management. BS ISO/IEC 17799:2000. 15 February 2001. ISBN 0 580 36958 7.

Cole, E. 2001. Hackers Beware. New Riders. ISBN 0735710090. pp290-291.

Davey, J, Furnell, S. and Gaunt, N. 2001. "The ISHTAR Security Guidelines", in Implementing Secure Healthcare Telematics Applications in Europe. The ISHTAR Consortium (Eds). Technology and Informatics 66, IOS Press: pp167-180.

DTI. 2002. Information Security Breaches Survey 2002. Department of Trade & Industry, April 2002. URN 02/318.

Ernst & Young. 2002. Global Information Security Survey 2002. Technology and Security Risk Services, Ernst & Young LLP.

Finch, J.W, Furnell, S.M, and Dowland, P.S. 2003. "Assessing IT Security Culture: System Administrator and End-User Perspectives", to appear in Proceedings of ISOneWorld 2003 conference and convention, Las Vegas, Nevada, USA, April 23-25, 2003.

Furnell, S.M., Gennatou, M. and Dowland, P.S. 2002. "A prototype tool for information security awareness and training", Logistics Information Management, vol. 15, no. 5/6: 352-357.

KPMG. 1998. Information Security Survey 1998. KPMG Information Risk Management, London, UK.

Learning Tree. 2002. Hands-On Training for IT Professionals and Managers, Learning Tree International catalogue, September 2002 – February 2003.

Lee, W.W. and Mamone, R.A. 1995. The Computer Based Training Handbook: Assessment, Design, Development, Evaluation. Englewood Cliffs, NJ: Educational Technology Publications.

NCC. 2000. The Business Information Security Survey 2000 (BISS 2000). National Computing Centre, Manchester, UK.

OECD. 2002. OECD Guidelines for the Security of Information Systems and Networks: Towards a Culture of Security. Organisation for Economic Co-operation and Development.

Warren, A. 2002. An Educational Tool for Information Security. MSc Thesis. University of Plymouth, Plymouth, UK.

# IDENTIFICATION AND INTEGRATION OF INFORMATION SECURITY TOPICS
*Applied in a Web Application Programming Course*

Justin Brown
*KAP*

**Abstract**: This paper discusses a unit of university study running within an Internet Computing degree aimed at second year undergraduate students. The unit is preparing for an update of the teaching material. Recent rises in security holes in web technologies has prompted the unit author to identify the critical security concepts that should be taught to web application developers and how such material can be integrated into a 12 week teaching schedule. Current course materials are examined, as are issues in teaching both theoretical and practical concepts of information security within a lecture/workshop arrangement.

**Key words**: Internet, World Wide Web, Application Development, Programming, Security, Hacking, Hackers, Vulnerability, Education, University

## 1. INTRODUCTION

Though the hype and financial impetus behind the World Wide Web have slowed in the wake of the 'dot com' collapse of 2000/2001, the requirement for tertiary level courses addressing this medium has not. Since 2000, as a part of an Internet Computing course, the School of Computer and Information Science at Edith Cowan University in Perth, Western Australia, has been running a unit of study called Interactive Web Development. This unit deals with both client and server side technologies, and requires students to exit the semester with identifiable skills in web application development.

Given the ever-changing nature of the Web and the technologies that drive it, this unit is obviously under constant revision, and though operating within its niche of web programming, the tools and technologies have changed markedly in only three years. As the unit is preparing for yet another curriculum update for semester 2, 2003, the issues of theory, and subsequent application of that theory must be addressed. Recently, while a list of new technologies for inclusion in the unit was being drawn up, it became apparent that there has been a more fundamental change in the environmental aspect of the web phenomenon, rather than a technical one. This change comes in the form of constant security threats against the web-servers that drive the web and the database-driven applications that provide the content. In an article discussing how to build more secure web sites, Microsoft authors Bollefer, et al, (2002, paragraph 1) highlight some of the most common vulnerabilities, including "cross-site scripting attacks, dynamic Web page source code disclosure, Web page defacement, posting malicious SQL commands to the databases, and theft of credit card data from the databases used". These are just some of the techniques used to exploit weaknesses in server configuration and application code, to say nothing of virus attacks and attempts to gain administrative access to server systems.

Considered the 'whipping boy' of lax web security in their server systems, Microsoft is now taking great pains to illustrate that their systems can be highly secure, but that "Every project is unique and will require work on the part of both the developers and the administrators to figure out the potential vectors of attack and how to guard against them" (Bollefer, et al, 2002, last paragraph). In the last quarter of 2002, the eWeek online technology news site ran a competition whereby Microsoft Corp and Oracle Corp were challenged to re-engineer a web application of eWeek's choice so as to make it as secure as possible using any platform and application development system the two companies preferred. Though the results were very detailed, as were descriptions of the test systems used, the interesting conclusion from this challenge revealed that;

> "Indeed, it's the little things that really matter in security: Each of the two successful cross-site scripting attacks was made possible by a single mistake on a single line of code in the test application" (Dyck, 2002. paragraph 5).

So, even though the servers and operating systems had been rigorously secured, a single mistake in coding practice allowed for an entry point into the system. It is exactly these types of security oversights that will, and must be, highlighted in the revamp of the Interactive Web Development unit. This author has been running web-servers in various fashions on various platforms since 1996, and until the year 2000/2001 experienced little or no problems with security or hacking. From early 2001, particularly with the coming of trojan attacks against insecure web-servers, the propensity for being 'hacked' in one way or another via the web has grown markedly, with

Trembly (2002, pg 18) stating that "security vulnerabilities have risen by 124 percent over the past two years".

Over the previous 18 months we have gone from a situation where regular updating of security patches to web-servers was an adequate defense to now requiring highly configured firewall solutions working in conjunction with patches to offer a modicum of protection. Though different operating systems and web server applications vary in their levels of vulnerability, the fact remains that web application developers must now realize that they need to be aware of these vulnerabilities, as they may be the person building and maintaining such servers.

## 2. UNIT STRUCTURE AND CONTENT

Currently, the unit provides instruction in interface design and implementation using client side technologies, such as HTML/XHTML/JavaScript/Macromedia Flash while focusing in the second half the semester on server-side technologies, such as scripting languages, web servers and databases. In the lecture program students are introduced to the evolution of the Internet and its' core technologies, such as HTML and web browsers. As the lectures progress the content becomes far more technical and covers server side coding solutions. Emphasis is given to how the scripting code works in conjunction with the web server in order to produce dynamically generated web pages. In the associated workshop or lab program, students actually develop client side code, then server side code in order to complete their assessments.

To date, there is a single lecture covering technologies involved in secure transactions, looking mainly at Secure Sockets Layer and Digital Certificates. Issues of public/private key management and basic concepts of cryptography are covered as well. Issues of web server security and possible vulnerabilities have not been covered in the program to date, aside from anecdotally, as the ability to perform 'hands on' web server construction in the workshop has not been available. The computers used by students in this unit are common across all courses within the School of Computer and Information Science, thus return to a default state upon rebooting. Along with the shared computing issue, the problem of security arises in that students in a web-connected workshop environment are not going to be given administrative rights over the machines, rights which are required to perform almost any change to the web servers' settings.

A solution of sorts has presented itself in the form of students downloading server software to their computers at home and running the systems there, with most students being able to dedicate a machine to that task alone. The current server-side scripting languages taught within the unit are PHP and Perl, both of which currently run across all the major operating systems and with almost any web server. Students can download Apache server and PHP/Perl and run them on almost any version of Microsoft Windows, or use them built into most distributions of Linux. The fact that students now have access to powerful server and development tools within their own homes creates the opportunity to attack web development security issues in a practical, hands-on way. It should be stated that the requirement for running web development systems at home is not forced upon students, but has come as a result of students doing this independently, so that they can work at home and on campus. Additionally, it is a requirement of all students within the Internet Computing and/or Computer Science degree to have a modern personal computer available to them at home.

In fact, this focus on issues of web security is more a necessity than an opportunity as many students install the servers/scripting environments with their default settings, which usually means the web server starts during the system boot process. If the students or other members of their household connect to the Internet using this machine and are unaware of the security risks, they may inadvertently bring an attack upon themselves, perhaps without even realizing such.

## 3.    POSITIONING OF WEB SECURITY CONTENT

As the teaching structure for Interactive Web Development currently stands, a 12-week teaching semester consists of 12 weeks worth of lectures, and associated workshops. In the first half of the semester, the lecture topics do not necessarily correlate to a direct workshop on that topic, though the lecture/workshop correlation increases markedly in the second part of semester. The structure as it currently stands looks like that shown in table 1.

Table 1: Current unit teaching structure

| Week | Lecture | Workshop |
|------|---------|----------|
| 1 | Unit Introduction: Background to Internet and World Wide Web 1 | Cascading Style Sheets and Macromedia Flash |
| 2 | Internet and World Wide Web 2 | JavaScript Cookies and Flash |
| 3 | HCI and Dynamic HTML | Calculations and arrays in Java Script |
| 4 | Linking browsers to applications | HTML Forms |
| 5 | Linking browsers to Perl | CGI (Perl) interface |
| 6 | Manipulating browser data with Perl | Processing HTML with the Perl CGI module |
| 7 | Persistent data and Perl | Using the Perl DBI Module for RDBMS access |
| 8 | PHP – Linking browsers | Sessions and authentication with Perl CGI |
| 9 | Manipulating browser data with PHP | PHP basics |
| 10 | PHP persistent data and sessions | PHP and MySQL |
| 11 | Web Dev and Project Management | Marinating persistent data using PHP |
| 12 | Secure Online Transactions | Assignment work in labs |

As the structure in Table 1 illustrates, the only current concession to security is that given in the lecture of week 12, with no associated workshop activity. When the new structure is created, the lectures dealing with web server security will be associated with a practical workshop where the student is tasked with performing some kind of security setup or auditing on their server. It is expected that the workshop element for the various security lectures will involve working on-campus in the computer labs, locating service and security patches for the web-server that the student runs at home, while also looking for known security weaknesses in their server/operating system environment. Students will take this material home and apply the updates/fixes as required, evidence of which can be brought to class in the form of screen shots or config files.

Making room in the current schedule for the new security content will be a challenge in itself, as those who have taught such units can testify. Most students would like to have nothing but 12 weeks of hands-on coding so that they can fully immerse themselves in the technology and become readily conversant in the development tools. However, as a more 'big-picture' approach is needed at a tertiary level, a balance must be identified between pure practical experience and an understanding of why the systems actually work as they do. Without a broader understanding of the underlying technology and the possibilities it presents, students are left with powerful construction tools but no idea what to build with them.

With this in mind, the unit as it currently stands needs to be re-developed in a way that allows for significant experience with the development tools, but also a non trivial interaction with web server setup, focusing on security weaknesses inherent in the way such systems operate. The order in which this is done is also going to be crucial, as issues of server security must be addressed early in the semester, as students tend to start working with the code at home well ahead of its place in the teaching structure. Logically, the workings of the web server need to be discussed followed by or, in conjunction with, the protocols that operate through the server and across the web. These protocols will be introduced early in the program and will replace the more introductory materials dealing with the history of the Internet.

Working on this basis, a decision has been made to drop three of the workshops pertaining to Perl, leaving only one such workshop as a demonstration of the language. The workshops will be 6 through 8. The lectures associated with these workshops will also be removed in favour of the new content, leaving a three week slice of the teaching schedule in which to deal with the topics of web server and application security. This gap will lead to the need for a program reshuffle, but before this reshuffle can take place, the key topics in web development security will need to be identified.

## 4.     IDENTIFICATION OF KEY TOPICS

As has been touched on earlier, there are many aspects to web application / web server environments, and many vulnerabilities that can be exploited by those with the technical known how. The aims of the current unit re-write, and the focus of this paper, is to find the crucial topics in security that need to be covered in the context of the web developer. As there is a limited amount of teaching space in the lecture and workshop program to cover what is a very broad subject area, the issues in security need to be those that fit into two main criteria:

1. Does the topic fall into the category of required knowledge, one that is essential for the day-to-day development of web applications and management of web server systems?
2. Can the topic be taught in a theoretical and practical situation to the level where students actually synthesize and understand the concepts and the underlying logic?

Given these criteria and the amount of room available in the teaching program, it would seem prudent to concentrate on three broad areas within the subject area, those being;

1. Know the most common attack methods
2. Secure systems and code against these common attacks
3. Audit system regularly and know system environment thoroughly

## 4.1    Know the Most Common Attack Methods

Currently, one of the most relentless and annoying security concerns with the web is automated IP address and port scanning by hackers with varying motives. According to UK Security Online (2002, paragraphs 7-11) these motivations can vary from industrial spying, thrill-seekers, self-styled gurus seeking respect or out and out criminals.

These scans take the form of networking software automatically ICMP pinging known address ranges, like those used by ISPs, attempting to gain access to the machine at the other end of the connection should a return ping be sent. If the machine receiving the ping is running a web server, identified using a port scan on port 80, the scanning software at the other end can interrogate that server to identify the server application type. Once compromised, a server can be used to serve as a remote hacking platform to other networks, as entry point into a network or as a victim of defacement. Defacement attacks are usually perpetrated by the hacker gaining administrative rights to the server, then uploading new source files in place of the existing, legitimate content, or by altering the content of database driven websites. Jim Wagner gives some indication of the frequency of these attacks when he states:

> "In the past two weeks, Zone-H.org proprietor Roberto Preatoni said defacements have increased to more than 500 separate attacks a day and more than 1,500 over weekends. A year ago, he said, his site got around 30 to 50 defacement notices a day from hackers." (2002, paragraph 2).

## 4.2    Secure Systems and Code Against These Common Attacks

There are numerous methods available for limiting the ability of hackers to enter a system and perform some of the violations discussed above. As this paper is focusing on issues of security that can be taught and comprehended in a class of developers rather than security experts, the type of solutions to these problems will be considered the most 'obvious' and 'minimum level'.

Below are the technologies and methodologies identified as being critical to a minimum level of defense for web applications and that also offer the possibility for integration into the learning process.

### 4.2.1    Firewalls and Protocalls

To begin with, students should be given a thorough understanding of TCP/IP and the most common protocols that sit on top of it, particularly http, FTP and SMTP. Along with a discussion of what these protocols do, a detailed description of the role of ports is also required. The reason for the focus on the protocols and their related ports is to create a foundation for instruction on the role of firewalls, software and hardware applications that can monitor protocols and ports in order to detect possible attacks. Most students understand that a firewall is a device that protects networks connected to the Internet, but little beyond this piece of common knowledge. By understanding the role of protocols in the functioning of the World Wide Web, students are better capable of understanding how firewalls actually work and their critical role in protecting web servers from unwanted attack. It is hoped that students will be able to identify the protocols that are necessary for the application they are developing and those that are not.

### 4.2.2    Web Server Setups

Anecdotal evidence from previous semesters teaching web technologies indicate that most students install pre-packaged server solutions, especially IIS under Windows 2000/XP Pro. Usually students select the basic install option, which usually includes an active SMTP and FTP server. As students do not understand what these systems do, they just leave them alone, running, with no tweaking of security settings. Given that a student develops an understanding of the role of such protocols, they can decide whether to keep them or not. Should they leave them enabled, they should then learn how to configure firewall applications in order to minimize chances of attack against them. In her example based on protecting university network systems, Olsen (2000, p. A40) eloquently states that

> "Universities should shut down services that they don't need to run. Network operating servers come, by default, with most services turned on when you install them. People need to configure these machines when they install them. If they absolutely don't need to have a particular service

running, they should shut it down, because if a service is running, it can be exploited."

A less is best approach will be instilled into students, along the lines of Olsen's beliefs, whereby http on port 80 is advised as the only open port to the outside world, given that this is the way web content is accessed and transferred. If FTP is essential for updates for web masters and web admins, it should be accessible only through the same domain (as is common with most ISPs), or through a secure connection, such as a VPN. If a web application requires the use of a mailing system using SMTP, that SMTP server should be limited to specific tasks, like only sending email within a set domain or disallowing bulk emails without verified addresses.

### 4.2.3    DMZs

Though it may be argued to be outside the purview of the budding web developer, the concept of network topology and domain numbering should be introduced for the purposes of discussing Demilitarized Zones (DMZs). A DMZ is used to separate a web server from the rest of the company/agency network, so that if the server is compromised, an access point to the rest of the network is not available. Once students understand that TCP/IP is a routable protocol, and that a method of translation is required when moving from one domain numbering system to another, they should be able to see the value of creating a special zone for servers only. At this point, the concept of using a hardware-based firewall/router can be introduced, so that students can see how a DMZ can be created between the outside world and the internal intranet without having to physically isolate the web server from the local network.

### 4.2.4    Patches

As well as running defense tools such as hardware/software firewalls, students need to be instructed on the importance of keeping both their operating systems and their web server system constantly up-to-date with security/application patches. When a security problem arises with a web server application, or an operating system or a server-side scripting tool, a patch is usually released by the software house that created the application. This patch will fix the current problem, and no further patches will be required until the next hole is found within the development environment. Students should become ingrained with the habit of checking for any type of update that is available for any of the tools they use in web development, particularly for web server and scripting applications. Checking for, downloading and installing product updates is considered a tedious use of valuable time, and while once is it was considered more optional than necessary, it is now essential for the protection of any web-facing server system. Students will be instructed that a firewall is one piece of the puzzle for managing server security, but that to cover only one flank in a battle is a perilous way of working indeed. The importance of patching is reiterated by Goldsborough (2001, p 51) when he puts forward "Whatever security approach you take, keep current by installing patches and upgrades as they become available".

### 4.2.5    Code

The concepts above have dealt more with the systems that reside outside the direct experience of the web developer, as they are software/hardware settings rather than code. However, students must be taught that even though their firewall may be running nicely, and their systems are fully patched, the imperative is upon them to write scripting code that does not open a door for entry into the system. As http is always going to be necessary in order to serve web pages, it is most likely to offer the first point of attack. Students need to identify possible security weak spots in their applications and propose methods of reducing such weakness. Use of scripts which have admin level usernames and passwords is to be highlighted as poor practice, as is the use of file-upload scripts that have full read-write-execute access to the file system. Scripts that do not perform adequate data validation upon submission may cause buffer overrun errors, crash the server or even open a gateway into the server. Code that accesses SMTP applications needs to be configured in such a way that hackers cannot exploit the system to their own gain. For example, a page that executes calls to an SMTP system could be configured to only be accessible from the current ip address of the server machine, receiving the required instructions from another page that the user sees, thus putting a small extra barrier between system and potential attacker.

## 4.3    Audit Systems Regularly and Know System Environment Thoroughly

Perhaps the most overlooked and unexciting of all the protection methods for web development systems is the monitoring of logfiles, from web server activity logs to operating system logs. Most web servers will detail where each 'hit' has originated from (IP address), what time the hit was made and on what port and using what protocol. This information can be very informative, as it can indicate trends that may be someone trying to attack the system. A classic (which this author has experienced *ad nauseum*) is a remote host attempting to log onto port 21 utilizing FTP, sending various combinations of usernames and passwords, hoping to find one with administrative rights. If the IP address of this individual is constant, indicating they are using a machine with a fixed IP, that IP number can be placed in an inclusion list of banned addresses, placed in either the web server if it supports this function, or even better, within the firewall's blocking list.

Unexpected changes to files are another indication that perhaps someone has illicitly gained access to the system and are altering content. Most file systems will allow a file listing that can be sorted according to when a file was last changed. If such a change occurs without the web developer actually making the change, investigation is warranted. This is obviously extremely difficult for large websites, especially where the content is dynamically generated from database systems. In order to make this problem more approachable, it may be decided that only certain files need to be closely monitored, such as server-side include type files which contain large number of code functions or configuration information for database connections. Though these files are not supposed to be accessible from sources external to the server, the assumption must be made that they are vulnerable. Software tools can be used to monitor changes to files, similar to the way most virus checkers work, though once again, maintaining change-tracking for large numbers of files on a big site is a time consuming, usually expensive undertaking.

By having a complete understanding of the current setup and structure of the web development environment, such as the operating system, web server, scripting tools, databases, user accounts and number of files/total size of site, the web developer is in a far better position to see where undesirable changes have occurred. If a suspected hack has occurred the web develop should dive straight into the log files for firewall/os/web server, at which point the breach should become apparent. Students should learn that these basic methods of problem monitoring and identification should be as much a part of web application development as writing code. Of course, choosing what to monitor requires some thought, as Posey (2002, paragraph 9) justifiably states

"It's better to just audit administrative actions such as account creations, password changes, and the assignment of permissions. Whatever you choose to audit, be sure to review the audit logs daily or even more often if you detect any suspicious activity."

# 5.     INTEGRATING THE SELECTED
#        TECHNOLOGIES INTO TEACHING PRACTICE

Having identified the topics considered to be required for teaching in the context of web development, the problem of integrating these technologies into the current course setup still remains. As well as the theoretical underpinnings, students need to be exposed, where possible, to practical examples of this security theory.

In order to achieve this, the unit, which as stated earlier is in need of an update, is to be re-structured quite rigorously, with some content being placed in a different part of the program, while other content, such as bulk of the Perl materials, will be discarded from the current teaching curriculum. As well as introducing the much needed materials on web development security, the course will be changing the base markup language to XHTML, whilst also introducing some materials on database design and analysis, focusing on practical database structures for web applications.

Some content regarding security and database systems will be introduced here, further enhancing the point of thinking about security in all aspects of web design. Table 2 on the following page contains the new-look structure for the unit.

Table 2: Proposed new unit teaching schedule inclusive of security content

| Week | Lecture | Workshop |
|---|---|---|
| 1 | Unit Introduction: Background to Internet and World Wide Web | Introduction to XHTML |
| 2 | Markup languages (HTML and XHTML) and the Document Object Model | XHTML and Cascading Style Sheets |
| 3 | Project Management for Web development | JavaScript Cookies |
| 4 | Internet / Web protocols and addressing systems | HTML Forms |
| 5 | Dynamic content generation – the role of server-side scripting languages | Processing XHTML with the Perl CGI module |
| 6 | Web servers and web server configuration: practice, problems and vulnerabilities | Examination and customization of web server configuration files |
| 7 | Enhancing web application security – the role of firewalls, smart coding and system auditing | Identification of security loopholes and possible solutions |
| 8 | Database design considerations – efficiency – reliability – scalability and security | Application of database design principles |
| 9 | PHP – Linking browsers | PHP basics |
| 10 | Manipulating browser data with PHP | PHP and MySQL |
| 11 | PHP persistent data and sessions | Marinating persistent data using PHP |
| 12 | Efficient coding practice and code reusability | Assignment work in labs |

Instead of concentrating the security topics into the newly created three week gap left by the Perl materials, the topics of security will be spread across 5 weeks, being integrated into the theoretical lecture materials, starting with week four. The proposed changed content and teaching methods are as follows;

**Week:**

1. LECTURE: Will cover the primary protocols used throughout the web and how they work in conjunction with the IP numbering system that allows for information transfer. Concepts such as different domain numbering systems and protocol port numbers will be addressed – WORKSHOP: Will be a normal markup language tutorial with no direct relation to the lecture material

2. LECTURE: Introductory information regarding the concepts of client-side vs server-side technology will be presented, along with in-depth discussion as to why server-side systems offer such functionality, yet such security risks – WORKSHOP: Will be a Perl code dynamically generating an XHTML document exercise, with a focus on how the server-side code produces client-side code for transport via the protocols discussed in week 4. The lab will end with a discussion of the role of the CGI-BIN directory with security.

3. LECTURE: The general functions of common web servers will be discussed, with in-depth analysis of all the key system settings, such as FTP (where the server supports it), SMTP, Sessions, Cookies, Timeouts, Root folder locations, Domain restrictions, Scripting Language support, Log file creation, File Upload capabilities and permissible user accounts – WORKSHOPS: Students will be shown a sample config file from a publicly available web server such as Apache. Students will be asked to change the config file to meet various criteria, such as restricting CGI-BIN to a specific folder, or allowing script-only processing, not executables. Student's work will be examined in class, and where possible, tested on a 'sacrificial' server.

4. LECTURE: This lecture will be a 'nuts and bolts' approach, illustrating to students many of the known attack methods and how they can be defended against. Examples from the press will be highlighted, as will the importance of firewalls, server and OS patching and writing secure code – WORKSHOP: Students will be given a number of scenarios, such as Company A wishes you to develop an application that performs this task using this database back-end and this development environment. Students will need to draw up a plan on the key technologies they will need to develop the application, what protocols they will need, what the level of security will need to be and how to best deliver that level of security.

5. LECTURE: Though this lecture will be based mainly on the concepts of database design and normalization, some mention will be made on issues in database security, such as encryption, access permissions, connections to and possible attack points depending upon the database in question – WORKSHOP: Students will actually begin designing the database system for their assignments, though the ability for them to create security accounts is yet to be seen.

The above breakdown of the new teaching materials should indicate that the course has gone from almost no reference to issues of security, say for a single lecture at the end of semester, through to a relatively thorough and hopefully practical exploration of key security topics.

## 6.     CONCLUSION

Most educators, especially educators of technology related content, wish they could fit into a schedule all the key points that they, from personal and professional experience, feel are essential to the student's understanding of the content. For the most part this is not possible, though it is perhaps possible to break these points down into a list of the absolutely necessary. It is hoped that this paper has shed some light on the thinking involved when re-engineering a tertiary web development unit to focus more heavily on the topic of security, for it is a topic that now falls into the category of 'essential'. In the same way that building architects must consider issues of safety and security, so must the developer of web applications, whatever their level of involvement in the process.

# REFERENCES

1. Bollefer, T, Chander, G, Johansson, J, Kass, M & Olson, E. (2002). Building and Configuring More Secure Web Sites. *Microsoft Corporation*. Retrieved December 29, 2002, from http://msdn.microsoft.com/library/en-us/dnnetsec/html/openhack.asp
2. Dyck, T. (2002). OpenHack Wrap. *eWeek*. Retrieved January 5, 2003, from http://www.eweek.com/article2/0,3959,743411,00.asp
3. Goldsborough, R. (2001 Nov 22). Protecting yourself against cyberterrorism. *Black Issues in Higher Education*, 18(20), p52. Retrieved December 19, 2002, from ProQuest Database.
4. Olsen, F. (2000). Logging in with...Thomas J. Talleur. *The Chronicle of Higher Education*, 46(45), p A40. Retrieved December 27, 2002, from ProQuest Database.
5. Posey, B. (2002, August 29). Basic strategies for securing Internet Information Server, CNETAsia. Retrieved December 30, 2002, from http://asia.cnet.com/itmanager/trends/0,39006409,39073946-2,00.htm
6. Trembly, A. (2002 Dec 16). Security woes go from bad to worse. *National Underwriter*, 106(50), p18-21. Retrieved January 4, 2003, from ProQuest Database
7. UK Security Online. (2002). Hacker Threat Analysed. *UK Security Online*. Retrieved January 3, 2003, from http://www.uksecurityonline.com/threat/hackers.php
8. Wagner, J. (2002 Oct 22). Web Vandalism on the Rise. *Internetnews.com*. Retrieved December 15, 2002, from http://www.Internetnews.com/dev-news/article.php/1485601

# A DEDICATED UNDERGRADUATE TRACK IN COMPUTER SECURITY EDUCATION

S. Azadegan, M. Lavine, M. O'Leary, A. Wijesinha, and M. Zimand
*Towson University*

Abstract: To better prepare our graduates to face the challenges in computer and information security, in Fall 2002, the authors launched an undergraduate track in computer security for the computer science majors at Towson University. This paper describes the motivation for this track and discusses its structure and requirements.

Keywords: Undergraduate Computer Security Education, Cryptography, Network Security, Operating Systems Security, Application Software Security, Computer Security Case Studies

## 1. INTRODUCTION

Our computer security track addresses the need for skilled personnel in the Computer Security field and provides an opportunity for our undergraduate students to be educated in this field. What is unique about this track is that at the time of its development, summer 2001, it was the only undergraduate track in computer security in the State of Maryland. Also, based on a preliminary search done on the Web, Towson University is one of the few Centers of Academic Excellence in Information Assurance Education with an undergraduate program in computer security. Another unique feature of this track is our capstone course, titled "Computer Security Case Studies". Students take this course as the last course in the track and collaborate with their classmates on real-world projects using their knowledge and skills gained in other courses of the track.

Students graduating with this track will have a strong background in the fundamental principles of computer security and its applications, plus hands-on experience with security tools commonly used in industry. This will better prepare them to join the 21$^{st}$ century workforce and to protect our national infrastructure and information assets, which is in keeping with the influential "Call to Action" document [1] that identified the lack of security skills as one of the top ten trends impacting security.

## 2.     GOALS AND OBJECTIVES

The objective was to develop a high-quality computer security track that uses and builds upon the courses that are already part of the computer science curriculum and allows students to finish their degree in four years. The courses in this track expose students to a wide range of security problems and vulnerabilities that exist in operating systems, application systems and networking protocols, and shows students how these vulnerabilities might be exploited by potential adversaries. The students will be given opportunities for hands-on experience with the tools and software used to secure systems.

At the present, the developed track is only available to our computer science majors and computer science and mathematics double majors. Both programs are accredited by Computer Science Accreditation Commission (CSAC) and the track allows students to join the program at any time before the start of their third year. We designed the track with the expectation that it will be accredited by the CSAC at their next visit scheduled for the AY 2003-2004.

The development of the track started over two years ago and the track was approved and made available to students as of Fall 2002. In spite of this short period of time, the track has become very popular among the students, to the extent that our computer information systems majors have been requesting the creation of a similar track for their program. Other institutions offering an accredited program in computer science can easily adopt this track.

## 3.     THE TRACK

Our computer Security track is our standard Computer Science program where upper level computer science electives are replaced by security courses. Most of our upper-level computer sciences courses run with fewer than 25 students. Table 1 below contains the Computer Science program and also illustrates the changes that were made to incorporate the security track.

*Table 1:* Changes in the Computer Science Program to Incorporate the Security Track

| Computer Science with a Track in Computer Security | Computer Science |
|---|---|
| **Required Core courses**<br>Computer Science I and II,<br>Computer Architecture,<br>Data & File Structure,<br>Computer Organization,<br>Operating Systems,<br>Programming Languages: Design &<br>Implementation,<br>Database Systems,<br>**Computer Ethics** | The same |
| Required Math courses<br>Calculus I, Calculus II<br>Discrete Math, and<br>Statistics | The same |
| Introduction to Cryptography | One additional upper level mathematics course |
| Science Requirement (12 credits) | The same |
| Introduction to Information Security,<br>Network Security,<br>Application Software Security,<br>Operating Systems Security,<br>Case Studies in Computer Security | Elective Computer Science courses (12-14 credits) |

The following seven courses are the key components of this track:
1. Computer Ethics
2. Introduction to Information Security
3. Introduction to Cryptography
4. Network Security
5. Application Software Security
6. Operating Systems Security
7. Case Studies in Computer Security

Although, there are other courses that could be included in a computer security track, e.g. computer forensics, biometrics, and communications law, we selected these courses focusing on our existing program and utilizing our expertise and strengths. Below we describe each of the courses that students in the computer security track have to complete.

## 3.1     Computer Ethics

This is a traditional computer ethics course and it is a required course for all students majoring in Computer Science. This course has been taught for many years and prepares students to deal as professionals with ethical questions and societal concerns related to the widespread uses of computers and resulting responsibilities of computer scientists. In this course, topics such as: intellectual property rights, privacy issues, computer crimes, codes of ethics and legislation regarding computer technology are covered. The textbooks for this course are *Readings in CyberEthics* by Richard A. Spinello and Herman T. Tavani [2] and *Morality and Machines: Perspective on Computer Ethics,* by Stacey L. Edgar [3].

## 3.2     Introduction to Information Security

This course provides students with a very broad understanding of the major technical and human components of information security. It focuses on information systems security threats, vulnerabilities, technologies and business requirements. Emphasis is placed on the human and technological aspects of IT security problems and issues relevant to the risks in which information systems are exposed and methods of dealing with such risks. The prerequisite for this course is junior standing and students are strongly encouraged to take this as the first course for the track. This course has been taught three times and is also available to undergraduate students in our computer information systems major as an elective.

The following is a summary of the major topics covered in this course:

* Identification, Authentication and Access Control;

* Security Threats and Vulnerabilities;

* Security Melsod, Security Requirements and Standards;

* The Security Kernel;

* Network and Distributed Systems Security;

* Internet Security and Cryptography;

* Operating System Security;

* Database Security; and

* Legal and Ethical Issues

We selected *Computer Security* by Gollmann [4], and *Security in Computing* by Pfleeger [5] as the required textbooks for this course. Both books have their own specific advantages from a instructional/teaching perspective and a diversity of subject matter point of view. The combination of these books seems to be highly effective for this type of course. A significant amount of extra course materials are distributed throughout the duration of the course. In addition, a considerable amount of recently published articles are circulated by the instructor. Furthermore, students are also encouraged to bring in related articles from web sites, practitioner journals, magazines and newspapers.

This is a rigorous course and includes a diverse set of coursework. In total, there are two examinations, two small applied/hands-on projects, various written homework assignments, a group research paper and a group presentation. The examinations are based on the topics and sub-topics of the course and are usually a combination of objective, multiple choice questions and short essay questions. One of the applied projects for this course deals with a comparison of SSH and Telnet. This project is effective for student learning about utility programs and control techniques, and also provides a useful comparison of the historical and current developments in information security. The other hands-on project is based on PC vulnerability scanning. To our students, this appears to be the more interesting and intriguing of the two applied projects., since it highlights a number of the common issues with protecting individual personal computers such as: primary password controls, unpatched operating systems, configuration issues, and user and administrator privileges.

The homework assignments tend to deal with current topics in Information Security such as Information Warfare, Cyberterrorism and Critical Infrastructure Protection. For the group research project, small groups of four to five students are required to submit a project proposal outlining the specific area of research that they would like to conduct. After instructor review and approval, these projects proceed as 'traditional' research papers of twenty to twenty five pages in length. These papers allow students to pursue an area of specific interest and have included a diverse set of topics as: wireless security, encryption techniques, PKI, firewall architecture and employee monitoring. The group presentation is included as a thirty-minute overview of the research paper to encourage teamwork and information sharing.

Another key component of this course are guest lecturers that primarily come from private industry and consulting organizations. In the most recent semester, two guest lecturers from a major consulting organization provided excellent individual lectures on Windows and UNIX security. Another example is where an Information Security Officer from a major IT corporation gave a guest lecture on Network and Internet Security. These guest lectures were very successful and the students in the course felt that this was one of the most important features of the course. In its totality, this course provides students with a strong understanding of the fundamental principles of computer and security and lays the foundation for the other courses in the academic track.

## 3.3    Introduction to Cryptography

The course gives a broad overview of the mathematical basis of modern cryptography and of the main cryptosystems currently in use. Students taking the course are exposed to relevant chapters of number theory and computational number theory at a level appropriate for undergraduates. The course covers the most important cryptosystems (e.g. DES, Rijndael and some other AES finalists, RSA, Diffie-Hellman key exchange. etc.) and the basic tools used in building security mechanisms. Some important methods for cryptanalysis are presented as well. The course also provides an overview of some important protocols having a strong cryptographic flavor. At the end of the course, students should have a good understanding of the theoretical foundations of cryptography and of the basic techniques in achieving different cryptographic services. Discrete math and junior standing are the prerequisites for this course. The course was taught for the first time in Fall 2002.

The following is a summary of the major topics covered in this course:

- **Basic concepts of cryptology:** (Historical ciphers, cryptanalysis of historical ciphers, one-time pad)

- **Modern Symmetric Cryptographic Systems:** (DES, differential cryptanalysis, triple DES, modes of operation (ECB, CBC, CFB, OFB), Advanced Encryption Standard - Rijndael, and brief coverage of the other finalists)

- **Basic Number Theory:** (Euclidean algorithm, modular arithmetic, Chinese Remainder Theorem, Fermat's Little Theorem and Euler's Theorem, primitive roots, quadratic residues, finite fields)

- **Public Key Cryptography:** (RSA , attacks on RSA, factoring and primality testing, implementation issues of RSA, discrete logarithms, ElGamal public key cryptosystem)

- **Data integrity and authentication:** (Diffie-Hellman key exchange protocol, digital signature schemes, hash functions, pseudo-random generators, security of hash functions and MACs, public-key infrastructure)

- **Protocols:** (secret sharing schemes, bit commitment schemes, 2-party and multi-party protocols for private distributed computation, )

- **Zero-Knowledge Techniques:** (Basic scheme, Feige-Fiat-Shamir identification scheme)

We chose *Introduction to Cryptography* by Wade Trappe and Larry Washington [6], as the textbook for this course. This book is quite comprehensive in its choice of topics and achieves a carefully crafted and intelligent balance between mathematical rigor and accessibility to students that have little background in number theory. Numerous handouts containing up-to-date information from a variety of sources are distributed throughout the course. Moreover, the students are encouraged to seek such information that can be shared with the whole class.

The coursework is diverse. There are two exams and a number of short quizzes, written homework assignments, lab activities, and a team project. The exam and the quiz questions are of the short-essay type and try to assess the level to which the students have grasped the main concepts.

A key component of the course is its laboratory exercises. A lab consists of a set of activities followed by a series of questions. The Labs are supported by software packages that have been written by us (partially inspired by similar lab software written by Kris Gaj [7 ] from George Mason University). Currently, such labs exist for DES and RSA, and some other labs are in different stages of design and implementation for Number Theory Concepts and Rijndael. For illustration, we reproduce one question from our RSA lab: "*Using the Prime Number Theorem, estimate the number of odd numbers that one has to check to find a prime number having 256 bits. Execute the demonstration program (option Demo-Find a Prime Number). Enter the number of bits (256 in this case). You will see two numbers. One is the randomly generated initial odd number and the other is the prime number that was found. You will see how many odd numbers were tested before the program obtained the prime number. Have you been lucky or unlucky in your search for prime numbers?*"

In addition to homework assignments, the students are asked to develop either a software project or an analytical project based on cryptographic techniques. Software projects typically involve writing a program in a high-level language (C, C++, Java, etc.). Analytical projects involve comparative analysis of competing algorithms, protocols, or implementations. They also may involve reviewing/surveying issues related to cryptology and some other field such as number theory, physics, or law.

Though the topic is open, students are offered a list of suggestions for their projects, and they need to first submit a proposal that has to be approved by the instructor. Typically, students are asked to research a cryptography application and to implement it in as realistic a setting as possible. The usual steps in realizing the project are: (1) survey the literature relevant to the protocol (the instructor provides a starting point), (2) implement the protocol in a distributed environment (multiple PCs for example), (3) provide a nice GUI and (4) write a report describing the problem, solutions from literature, current solution, and implementation issues.

## 3.4    Network Security

The course provides students with a thorough understanding of the concepts underlying all aspects of network security with an emphasis on applications. It covers network security principles and applications. Topics include authentication applications, IP security, Web security, network management security, wireless security, and system security. The prerequisites for this course are computer networks, a required course for our computer science majors, and cryptography. We have chosen *Network Security Essentials* [8] by William Stallings, as the textbook for this course. This course will be taught for the first time in Spring 2003.

The following is a summary of the major topics covered in this course:

- **Introduction to Network Security:** Security Architecture, Attacks, Services and Models; Recent Developments

- **Review of Cryptography:** Encryption, Public-key Cryptography and Message Authentication

- **Authentication Applications:** Kerberos, X.509 Authentication Service

- E-mail Security: PGP, S/MIME

- **IP Security:** IPSec, Virtual Private Networks, IPv6 Security, Mobile IP Security

- **Web Security:** Secure Sockets Layer and Transport Layer Security, Secure Electronic Transaction

- **Network Management Security:** SNMP Security

- **Wireless Security:** Wireless LAN, Bluetooth, and GSM Security

- **System Security Overview:** Intrusion and Intrusion Detection, Viruses and Worms, Firewalls, Denial of Service, Honeypots

The students in this course, working in small groups, will be given 4 or 5 computer assignments (some will involve programming) that deal with network security applications and tools. A sample assignment involves the use of the Snort package [9]. The objective is to introduce students to a popular security tool and its major features. In particular, students will gain experience with Snort's capabilities as a sniffer, a logger, and an intrusion detection system. The assignment requires students to become familiar with Snort commands and alerts, and to write their own Snort rules. At the end, students will study the effect of modifying the rules, examine packets in the log files, and analyze the results.

## 3.5     Operating System Security

This course allows students to gain an in-depth knowledge of security threats, different types of malicious codes, and access control problems in the context of operating systems. We will discuss intrusion detection techniques and the design of trusted operating systems along with their cost and performance analysis. The prerequisite for this course is operating systems, a required course for our computer science majors. The prerequisite provides the theoretical foundations and this course will be more applied and topics will be discussed in the context of Linux and Windows NT operating systems. We have selected *Maximum Linux Security* [10], Anonymous, and *Window NT Security* [11] by Michael McInerney, as the textbooks for this course. This course is under development and will be offered in Fall 2003.

The following is a summary of the major topics covered in this course:

- Overview of the Linux Operating System

- Linux Security Basics: (User accounts, Discretionary Access Control, Network Access Control, Intrusion Detection)

- Linux User Security: (Password Attacks, Data Attacks)

- Linux Network Security: (Malicious Code, Sniffers and electronic eavesdropping, Scanners, Spoofing)

- Overview of the Windows NT Operating Systems

- Windows NT Security Architecture Overview: (Layered approach to securing your network, Modules of NT Security Architecture, Security implementation overview)

- File and Directory Security: (Disk Partition, File & directory permission, File & directory security, Share permission)

- User Profile: (Overview, Profile permissions, Default profile)

- Registry: (Registry Structure, Registry Tree permission, Registry editing tools)

Similar to the Network Security course, students will work on small bi-weekly programming projects to gain hands-on experience with the security issues covered in class. As mentioned earlier we are using VMWare products that allow running of multiple operating systems on the same machine. Moreover, students can get root access to the virtual operating system without compromising the security of the underlying machine. In this setting, students can become familiar with the privileges and responsibilities of both an administrator and a user.

## 3.6     Application Software Security

This course studies the security concepts in developing software applications. It discusses design principles for secure software development, and some of the security issues in current programming and scripting languages, database systems and web servers. The *Survey of Programming Languages* course is the prerequisite and the *Database Systems* course is the co-requisite for this course. We have chosen "*Building Secure Software: How to avoid Security Problems the Right Way* [12], by John Viega and Gary McGraw as the textbook for this course. This course is under development and will be offered in Spring 2004.

The following is a summary of the major topics covered in this course:

- **Software Security:** (Security Goals, Common Software Security Pitfalls, Overview of Software Risk Management for Security, Software Security Principles, Auditing Software, Selecting a language)

- **Java Security:** (Java Virtual Machine, Byte code Verifier, Java Sandbox, Java Language security constructs, The Class loader, Class accessibility, Java Cryptography architecture)

- **Secure CGI/API Programming**

- **Buffer Overflows:** (Overview, Defending against Buffer Overflow, Internal Buffer Overflows, Heap Overflows, Stack Overflows, Attack Code)

- **Database Security:** (Security Problems in Databases, Secure DBMS Design, Security Controls, Using Views for Access Control, Field Protection, Statistical Database Protection, Statistics Concepts and Definitions, Security against Statistical Attacks)

- **Client-side Security:** (Traditional Threats, Using SSL, Browser as a security hole)

- **Server-side Security:** (Current Major Host Security Problems, Minimizing Risk by Minimizing Services, Secure Content Updating, Physical Security, Access Control Strategies)

- **Firewall:** (Basic Architecture, Client Proxies, Server Proxies)

As apparent by the topic selection, the students in this course will get a chance to explore the security issues relevant to web-based technologies. In this course, in addition to small projects, students will work on a team project, which allows them to integrate and use their knowledge about Java security, database security, client-side and server-side security in a real-world E-Commerce project.

## 3.7    Computer Security Case Studies

This is a capstone course that allows students to work on comprehensive security-related projects. Currently in development, it will provide students with an in-depth study of the practical aspects of computer security vulnerabilities in a hands-on laboratory setting. The prerequisites for this course are Network Security and Operating Systems Security. Course work will consist primarily of computer laboratory projects. There will be no exams. Course assignments will consist of 6 to 8 projects, some smaller homework assignments, and a final paper. Towards the end of the semester, speakers from industry and government will be invited to present topics of particular interest to them in the areas of computer and network security, computer ethics, public policy for computing and security. This interaction between students and industry and government representatives would allow them to get first-hand knowledge about real projects and problems. It will provide students the opportunity to establish connections with their potential future employers. This course will be first offered in Spring 2004.

**Case Studies:**

- **Case Study 1:** Services (FTP, Mail, Telnet / SSH, Web Servers, File Sharing, Finger, WebDAV)

- **Case Study 2:** Hardening a Server (Linux / UNIX, NT / 2000 / XP)

- **Case Study 3:** Sniffers & Spoofing (Hubs vs. Switches, Detecting Sniffers, IP Spoofing, ARP Spoofing, DNS Spoofing, EMail Spoofing, Web Spoofing)

- **Case Study 4:** Session Hijacking & Anonymity

- **Case Study 5:** Firewalls & Scanners

- **Case Study 6:** Intrusion Detection Systems (SNORT, TripWire, Logging and Audit Tools, Web Server, Tools for Analyzing Log Files)

- **Case Study 7:** Password Attacks & Encryption (Password Management, NT / 2000 Password Implementation, UNIX / LINUX Password Implementation, Web Server Passwords, Application Passwords, PGP, Steganography, Password Cracking Tools)

- **Case Study 8:** DoS Attacks (Email floods, Network DoS, Network DDoS)

- **Case Study 9:** Malicious Code (Viruses, & Worms, Detection & Removal, Policies and Procedures).

## 4.     ISOLATED COMPUTER SECURITY LABORATORY

For the track to be successful, it is necessary to provide an environment that facilitates active learning and allows maximum opportunity for hands-on experiences for the students. Moreover, the nature of the experiments and projects does not allow the use of a general-purpose computer laboratory. Computers used for computer security experiments can never be considered to be in a 'safe' configuration for general use. Further, the configuration of these systems will be constantly changed, based on the needs of a particular laboratory exercise. Therefore, such systems cannot be maintained in a consistently configured state for general use. We are creating an isolated computer security laboratory. Access to this lab will be limited to the students who are taking the course and they will be closely supervised. Security measures will be implemented to prevent any unauthorized and inappropriate access. Students taking the security track, will be given a document describing the code of conduct and general responsibilities of the students [13]. They will be also be asked to sign an agreement acknowledging that they have read and understood the code of conduct of the computer security track and will act at all times with accordance with that code. We are in process of creating the laboratory and will be able to report on its status at the conference. In this laboratory, we plan to use the VMWare™ Workstation 3.2 [14] software product to allow running of multiple operating systems and easy re-configurability of the machines.

## 5.     CONCLUSION

In this paper, we presented a track in computer security that can be easily incorporated into any computer science program and described its courses in detail. At Towson University, the track was made available to our students, as of Fall 2002. During the fall semester, Introduction to Information Security and Introduction to Cryptography courses were offered. The Network Security course is scheduled for the Spring 2003 semester and the remaining three courses will be offered next academic year. The track has already attracted many students, and we are getting requests from our Computer Information Systems majors to either allow them to take this computer science track or to offer a similar track for them.

## ACKNOWLEDGMENTS

This acknowledgments work was supported by the National Science Foundation under grant No. DUE-0113783. We express our thanks to the academic and industry consultants and evaluators Dr. Deborah Frincke and Dr. Ronald Gove.

## REFERENCES

http://www.cerias.purdue.edu/events/accenture_cta_1q2001.pdf

Spinello, Richard A., Tavani, Herman T., Eds., "Readings in CyberEthics," Jones & Barlett, 2001.

Edgar, Stacy L., *"Morality and Machines,"* Second Edition, Jones and Barlett, 2002.

Dieter Gollmann, *"Computer Security,"* John Wiley & Sons, 1999.

Charles P. Pfleeger, *"Security in Computing,"* Second Edition, Prentice Hall PTR, 1997.

Wade Trappe, Larry Washington , *"Introduction to Cryptography,"* Prentice Hall, 2002.

Kris Gaj, Web page for Cryptography and Computer Network Security course, http://ece.gmu.edu/courses/ECE543/index.htm

William Stallings, *"Network Security Essentials,"* 2nd Edition, Prentice Hall, 2003.

The Open Source Network Intrusion Detection System, Web page for Snort, http://www.snort.org/

Anonymous, *"Maximum Linux Security,"* Second Edition, SAMS, 2001.

Michael McInerney, *"Window NT Security,"* Prentice Hall, 2000.

John Viega and Gary McGraw, " *Building Secure Software: How to Avoid Security Problems the Right Way,"* Addison Wesley, 2002.

Julie J. C. H. Ryan, Daniel J. Ryan, "Institutional and Professional Liability in Information Assurance Education, " George Washington University.

VMware, Web page for VMWare products, http://www.vmware.com/products

# Index of Keywords